VOGUE
FASHION KNITTING

VOGUE
FASHION KNITTING

Christina Probert

PHOTOGRAPHS BY PERRY OGDEN

STYLED BY SOPHIE HICKS

PEERAGE BOOKS

To my mother Mary

First published in Great Britain in 1983 by
David & Charles (Publishers) Limited under the
title *Knitting in Vogue Number 2*

This edition published in 1987 by
Peerage Books
59 Grosvenor Street
London W1

ISBN 1 85052 096 8

Printed in Hong Kong

Acknowledgements

Once again, I am indebted to all Vogue's knitting editors, past and present, who first commissioned the designs in this book, and to all the knitting yarn companies and individuals who were so co-operative in revising and reknitting the patterns, namely Art Needlework Industries, Chat Botte, Emu Wools, Christian de Falbe, Hayfield Textiles Ltd, Jaeger Handknitting, Lister-Lee (George Lee & Sons Ltd), Karen Naismith-Robertson, The Natural Dye Company, Patons and Baldwins Ltd, Phildar, Laines Picaud and Browns Woolshop, Pingouin (French Wools Ltd), Richard Poppleton and Sons Ltd, Sunbeam (Richard Ingham & Co Ltd), James Templeton and Son Ltd, 3 Suisses, H G Twilley Ltd, Wendy International and The Yarn Store. I should like to thank Alex Kroll for his guidance throughout, Anne Matthews and Lizzie Aitken, Essie Page, Montse Stanley for their help with pattern checking, Liz Prior for the book's design and her generous help, without which the book would not have appeared, and my parents for their excellent nursing of both the book and myself.

Colour photographs by Perry Ogden, styled by Sophie Hicks.
Details: Steve Kibble 32, 55, 58, 66, 94, 99, 104, 108, 110, 112, 132; Dudley Mountney 144.
Black and white photographs: Bailey 22; Baker 32; Descellers 34; Ogden 11, 39, 42, 86, 108, 137; Rand 94; Reinhardt 70; Scavullo 16; Schall 46; Schatzberg 134; Schiavone 59; Silverstein 73; Testino 111; Vernier 123. Charts by Andy Ingham. Drawings by Barbara Firth and Marion Appleton.

Hair by Kerry Warn, make-up by Fran Cooper, both of New York on pages 10, 13, 15, 17, 19, 21, 24, 27, 29, 33, 37, 38, 43, 49, 50, 57, 61, 63, 71, 72, 75, 79, 80, 83, 87, 91, 93, 98, 103, 105, 107, 113, 119, 121, 122, 127, 129, 130, 136, 140, 142; hair by Nicky Clarke and Ashley Russell, both of John Frieda, make-up by Mark Hayles on pages 30, 35, 40, 45, 53, 54, 59, 64, 69, 77, 85, 89, 96, 100, 109, 114, 116, 133, 135, 139.

Clothes and accessories by Sheridan Barnett, Browns, Lawrence Corner, Paul Costelloe, Courtenay, Crolla, Perry Ellis, Flip, Margaret Howell, Herbert Johnson, Joseph, Kir, Calvin Klein, Lana Lino, New & Lingwood, MaxMara, Mulberry, Benny Ong, Maxfield Parrish, N Peal, Pollen, Marco Polo, Scotch House, Paul Smith, Tessiers, Patricia Underwood, Whistles, Zoran.
International Textile Care Labelling Code courtesy of the Home Laundering Consultative Council.

Contents

KNITTING KNOW-HOW

INTERNATIONAL INFORMATION

Introduction

Since the twenties, knitters have looked to Vogue for the very best handknitting patterns. Always highly fashionable and easy to follow, their strength of design has made each garment an almost timeless classic. Just as wearable now, in fact, as when they were originally published. Here are sixty-six of the best Vogue designs, for men as well as women, dating from the twenties to the eighties, for you to knit now.

Vogue began to publish knitting patterns in the twenties, when designers like Lanvin, Patou and Schiaparelli started a new trend for handknitted, geometric and picture-patterned sportswear. Sports, as well as more formal, patterns appeared intermittently in the magazine until the launch of the Vogue Knitting Book, in 1932: the first of a highly successful series which was to run for over thirty years.

The arrival of World War II brought a spate of issues devoted to comforts for the forces, and to the art of unravelling old woollies ready for reknitting into new essentials. Coupon control extended to handknitting yarns, and Vogue rallied round to produce a range of designs in 'standard', interchangeable, yarns.

The fifties were handknitting's heyday: demand for new designs was constant and the Knitting Book became fatter and fatter with each issue. After the necessity for skimpy cut and standard-weight yarns during most of the previous decade, the long, loose fifties' shapes in thick, Icelandic wools, mohairs and angoras were really luxurious. Widespread interest in handknitting faded in the early sixties, as the skill itself became unfashionable and machine-knitted clothes in fine, often man-made, yarns, took over. But hot on the heels of the chameleon sixties came a return to things natural, and to knitting. Vogue started to publish country-look patterns in the magazine, and soon knitting had re-established itself as a regular feature.

Now knitting has once again become highly popular: more and more men and women are learning to knit, and new, young designers are appearing. Interestingly enough, there is a distinct nostalgia for the shapes of the twenties, blended with modern design, in recent knitting patterns.

This book is both nostalgic and yet very practical. Before World War II, it seems, knitters were far more skilled than we are now. The reason is, of course, that many women, who form the bulk of the knitting population, now have full-time jobs and thus less time to devote to the niceties of knitting skill. So, although the designs themselves are unaltered, in many cases their instructions have been considerably amplified.

The selection of Vogue originals in this book caters for knitters of every standard, and has been categorised as follows: patterns marked ★ are suitable for beginners, ★★ for knitters with some previous experience, and ★★★ for experienced knitters. There is a knitting know-how section, at the back of the book, to help beginners and to remind more experienced knitters of the various knitting processes. To assist you in your choice of patterns, each garment has been fashionably accessorised, and rephotographed in colour. The original fashion shot, in black and white, is shown, too, with a colour stitch detail where necessary, and a description of the design's construction.

For perfect results, you must achieve the knitting tension specified in the pattern. Yarns have been chosen to correspond in character and weight to those originally used, and to produce the correct tensions. The manufacturers of the yarns chosen for the patterns cannot take any responsibility for their success unless you use the correct yarn and work to the given tension. If the suggested yarn is not available, or if you are an experienced knitter and want to use a different yarn, test your tension carefully. If the tension is wrong, the garment will be out of proportion.

Read through your pattern carefully before you begin to knit. Note that sizes are given in increasing order throughout the pattern: where only one instruction is given, this applies to all sizes. It is often helpful to mark each instruction for the size which you are knitting, in pencil.

Garment length measurements are taken from shoulder to hem, unless otherwise specified. Alterations to body and sleeve lengths can be undertaken by experienced knitters, but be careful to mark all affected sections of the garment before you begin. On plain, unshaped designs, these alterations can usually be made after the welt and increases have been completed. Garments with a complicated self-pattern or Fair Isle design can be difficult to alter. Note also that lengthening increases your yarn requirement.

From softest cashmere to textured cotton, sparkling evening wear to active sportswear, multicoloured Fair Isles to traditional Aran designs, whatever your ability and style, Knitting in Vogue Number 2 is packed with patterns to give you that distinctive Vogue look.

Textured shawl 1956. Instructions on page 149

Boat-necked Summer Tunic

Deep boat-necked tunic in broad rib, with three-quarter length sleeves, grafted shoulder seams and dropped armhole

★ Suitable for beginners

MATERIALS

Yarn
Pingouin Fil d'Ecosse 5
8(9) × 50g. balls

Needles
1 pair 3mm.
1 crochet hook 3mm.

MEASUREMENTS

Bust
82–87(92–97) cm.
32–34(36–38) in.

Length
65(67) cm.
25½(26) in.

Sleeve Seam
39(41) cm.
15½(16) in.

TENSION

31 sts. and 36 rows = 10 cm. (4 in.) square over patt. on 3mm. needles. If your tension square does not correspond to these measurements, see page 156 for adjustment instructions.

ABBREVIATIONS

k. = knit; p. = purl; st(s). = stitch(es); inc. = increas(ing) (see page 156); dec. = decreas(ing) (see page 157); beg. = begin(ning); rem. = remain(ing); rep. = repeat; alt. = alternate; tog. = together; sl. = slip stitch (transfer one stitch from left needle, knitwise unless otherwise stated, to right hand needle.); cont. = continue; patt. = pattern; foll. = following; folls. = follows; mm. = millimetres; cm. = centimetres; in. = inch(es); st.st. = stocking stitch; m.1 = make 1 st.: pick up thread lying before next st., from row below, and k. into back of it.

BACK

Cast on 153(163) sts. with 3mm. needles and work in patt. as folls.:
1st row: p.6(21), * k.1, p.19, rep. from * to last 7(22) sts., k.1, p.6(21).
2nd row: k.6(21), * p.1, k.19, rep. from * to last 7(22) sts., p.1, k.6(21).
These 2 rows form the patt.
Work in patt. until work measures 42(43) cm. (16½(16¾) in.) from cast on edge.

Shape Armholes

Keeping patt. straight, shape armhole as folls.:
Next row: work 1 st., m.1, work to last st., m.1, work 1 st.
Work 1 row. Rep. these two rows once more.
Now m.1 st. at each end of next 7 rows. [171(181) sts.]
Cont. straight in patt. until work measures 13(14) cm. (5(5½) in.) from beg. of armhole shaping, ending with a wrong side row.

Shape Neck

Keeping patt. straight, work as folls.:
Next row: k.65(69) and leave on st. holder, cast off centre 41(43) sts., k. to end.
Work 1 row.
Cast off 3 sts. at neck edge on next and foll. 3 alt. rows, then dec. 1 st. at neck edge on foll. 10 rows. [43(47) sts.]
Work 18(20) rows straight.
Leave these sts. on a st. holder.
Rejoin yarn to armhole edge of sts. for other side, and work to match first side, reversing shapings.

FRONT

Work as for back.

SLEEVES

Cast on 79(83) sts. with 3mm. needles and work in patt. as folls.:
1st row: p.9(11), * k.1, p.19, rep. from * to last 10(12) sts., k.1, p.9(11).
2nd row: k.1, m.1, k.8(10), * p.1, k.19, rep. from * to last 10(12) sts., p.1, k.8(10), m.1, k.1.
3rd row: p.10(12), * k.1, p.19, rep. from * to last 11(13) sts., k.1, p.10(12).
4th row: k.10(12), * p.1, k.19, rep. from * to last 11(13) sts., p.1, k.10(12).
Work 3rd and 4th rows once more.
Now cont. working in patt. as set in 3rd and 4th rows, and making 1 st. in manner set in 2nd row, at each end of next row and every foll 6th row, until there are 125(131) sts., working new sts. into patt.
Work 5 rows straight.
Cast off.

MAKING UP AND NECK BORDER

Press all pieces on wrong side.

Graft Right Shoulder Seam

Place front and back with right sides together.

Beg. at end of right shoulder seam with no rem. tail of yarn (neck edge), using crochet hook, take off first st. from holder at front of work onto hook.
Now take off first st. from holder at back of work and draw through the st. already on the crochet hook.
Next take the second st. from the front of the work and draw this through the first st. from the back of work which is on crochet hook, as before.
Cont. in this manner, taking alternate sts. from front and back to end of seam. Cast off by pulling tail of yarn through last st.

Work Neck Border

With 3mm. needles and right side facing, pick up and k. 41(43) sts. down left side of front neck, 41(43) sts. across centre front cast off sts., 82(86) sts. up right side of front neck and down right side of back neck, 41(43) sts. across cast off sts. of centre back neck and 41(43) sts. up left side of back neck. [246(258) sts.]
Turn and cast off.

Graft Left Shoulder Seam

Work as for grafting right shoulder seam.
Sew in end left by neck casting-off neatly.

Finishing

Sew cast off edge of sleeve to straight edge of armhole.
Sew up sleeve and side seams.
Press seams.

Chunky, Ribbed, Country Sweater

1968

Soft, roomy sweater with saddle shoulders, in textured rib pattern, with single-rib lower edge, cuff and hemmed neck welts

★★ Suitable for knitters with some previous experience

MATERIALS

Yarn
Hunter Embo 3 ply (Heavyweight yarn)
11(12:13:13:14) × 112g. hanks

Needles
1 pair 5mm.
1 pair 6mm.

MEASUREMENTS

Chest
92(97:102:107:112) cm.
36(38:40:42:44) in.

Length
66(67:69:70:71) cm.
26(26¼:27¼:27½:28) in.

Sleeve Seam
46(46:47:47:48) cm.
18(18:18½:18½:19) in.

TENSION

18 sts. and 20 rows = 10 cm. (4 in.) square over patt. on 6mm. needles. If your tension square does not correspond to these measurements, see page 156 for adjustment instructions.

ABBREVIATIONS

k. = knit; p. = purl; st(s). = stitch(es); inc. = increas(ing) (see page 156); dec. = decreas(ing) (see page 157); beg. = begin(ning); rem. = remain(ing); rep. = repeat; alt. = alternate; tog. = together; sl. = slip stitch (transfer one stitch from left needle, knitwise unless otherwise stated, to right hand needle.); cont. = continue; patt. = pattern; foll. = following; folls. = follows; mm. = millimetres; cm. = centimetres; in. = inch(es); st.st. = stocking stitch; m.1 = make 1 st.: pick up horizontal loop lying before next st. and work into back of it; tw.2 = twist 2: k. into back of 2nd st., then front of first st. on left-hand needle and sl. 2 sts. off needle tog.

BACK

** Cast on 80(86:90:96:100) sts. with 5mm. needles and work in k.1, p.1 rib for 8 cm. (3¼ in.).
Next row: rib 5(2:5:3:5), m.1, rib 7(9:8:10:9), m.1 10(9:10:9:10) times, rib to end. [91(96:101:106:111) sts.]
Change to 6mm. needles and work in patt. as folls.:
1st row: (right side): k.2, * tw.2, k.1, p.1, k.1, rep. from * to last 4 sts., tw.2, k.2.
2nd row: k.2, * p.2, k.3, rep. from * to last 4 sts., p.2, k.2.
These 2 rows form patt.
Cont. in patt. until back measures 44 cm. (17¼ in.), ending with a wrong side row.

Shape Armholes
Cast off 6(6:6:7:7) sts. at beg. of next 2 rows.
Dec. 1 st. at each end of next and every row until 69(72:75:78:81) sts. rem.
Work straight until armholes measure 17(18:20:21:22) cm. (6½:7:7¾:8¼:8½) in.), ending with a wrong side row. **

Shape Shoulders
Cast off 4 sts. at beg. of next 10(8:8:6:4) rows, then 5 sts. at beg. of foll. 0(2:2:4:6) rows.
Cast off rem. 29(30:33:34:35) sts.

FRONT

Work as for back from ** to **.

Shape Shoulders and Front Neck
Next row: patt. 27(28:28:29:30), cast off 15(16:19:20:21) sts., patt. to end.
Cont. on these sts. for first side.
1st row: cast off 4 sts., patt. to last 2 sts., k.2 tog.
2nd row: k.2 tog., patt. to end.
Rep. last 2 rows once more.
Next row: cast off 4(4:4:4:5) sts., patt. to last 2 sts., k.2 tog.
Next row: k.2 tog., patt. to end.

Next row: cast off 4(4:4:5:5) sts., patt. to last 2 sts., k.2 tog.
Next row: patt.
Cast off rem. 4(5:5:5:5) sts.
With wrong side facing, rejoin yarn to rem. sts. and work to match first side, reversing shapings.

SLEEVES

Cast on 38(38:40:40:42) sts. with 5mm. needles and work in k.1, p.1 rib for 8 cm. (3¼ in.).
Next row: rib 8(8:2:2:1), m.1, rib 11(11:7:7:5), m.1 2(2:5:5:8) times, rib to end. [41(41:46:46:51) sts.]
Change to 6mm. needles and, working in patt. as given for back, shape sides by inc. 1 st. at each end of 3rd and every foll. 4th row until there are 71(71:76:76:81) sts., taking inc. sts. into patt.
Work straight until sleeve seam measures 46(46:47:47:48) cm. (18(18:18½:18½:18¾) in.), ending with a wrong side row.

Shape Top
Cast off 6(6:6:7:7) sts. at beg. of next 2 rows.
Dec. 1 st. at each end of next and every foll. alt. row until 37(33:34:26:31) sts. rem.
Work 1 row.
Dec. 1 st. at each end of every row until 17(17:18:18:19) sts. rem.
Work 22(24:24:24:26) rows on these sts. for saddle shoulder.
Cast off.

MAKING UP AND NECK BORDER

Sew saddles to shoulders, leaving left back shoulder open.

Neck Border
With right side facing and 5mm. needles, k. up 15(15:16:16:17) sts. from left saddle shoulder, 9 sts. down left side of neck, 15(16:19:20:21) sts. from the front, 9 sts. up right side of neck, 15(15:16:16:17), sts. from right saddle shoulder, 27(28:31:32:33) sts. from back. [90(92:100:102:106) sts.]
Work in k.1, p.1 rib for 15 cm. (6 in.).
With a 6mm. needle, cast off loosely in rib. Sew up left back saddle seam and neck border.
Fold neck border in half to wrong side and slip-hem in position.
Sew up side and sleeve seams.
Set in sleeves.
Press seams.

Moss-stitch, Crew-neck Sweater 1981

Hip-length, nubbly sweater in moss stitch, with roomy crew neckline, set-in sleeves and ribbed welts

★ Suitable for beginners

MATERIALS

Yarn
Sunbeam Aran Tweed
13(14:15) × 50g. balls

Needles
1 pair 5mm.
1 pair 6mm.

MEASUREMENTS

Bust
82(87:92) cm.
32(34:36) in.

Length
59(59:60) cm.
23¼(23¼:23½) in.

Sleeve Seam
46 cm.
18 in.

TENSION

8 sts. and 12 rows = 5 cm. (2 in.) square over moss stitch on 6mm. needles. If your tension square does not correspond to these measurements, see page 156 for adjustment instructions.

ABBREVIATIONS

k. = knit; p. = purl; st(s). = stitch(es); inc. = increas(ing) (see page 156); dec. = decreas-(ing) (see page 157); beg. = begin(ning); rem. = remain(ing); rep. = repeat; alt. = alternate; tog. = together; sl. = slip stitch (transfer one stitch from left needle, knit-wise unless otherwise stated, to right hand needle.); cont. = continue; patt. = pattern; foll. = following; folls. = follows; mm. = millimetres; cm. = centimetres; in. = inch(es); st.st. = stocking stitch.

BACK

Cast on 63(65:67) sts. with 5mm. needles.
1st row: k.1, * p.1, k.1, rep. from * to end.
2nd row: p.1, * k.1, p.1, rep. from * to end.
Rep. these 2 rows until work measures 10 cm. (4 in.), ending with a 1st row.
Next row: p., inc. 6(8:10) sts. evenly across row. [69(73:77) sts.]
Change to 6mm. needles and cont. in moss st. as folls.:
1st row (right side): k.1, * p.1, k.1, rep. from * to end.
2nd row: as 1st row.
These 2 rows form the patt.

Cont. in moss st. until work measures 40 cm. (15¾ in.) from beg., ending with 2nd row (right side facing).

Shape Armhole
Cont. in moss st. and at the same time cast off 4 sts. at beg. of next 2 rows, then dec. 1 st. at both ends of next and foll. 6(7:8) alt. rows. [49(51:53) sts.]
Work straight in moss st. until back measures 59(59:60) cm. (23¼(23¼:23½) in.) from beg.
Cast off.

FRONT

Work as for back until front measures 51(51:52) cm. (20(20:20½) in.) from beg., ending with right side facing for next row.

Shape Neck
Cont. in moss st., patt. 17(18:19) sts. and leave these sts. (right front) on spare needle or holder. Cast off 15 sts., patt. to end.
Cont. patt. on these 17(18:19) sts. for left front.
1st row: patt. to last 2 sts., dec. 1 st.
2nd row: patt.

Rep. these 2 rows twice more. [14(15:16) sts.]
Work straight in moss st. until front measures 59(59:60) cm. (23¼(23¼:23½) in.).
Cast off.
Rejoin wool at neck edge of right front and cont. in patt., dec. on neck edge as folls.:
1st row: dec. 1 st., patt. to end.
2nd row: patt.
Rep. these 2 rows twice more. [14(15:16) sts.]
Complete to match left front.

SLEEVES

Cast on 37(39:41) sts. with 5mm. needles.
1st row: k.1, * p.1, k.1, rep. from * to end.
2nd row: p.1, * k.1, p.1, rep. from * to end.
Rep. these 2 rows until work measures 10 cm. (4 in.), ending with 1st row.
Next row (with wrong side facing): p., inc. 1 st. at both ends of row. [39(41:43) sts.]
Change to 6mm. needles and cont. in moss st. as front, inc. 1 st. at both ends of every 10th row 3 times. [45(47:49) sts.]
Work straight in moss st. until sleeve seam measures 46 cm. (18 in.) from beg. ending with right side facing.

Shape Top
Cast off 4 sts. at beg. of next 2 rows, then dec. 1 st. at both ends of next and every alt. row until 11 sts. rem.
Cast off.

NECKBAND

Sew up right shoulder seam, backstitch-ing cast-off sts. on right shoulder with equivalent number on back cast-off edge. With right side of work facing, using 5mm. needles, pick up and k.18 sts. down left front neck shaping, 15 sts. across centre front neck, 18 sts. up right front neck shaping and 31 sts. across back neck. [82 sts.]
Cont. in rib.
1st row: k.1, p.1, to end of row.
2nd row: p.1, k.1, to end of row.
Rep. these rows once more.
Cast off loosely in rib.

MAKING UP

Join left shoulder seam, and invisibly join ribbing on neckband. Sew in sleeves, gathering any fullness at top of sleeve into shoulder. Sew up side and sleeve seams. Press all seams lightly on wrong side with a warm iron and damp cloth.

Bainin Sailing Sweater

Cable-within-cable patterned sweater, in thick Bainin, with set-in sleeves, ribbed welts and yoke with wide, faced, neck opening

★★ Suitable for knitters with some previous experience

MATERIALS

Yarn
3 Suisses Gaelic Bainin
15(16:16:17:17:18) × 50g. balls.

Needles
1 pair 3¾mm.
1 pair 4mm.
1 pair 4½mm.
1 cable needle

MEASUREMENTS

Bust
82(87:92:97:102:107) cm.
32(34:36:38:40:42) in.

Length
60(61:62:62:63:64) cm.
23½(24:24¼:24¼:24¾:25) in.

Sleeve Seam
46(46:46:47:47:47) cm.
18(18:18:18½:18½:18½) in.

TENSION

One cable plus p.4 (14 sts.) = 5·75 cm. (2¼ in.), 24 rows = 10 cm. (4 in.) over pattern on 4½mm. needles. If your tension does not correspond to these measurements, see page 156 for adjustment instructions.

ABBREVIATIONS

k. = knit; p. = purl; st(s). = stitch(es); inc. = increas(ing) (see page 156); dec. = decreas-(ing) (see page 157); beg. = begin(ning); rem. = remain(ing); rep. = repeat; alt. = alternate; tog. = together; sl. = slip stitch (transfer one stitch from left needle, knit-wise unless otherwise stated, to right hand needle.); cont. = continue; patt. = pattern; foll. = following; folls. = follows; mm. = millimetres; cm. = centimetres; in. = inch(es); st.st. = stocking stitch; cable 10 back = slip next 5 sts. onto cable needle, leave at back, k.5, then k.5 from cable needle; cable 4 back = slip next 2 sts. onto cable needle, leave at back, k.2, then k.2 from cable needle; incs. = increases; decs. = decreases.

BACK

Cast on 95(99:103:107:111:115) sts. with 3¾mm. needles and work in single rib beg. and ending right side rows with p.1 and wrong side rows with k.1.

Cont. until work measures 5 cm. (2 in.) from beg., ending with a right side row, then work 1 more row in rib working 14(15:18:18:19:19) incs. evenly spaced. [104(114:121:125:130:134) sts.]

Change to 4½mm. needles and patt.

1st row: p.4(3:3:5:4:6), * k.10, p.3(4:5:5:6:6), rep. from * 6 times more, k.10, p.4(3:3:5:4:6).

2nd row: k.4(3:3:5:4:6), * p.10, k.3(4:5:5:6:6), rep. from * 6 times more, p.10, k.4(3:3:5:4:6).

3rd row: p.4(3:3:5:4:6), * cable 10 back, p.3(4:5:5:6:6), rep. from * 6 times more, cable 10 back, p.4(3:3:5:4:6).

4th row: k.4(3:3:5:4:6), * p.2, k.1, p.4, k.1,

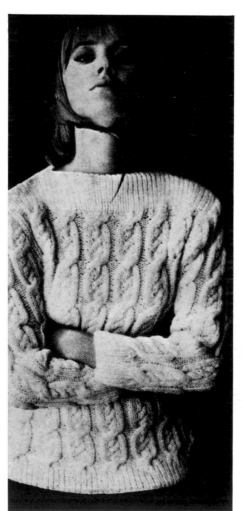

p.2, k.3(4:5:5:6:6), rep. from * ending last rep. with k.4(3:3:5:4:6).

5th row: p.4(3:3:5:4:6), * k.2, p.1, k.4, p.1, k.2, p.3(4:5:5:6:6), rep. from * ending last rep. with p.4(3:3:5:4:6).

6th row: as 4th.

7th row: p.4(3:3:5:4:6), * k.2, p.1, cable 4 back, p.1, k.2, p.3(4:5:5:6:6), rep. from * ending last rep. with p.4(3:3:5:4:6).

8th row to 17th row: rep. from 4th row to 7th row twice then 4th and 5th rows again.

18th row: as 2nd.

These last 16 rows form one patt. Cont. in patt. until work measures 42 cm. (16½ in.) from beg., ending with a wrong side row.

Shape Armholes

Cast off 3 sts. at beg. of next 2 rows, 2 sts. at beg. of next 6(6:6:8:8:10) rows and 1 st. at beg. of next 8(8:10:10:12:10) rows.

Cont. on rem. 83(88:93:93:96:98) sts. until you have worked 117 rows in patt.

Now work 1 more row in patt. working 12(13:14:14:15:15) decs. evenly spaced. [71(75:79:79:81:83) sts.]

Change to 4mm. needles and work in rib as on welt until armholes measure 18(19:20:20:21:22) cm. (7(7½:7¾:7¾:8¼:8½) in.) measured on the straight, ending after a wrong side row.

Shape Shoulders

Cast off in rib 4(5:5:5:5:5) sts. at beg. of next 4 rows and 5(5:7:7:7:8) sts. at beg. of next 2 rows. [45(45:45:45:47:47) sts.]

Cont. in rib for neck facing: work 1 row straight then inc. 1 st. at both ends of next 5 rows. Cast off loosely ribwise.

FRONT

Work exactly as for back.

SLEEVES

Cast on 45(45:47:49:49:53) sts. with 3¾mm. needles and work in rib as on welt for 8 cm. (3¼ in.), ending with a right side row.

Now rib 1 more row working 12(13:14:16:17:17) incs. evenly spaced. [57(58:61:65:66:70) sts.]

Change to 4mm. needles and patt.

1st row: p.4(3:3:5:4:6), rep. from * in 1st patt. row of back 3 times, k.10, p.4(3:3:5:4:6).

Cont. in patt. as now set: for each size patt. is arranged as on back, but with 4 patts. fewer.

Work 3 rows straight then inc. 1 st. at both ends of next row, then every foll. 6th row 12(13:11:11:9:9) times more, then at both ends of every foll. 4th row 0(0:3:3:6:6) times, working sts. into patt. For each size patt. will fit as before with 2 more patt. repeats.

Cont. on these 83(86:91:95:98:102) sts. until work measures 46(46:46:47:47:47) cm. (18(18:18:18½:18½:18½) in.) from beg.

Shape Top

Cast off 3 sts. at beg. of next 2 rows, 2 sts. at beg. of next 6(6:6:8:8:10) rows, 1 st. at beg. of next 8(8:10:10:12:12) rows, 2 sts. at beg. of next 6(8:10:10:10:10) rows, and 4 sts. at beg. of next 4 rows.

Cast off rem. 29(28:27:27:28:28) sts.

MAKING UP

Sew up shoulder seams, backstitching these and all seams.

Press all seams lightly on wrong side with warm iron and damp cloth, using point of iron on ribbed parts.

Patt. parts may be pressed lightly if desired.

Leave ends of neck facing open.

Sew in sleeves, then sew up side and sleeve seams.

Fold neck facings to inside and slipstitch loosely in place.

Sew up shaped ends with a flat seam and slipstitch to inside of shoulder seams.

Cable and Rib Sweater

Chunky sports sweater with set-in sleeves, knitted in alternating bands of cable stitch and ribbing

★★ Suitable for knitters with some previous experience

MATERIALS

Yarn

Jaeger Luxury Spun DK
11(11:12:12:13) × 50g. balls.

Needles

1 pair 3mm.
1 pair 3¾mm.
1 cable needle

MEASUREMENTS

Chest

92(97:102:107:112) cm.
36(38:40:42:44) in.

Length

65(66:67:68:69) cm.
25½(26:26¼:26¾:27¼) in.

Sleeve Seam

48(48:49:49:50) cm.
18¾(18¾:19¼:19¼:19½) in.

TENSION

29 sts. and 27 rows = 10 cm. (4 in.) square over patt. on 3¾mm. needles, slightly flattened as in wear. If your tension square does not correspond to these measurements, see page 156 for adjustment instructions.

ABBREVIATIONS

k. = knit; p. = purl; st(s). = stitch(es); inc. = increas(ing) (see page 156); dec. = decreas-(ing) (see page 157); beg. = begin(ning); rem. = remain(ing); rep. = repeat; alt. = alternate; tog. = together; sl. = slip stitch (transfer one stitch from left needle, knit-wise unless otherwise stated, to right hand needle.); cont. = continue; patt. = pattern; foll. = following; folls. = follows; mm. = millimetres; cm. = centimetres; in. = inch(es); st.st. = stocking stitch; p.f.b. = p. into front and back of ext st.; C10B = cable 10 back: sl. next 5 sts. onto cable needle, leave at back, k.5, then k.5 from cable needle.

BACK

Cast on 117(127:135:145:153) sts. with 3mm. needles and work in single rib beg. and ending right side rows with p.1 and wrong side rows with k.1.

Cont. until work measures 8 cm. (3¼ in.) from beg., ending with a right side row.

Inc. row: (k.1, p.1) 8(9:11:12:11) times, k.1, * p.f.b. 5 times, (k.1, p.1) 10(11:11:12:14) times, k.1, rep. from * to last 22(24:28:30: 28) sts., p.f.b. 5 times, (k.1, p.1) 8(9:11:12: 11) times, k.1. [137(147:155:165:173) sts.]

Change to 3¾mm. needles and patt.

1st row: rib 17(19:23:25:23), thus ending p.1, * k.10, rib 21(23:23:25:29), rep. from * to last 27(29:33:35:33) sts., k.10, rib 17(19: 23:24:23).

2nd row: rib 17(19:23:25:23), * p.10, rib 21(23:23:25:29), rep. from * to last 27(29: 33:35:33) sts., p.10, rib 17(19:23:25:23).

Rep. these 2 rows twice more.

7th row: rib 17(19:23:25:23), * C10B, rib 21(23:23:25:29), rep. from * to last 27(29:33:

35:33) sts., C10B, rib 17(19:23:25:23).

8th row: as 2nd.

9th row to 12th row: rep. 1st to 2nd rows twice more.

These 12 rows form one patt.

Cont. in patt. until work measures 43(44:44:45:45) cm. (16¾(17¼:17¼:17¾: 17¾) in.) from beg., ending with a wrong side row.

Shape Armholes

Cast off 4 sts. at beg. of next 2 rows.

Cast off 2 sts. at beg. of next 6(6:8:10:12) rows.

Cast off 1 st. at beg. of next 8(12:12:12:12) rows.

Cont. on rem. 109(115:119:125:129) sts. until armholes measure 22(22:23:23:24) cm. (8½(8½:9:9:9½) in.) measured on the straight, ending with a wrong side row.

Shape Shoulders

Cast off 8(8:8:9:9) sts. at beg. of next 6 rows, then cast off 7(9:11:10:12) sts. at beg. of next 2 rows.

Cast off rem. 47(49:49:51:51) sts.

FRONT

Work as for back until you have worked 22 rows fewer that on back to start of shoulder, ending with a wrong side row.

Shape Neck and Shoulders

Next row: patt. 47(49:51:53:55) sts. and leave these sts. of left front on a spare needle, cast off next 15(17:17:19:19) sts., patt. to end.

Cont. on 47(49:51:53:55) sts. now rem. on needle for right front and work 1 row straight.

** Cast off 4 sts. at beg. of next row, 2 sts. at same edge on next 3 alt. rows and 1 st. on next 6 alt. rows.

Work 2 rows on rem. 31(33:35:37:39) sts., thus ending at armhole edge.

Cast off 8(8:8:9:9) sts. at beg. of next row and next 2 alt. rows.

Work 1 row, then cast off rem. 7(9:11:10:12) sts.

Rejoin yarn to neck edge of left front sts. Complete as for right front from * to end, reversing shapings.

SLEEVES

Cast on 57(59:63:65:65) sts. with 3mm. needles and work in rib as on back welt for 8 cm. (3¼ in.), ending with a right side row.

Inc. row: rib 13(13:15:15:13), * p.f.b. 5 times, rib 21(23:23:25:29), p.f.b. 5 times, rib 13(13:15:15:13). [67(69:73:75:75) sts.]

Change to 3¾mm. needles and patt.

1st row: rib 13(13:15:15:13), k.10, rib 21(23:23:25:29), k.10, rib 13(13:15:15:13).

Cont. in patt. as now set, working cables over the 2 groups of 10 sts., but at same time work 4 more rows straight, then inc. 1 st. at both ends of next row, then every foll. 6th row 5(7:5:7:2) times, then inc. at both ends of every foll. 4th row 16(13:16: 13:21) times keeping all extra sts. in rib. Cont. on these 111(111:117:117:123) sts. until work measures 48(48:49:49:50) cm. (18¾(18¾:19¼:19¼:19½) in.) from beg.

Shape Top

Cast off 4 sts. at beg. of next 2 rows, 2 sts. at beg. of next 6(6:8:10:12) rows, 1 st. at beg. of next 8(12:12:12:14) rows, 2 sts. at beg. of next 8(6:6:4:6) rows, 4 sts. at beg. of next 8(6:6:6:4) rows and 5 sts. at beg. of next 2(2:4:4:6) rows.

Cast off rem. 25 sts.

NECKBAND

Sew up right shoulder seam matching patt. With right side of work facing you and 3mm. needles, pick up and k.71(73: 73:75:75) sts. round front neck edge and 42(44:44:46:46) sts. across back neck.

Work in rib as on welt for 9 rows.

Cast off loosely ribwise.

MAKING UP

Sew up left shoulder seam and ends of neckband.

Sew in sleeves, then sew up side and sleeve seams.

Fern-pattern Cardigan

1964

Two-tone, round-neck cardigan in diamond and fern pattern, with hemmed borders in main colour

★★ Suitable for knitters with some previous experience

MATERIALS

Yarn

3 Suisses Suizy DK

6(6:7:7) × 50g. balls (Main Col. A)

6(6:7:7) × 50g. balls (Contrast Col. B)

Needles

1 pair 3mm.

1 pair 4mm.

1 circular 3mm. (med. length)

1 circular 4mm. (med. length)

Buttons

6

MEASUREMENTS

Bust

82(92:102:112) cm.

32(36:40:44) in.

Length

62(63:65:66) cm.

24¼(24¾:25½:26) in.

Sleeve Seam

44(44:45:45) cm.

17¼(17¼:17¾:17¾) in.

TENSION

25 sts. and 24 rows = 10 cm. (4 in.) square over stocking stitch on 4mm. needles. If your tension square does not correspond to these measurements, see page 156 for adjustment instructions.

to these measurements, see page 156 for adjustment instructions.

ABBREVIATIONS

k. = knit; p. = purl; st(s). = stitch(es); inc. = increas(ing) (see page 156); dec. = decreas-(ing) (see page 157); beg. = begin(ning); rem. = remain(ing); rep. = repeat; alt. = alternate; sl. = slip stitch (transfer one stitch from left needle, knit-wise unless otherwise stated, to right hand needle.); cont. = continue; patt. = pattern; foll. = following; folls. = follows; mm. = millimetres; cm. = centimetres; in. = inch(es); st.st. = stocking stitch; t.b.l. = through back of loop.

MAIN PART

This is worked in one piece up to the armholes, beg. with the hem section.

Cast on 203(225:247:269) sts. with 3mm. circular needle and A.

Beg. with a p. row work in st.st., but after working 1st row inc. 1 st. at both ends of next 7 rows. You have ended with a k. row.

Next row: k. all sts. t.b.l. making a ridge on right side for hemline. Cont. in st.st. and k.1 row straight, then dec. 1 st. at both ends of next 7 rows.

K.1 row on 203(225:247:269) sts.

On next row k. every st. t.b.l. This makes another ridge for top of hem; all measurements are taken from the *first* (i.e. hem) ridge.

The right side of work is now facing you. Change to 4mm. circular needle, join in B and, working in st.st., work patt. from chart; B is the background colour with patt. in A. *N.B.:* for each size there is 1 edge st. at each end of row not shown on chart which can be worked in either colour.

Cont. in patt. until work measures 44(44:45:45) cm. (17¼(17¼:17¾:17¾) in.) from hemline ridge, ending with a p. row. Now divide work for armholes.

Next row: patt. 48(53:58:63) and leave these sts. of right front on the circular needle, cast off next 5(6:7:8) sts., patt. until there are 97(107:117:127) sts. on needle after first armhole, leave these for back, cast off next 5(6:7:8) sts., patt. to end.

Cont. on last set of 48(53:58:63) sts. for left front with pair 4mm. needles.

** Dec. 1 st. at armhole edge on next 3(3:4:4) rows, then dec. 1 st. at same edge on next 3(4:4:5) alt. rows.

Cont. in patt. on rem. 42(46:50:54) sts. until work measures 13(14:15:16) cm. (5(5½:5¾:6¼) in.) from beg. of armhole, ending at front edge after a k. row.

Shape Neck and Shoulder

Cast off 7(7:8:8) sts. at beg. of next row, 2 sts. at same edge on next 3 alt. rows and 1 st. on next 3 alt. rows. You have ended at armhole edge. [26(30:33:37) sts.]

Cast off for shoulder 6(7:8:9) sts. at beg. of next row and next 2 alt. rows.

Work 1 row then cast off rem. 8(9:9:10) sts.

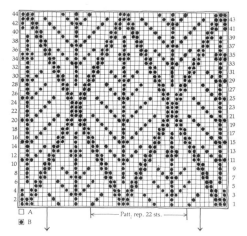

BACK

With wrong side facing, rejoin yarns to sts. of back.

Cont. in patt., dec. 1 st. at both ends of next 3(3:4:4) rows then at both ends of next 3(4:4:5) alt. rows.

Cont. in patt. on rem. 85(93:101:109) sts. until work matches left front to start of shoulder, thus ending with a p. row.

Shape Shoulders

Cast off 6(7:8:9) sts. at beg. of next 6 rows and 8(9:9:10) sts. at beg. of next 2 rows.

Cast off rem. 33(33:35:35) sts. for back neck.

FRONT

With wrong side facing, rejoin yarns to armhole edge of right front sts.

Complete as for left front from ** to end, all shapings being worked at opposite edges, and thus beg. neck shaping 1 row after that of left front.

SLEEVES

Cast on 49(49:59:59) sts. with 3mm. needles and A.

Beg. with a p. row, work 8 rows in st.st.
Next row: k. each st. t.b.l. for hemline.

Work a further 9 rows in st.st., beg. with a k. row.

Next row: k. each st. t.b.l.

The right side is now facing you.

Change to 4mm. needles and work in patt., arranging sts. as on chart but still with an edge st. at each end.

Inc. 1 st. at both ends of every foll. 4th row 20(22:19:21) times, working sts. into patt. as on main part up to armhole.

Top Shaping

Cast off 3(3:4:4) sts. at beg. of next 2 rows. Dec. 1 st. at both ends of next 3(3:4:4) rows.

Cast off 1 st. at beg. of next 6(8:8:10) rows, 2 sts. at beg. of next 6 rows, 3 sts. at beg. of next 8 rows and 4 sts. at beg. of next 4 rows.

Cast off rem. 19(21:21:23) sts.

BORDERS

All worked with 3mm. needles and A.

With right side facing, pick up and k.123(126:131:134) sts. along front edge of left front, beg. at neck edge and ending just above the second ridge.

1st row (wrong side): k. all sts. t.b.l.

K.1 row on right side, then cont. in st.st., inc. 1 st. at both ends of next 7 rows.

K.1 row then on foll. row (wrong side) k. all sts. t.b.l. to make a ridge for foldline.

Cont. in st.st. and k.1 row straight, then dec. 1 st. at both ends of foll. 7 rows.

Work 1 row.

Cast off.

On right front pick up same number of sts. beg. just above the second ridge and ending at neckline.

Work first 5 rows as for left front border, [129(132:137:140) sts.], then make buttonholes as folls.:

6th row: inc. in 1st st., k.23(23:24:24), cast off 3 sts., (k. until you have 23(24:25:26) sts. on right needle after buttonhole, cast off 3 sts.) 3 times, inc. in last st.

On foll. row inc. at each end and cast on 3 sts. over each buttonhole.

Cont. working as for left front border, but on the facing section make 4 more buttonholes on 15th and 16th rows, placing them above previous ones.

Complete as for left front border.

NECKBAND

Sew up shoulder seams, using backstitch for these and all seams.

Press seams very lightly on wrong side with barely warm iron and slightly damp cloth. Patt. may also be pressed in same way.

With right side of work facing you and using 3mm. needles and A, pick up and k.23(23:24:24) sts. up left front neck edge leaving front border free, 33(33:35:35) sts. across back neck and 23(23:24:24) sts. down left front neck.

Work as for left front border but on 7th row work 8 decs. evenly spaced and on 15th row work 8 incs. above the decs.

Complete as for left front border.

MAKING UP

Sew mitred edges at neck and lower corners, leaving a space in these seams at top and bottom of right front border both on the upper and facing sections, to form buttonholes.

Fold facings and hems to inside and slip-stitch edges in place.

Sew up sleeve seams and sew in sleeves.

Buttonhole-st. around edge each double buttonhole and sew on buttons.

Diamond-patterned Twin Set

Cardigan and short-sleeved sweater with contrast bands, neck and hem welts, diamond pattern on sweater front, cardigan hem

★★★ Suitable for experienced knitters

MATERIALS

Yarn
Sunbeam 2 ply
Cardigan and sweater:
15(16:16:17) × 25g. hanks Main Col. A
3(3:4:4) × 25g. hanks Contrast Col. B

Needles
1 pair 3mm.
1 pair 3¾mm.

Buttons
9

MEASUREMENTS

Bust (both)
87(92:97:102) cm.
34(36:38:40) in.

Length (both)
66(67:67:69) cm.
26(26½:26½:27) in.

Sleeve Seam (sweater)
11·5 cm.
4½ in.

Sleeve Seam (cardigan)
42(43:43:44) cm.
16½(16¾:16¾:17¼) in.

TENSION

26 sts. and 34 rows = 10 cm. (4 in.) square over stocking stitch on 3¾mm. needles. If your tension square does not correspond to these measurements, see page 156 for adjustment instructions.

ABBREVIATIONS

k. = knit; p. = purl; st(s). = stitch(es); inc. = increas(ing) (see page 156); dec. = decreas-(ing) (see page 157); beg. = begin(ning); rem. = remain(ing); rep. = repeat; alt. = alternate; tog. = together; sl. = slip stitch (transfer one stitch from left needle, knit-wise unless otherwise stated, to right hand needle.); cont. = continue; patt. = pattern; foll. – following; folls. = follows; mm. = millimetres; cm. = centimetres; in. = inch(es); st.st. = stocking stitch.

SWEATER BACK

Cast on 121(127:133:139) sts. with 3mm. needles and A.
Work 6 cm. (2 in.) in k.1, p.1 rib.
Change to 3¾mm. needles and st.st.
Cont. straight until work measures 42(43:43:44) cm. (16½(16¾:16¾:17¼) in.).

Shape Armholes
Cast off 8(9:9:10) sts. at beg. of next 2 rows.
Dec. 1 st. at each end of next 6 rows, then dec. 1 st. at each end of every alt. row until 89(93:99:103) sts. rem.
Cont. straight until work measures 62(63:63:65) cm. (24¼(24¾:24¾:25½) in.)

Shape Shoulders
Cast off 9(10:10:11) sts. at beg. of next 4 rows.
Cast off 10(10:11:11) sts. at beg. of next 2 rows.
Cast off rem. 33(33:37:37) sts.

SWEATER FRONT

Work as back until work measures 52(53·5:53·5:55) cm. (20½(21:21:21½) in.). Now work from Chart A.
[Note: Chart shows half of design. To complete the row follow chart across from right to left, beg. at point marked for size being worked then omitting centre st., follow chart back across same row to beg. Always twist yarns when changing colours to prevent holes.]
Work until you have completed row 26.
27th row: now, keeping pattern correct throughout, work 32(34:35:37) sts., work 2 tog., turn.
28th row: work 2 tog., work to end of row.
29th – 32nd rows: work 4 more rows, dec. 1 st. at neck edge on each row.
33rd row: cast off 9(10:10:11) sts., work to end.
34th row: work to end.
Using A only, cast off 9(10:10:11) sts., work to end. Work one row.
Next row: cast off rem. sts.
Return to sts. on needle and slip centre 21(21:25:25) sts. onto pin holder for neck. Rejoin wool to rem. 34(36:37:39) sts. and work in patt., starting at point marked B for size you are making, working between markers, work row 27 from left to right, 28 from right to left, etc.
Next row: work 2 tog., work to end of row.
Work 5 more rows, dec. 1 st. at neck edge on each row.

Chart A

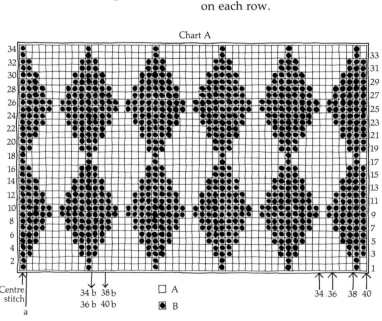

Centre stitch
a
34 b 38 b
36 b 40 b
□ A
◼ B
34 36 38 40

Work 1 row.
Cast off 9(10:10:11) sts. at beg. of next 2 alt.
rows.
Work 1 row.
Cast off rem. sts.

SWEATER SLEEVES

Cast on 78(80:82:84) sts. with 3mm.
needles and A.
Work in k.1, p.1 rib for 2·5 cm. (1 in.).
Change to 3¾mm. needles and st.st. and
inc. 1 st. at each end of 5th and then every
6th row until there are 86(88:90:92) sts.
Cont. straight until work measures 11 cm.
(4½ in.).

Shape Top

Cast off 8(9:9:10) sts. at beg. of next 2 rows.
Work 2 tog. at each end of every alt. row
until 36 sts. rem.
Cast off 3 sts. at beg. of next 4 rows.
Cast off rem. sts.
Finishing: sew right shoulder seam.

NECKBAND

With B and 3mm. needles and with right
side of work facing, pick up and knit
89(93:93:97) sts. including sts. on holder.
Work in k.1, p.1 rib for 5 cm. (2 in.).
Cast off very loosely in rib. Sew up rem.
shoulder seam.
Turn down and stitch neckband.

CARDIGAN BACK

Cast on 121(127:135:141) sts. with 3mm.
needles and work 5 cm. (2 in.) in k.1, p.1
rib.
Change to 3¾mm. needles and st.st.
Work Chart B from bottom to top, working
each row from right to left beg. at size marker and back from point B to size marker
on the right, as before.
With A only, cont. straight until work
measures 43(44:44:45) cm. (16¾(17¼:
17¼:17¾) in.).

Shape Armholes

Cast off 8(9:9:10) sts. at beg. of next 2 rows.
Dec. 1 st. at each end of next 6 rows, then
dec. 1 st. at each end of every alt. row until
89(93:101:105) sts. rem.
Cont. straight until work measures
65(66:66:67) cm. (25½(26:26:26¼) in.).
Cast off 9(10:10:11) sts. at beg. of next 4
rows.
Cast off 10(10:11:11) sts. at beg. of next 2
rows.
Cast off rem. sts.

CARDIGAN LEFT FRONT

Cast on 71(75:77:81) sts. with 3mm.
needles and B and work 5 cm. (2 in.) in
k.1, p.1 rib. Change to 3¾mm. needles,
and st.st. Now follow Chart C, starting at
size marker and working left to right on
1st row, right to left on 2nd row etc. On 1st
row work across 60(64:66:70) patt. sts.
Place 11 sts. left after working across patt.
sts. on a holder for front band, to be worked later.
Cont. working to top of Chart C.
With A only, cont. straight until work
measures 43(44:44:45) cm. (16¾(17¼:

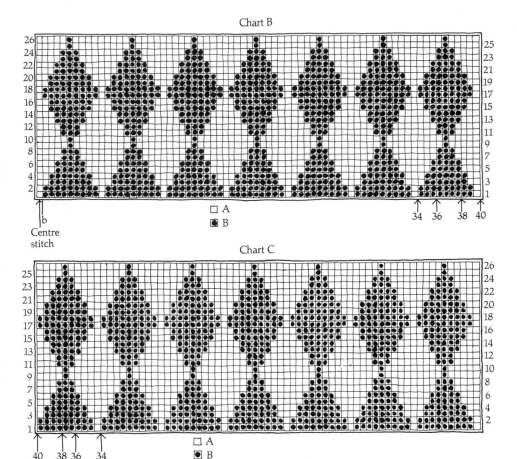

Chart B

□ A
● B

Centre stitch

34 36 38 40

Chart C

□ A
● B

40 38 36 34

17¼:17¾) in.), finishing at side edge.
Cast off 8(9:9:10) sts. at beg. of next row.
Work one row.
Dec. 1 st. at armhole edge on next 6 rows.
Then dec. 1 st. at armhole edge of next 2
alt. rows. [44(47:49:52) sts.]
Now work straight until work measures
60(61:61:62) cm. (23½(24:24:24¼) in.)
finishing at neck edge.
Next row: work next 8(9:9:10) sts. and place
these on a holder, work to end of row.
Now dec. 1 st. at neck edge on next
2(2:3:3) rows, then at neck edge of every
alt. row until 28(30:31:33) sts. rem.
Cont. straight until work measures same
as back to shoulder shaping, finishing at
armhole edge.
Cast off 9(10:10:11) sts. at beg. of next 2 alt.
rows.
Cast off rem. 10(10:11:11) sts.

Buttonband

Place the 11 sts. from holder on 3mm.
needles and with B work in k.1, p.1 rib
until band is long enough to fit along front
edge when very slightly stretched.
Place sts. on holder. Mark position of 9
buttons placing first one 1 cm. (½ in.) from
lower edge and allowing for last one to be
in the centre of the 2 cm. (1 in.) neckband,
which is worked later.

CARDIGAN RIGHT FRONT

Work as for left front reversing shapings
and chart and working buttonholes to correspond to position of buttons on button-
band each worked as folls.:
Work 4 sts., cast off 3 sts., work 3 sts.

Next row: work across row, casting on 3
sts. over cast off sts.

CARDIGAN SLEEVES

Cast on 64(66:70:72) sts. with 3mm.
needles using A and work 6 cm. (2¼ in.)
in k.1, p.1 rib.
Change to 3¾mm. needles and st.st. and
inc. 1 st. at each end of 5th and every foll.
6th row until there are 76(82:86:90) sts.
Then inc. 1 st. at each end of every 8th row
until there are 94(96:98:100) sts.
Cont. straight until work measures
42(43:43:44) cm. (16½(16¾:16¾:17¼) in.).

Shape Top

Cast off 8(9:9:10) sts. at beg. of next 2 rows.
Work 2 sts. tog. at each end of every alt.
row until 40 sts. rem.
Cast off 3 sts. at beg. of next 6 rows.
Cast off rem. sts.

CARDIGAN NECKBAND

With B and 3mm. needles and with right
side of work facing, pick up and
k.113(115:117:119) sts. around neck edge
including sts. on holder from bands.
Work in k.1, p.1 rib for 5 cm. (2 in.),
remembering to make a buttonhole twice
on both front and back of neckband,
which is later folded over.
Cast off very loosely in rib and turn down
neckband and stitch.

MAKING UP

Sew seams.
Set in sleeves.
Sew bands in place.

Wartime Forces' Polo-neck Sweater 1942

Simplest, unisex, stocking-stitch, polo-neck sweater with set-in sleeves and ribbed welts, designed as forces' wartime comfort

★ Suitable for beginners

MATERIALS

Yarn
Patons Clansman 4 ply
8(8:9:9:9) × 50g. balls

Needles
1 pair 2¾mm.
1 pair 3¼mm.
1 set of 4 double-pointed 2¾mm.

MEASUREMENTS

Chest
92(97:102:107:112) cm.
36(38:40:42:44) in.

Length
63(65:66:67:69) cm.
24¾(25½:26:26¼:27) in.

Sleeve Seam
46(46:47:47:48) cm.
18(18:18½:18½:18¾) in.

TENSION

28 sts. and 36 rows = 10 cm. (4 in.) square over st.st. on 3¼mm. needles. If your tension square does not correspond to these measurements see page 156 for adjustment instructions.

ABBREVIATIONS

k. = knit; p. = purl; st(s). = stitch(es); inc. = increas(ing) (see page 156); dec. = decreas(ing) (see page 157); beg. = begin(ning); rem. = remain(ing); rep. = repeat; alt. = alternate; tog. = together; sl. = slip stitch (transfer one stitch from left needle, knitwise unless otherwise stated, to right hand needle.); cont. = continue; patt. = pattern; foll. = following; folls. = follows; mm. = millimetres; cm. = centimetres; in. = inch(es); st.st. = stocking stitch.

BACK

Cast on 127(135:141:149:155) sts. with 2¾mm. needles.
1st row: k.2, * p.1, k.1, rep. from * to last st., k.1.
2nd row: k.1, * p.1, k.1, rep. from * to end.
These 2 rows form rib.
Cont. until work measures 10 cm. (4 in.), ending after 2nd row and inc. 6 sts. during last row. [133(141:147:155:161) sts.]

Change to 3¼mm. needles and st.st., beg. with a k. row.
Cont. until work measures 42 cm. (16½ in.), ending after a p. row.

Shape Armholes
Cast off 8(9:10:11:12) sts. at beg. of next 2 rows.
Dec. 1 st. at each end of next 7(7:7:9:9) rows, then at each end of every alt. row until 95(99:103:107:111) sts. rem. **
Cont. straight until back measures 63(65:66:67:69) cm. (24¾(25½:26:26¼:27) in.) at centre, ending after a p. row.

Shape Shoulders
Cast off 9(10:10:10:11) sts. at beg. of next 4 rows, then 10(9:10:11:10) sts. at beg. of next 2 rows.
Leave rem. 39(41:43:45:47) sts. on a spare needle.

FRONT

Work as back to **.
Work straight until front measures 54(56:57:57:58) cm. (21¼(22:22¼:22¼:22¾) in.) at centre, ending after a p. row.

Shape Neck
Next row: k.33(34:35:36:37), turn. Cont. on this group.
Dec. 1 st. at neck edge on next 5 rows. [28(29:30:31:32) sts.]
Work straight until front measures same

as back to shoulder, ending at armhole edge.

Shape Shoulder
Cast off 9(10:10:10:11) sts. at beg. of next row and foll. alt. row.
Work 1 row. Cast off.
With right side facing, slip centre 29(31:33:35:37) sts. onto a spare needle.
Rejoin yarn to sts. left for other side and complete to match first half.

SLEEVES

Cast on 59(61:63:65:67) sts. with 2¾mm. needles and work 10 cm. (4 in.) in k.1, p.1 rib as for back, ending after a 1st row.
Next row: rib 5(3:4:2:3), * inc. in next st., rib 11(8:8:5:4), rep. from * to last 6(4:5:3:4) sts., inc. in next st., rib to end. [64(68:70:76:80) sts.]
Change to 3¼mm. needles and st.st.
Inc. 1 st. at each end of 9th row, then at each end of every foll. 6th row until there are 84(88:94:100:108) sts., then at each end of every foll. 8th row until there are 96(100:106:110:116) sts.
Cont. straight until work measures 46(46:47:47:48) cm., (18(18:18½:18½:18¾) in.), ending after a p. row.

Shape Sleeve Top
Cast off 8(9:10:11:12) sts. at beg. of next 2 rows.
Work 2(4:4:6:6) rows straight.
Dec. 1 st. at each end of every k. row until 42 sts. rem.
Dec. 1 st. at each end of every row until 28 sts. rem.
Cast off.

POLO COLLAR

Sew up shoulder seams.
With set of 2¾mm. needles, k. across back sts., pick up and knit 29(29:29:33:33) sts. down left side of front, knit across the sts. on spare needle, pick up and knit 29(29:29:33:33) sts. up right side of front. [126(130:134:146:150) sts.]
Work 19 cm. (7½ in.) in k.1, p.1 rib.
Cast off loosely in rib.

MAKING UP

Omitting ribbing, press, following instructions on the ball band.
Sew up side and sleeve seams.
Set in sleeves. Press seams.

Raised Rib-pattern Slipover

Informal, easy-to-wear slipover in raised-rib pattern, with single rib welts, neck and armhole borders

★★ Suitable for knitters with some previous experience

MATERIALS

Yarn
Emu Superwash 4 ply
6(6:6:7:7) × 50g. balls

Needles
1 pair 2¾mm.
1 pair 3¼mm.

MEASUREMENTS

Chest
92(97:102:107:112) cm.
36(38:40:42:44) in.

Length
59(59:60:61:62) cm.
23¼(23¼:23½:24:24½) in.

TENSION

30 sts. and 38 rows = 10 cm. (4 in.) square over slightly stretched pattern on 3¼mm. needles. If your tension square does not correspond to these measurements see page 156 for adjustment instructions.

ABBREVIATIONS

k. = knit; p. = purl; st(s). = stitch(es); inc. = increas(ing) (see page 156); dec. = decreas(ing) (see page 157); beg. = begin(ning); rem. = remain(ing); rep. = repeat; alt. = alternate; tog. = together; sl. = slip stitch (transfer one stitch from left needle, knitwise unless otherwise stated, to right hand needle.); cont. = continue; patt. = pattern; foll. = following; folls. = follows; mm. = millimetres; cm. = centimetres; in. = inch(es); st.st. = stocking stitch; p.s.s.o. = pass the slipped stitch over.

BACK

Cast on 145(151:163:169:175) sts. with 2¾mm. needles.
1st row: k.1, * p.1, k.1, rep. from * to end.
2nd row: p.1, * k.1, p.1, rep. from * to end.
Rep. these 2 rows until work measures 10 cm. (4 in.), ending with 2nd row and inc. 1 st. on last st. of last row. [146(152:164:170:176) sts.]
Change to 3¼mm. needles.
Now work in patt.
1st row: p.2, * k.1, k. next 2 sts., knitting 2nd st. before 1st st. with the needle taken across front of 1st st., k.1, p.2, rep. from * to end.
2nd row: k.2, * p.4, k.2, rep. from * to end.
These 2 rows form the patt.
Cont. in patt. until work measures 34 cm. (13½ in.), ending with 2nd row.

Shape Armholes
Cast off 7 sts. at beg. of next 2 rows.
Cast off 6 st. at beg. of foll. 2 rows.
Cast off 4 sts. at beg. of foll. 4 rows.
Dec. 1 st. at each end of every alt. row 3 times. [98(104:116:122:128) sts.]
Cont. straight until work measures 23(23:24:25:26) cm. (9(9:9½:9¾:10¼) in.) from beg. of armhole shaping, ending with 2nd row.

Shape Shoulder
Cast off 7(7:8:9:9) sts. at beg. of next 2 rows.
Cast off 7(8:9:9:10) sts. at beg. of foll. 4 rows.
Cast off 7(7:9:10:10) sts. at beg. of next 2 rows.
Cast off rem. 42(44:46:48:50) sts.

FRONT

Work as given for back to end of armhole shaping, ending with 2nd row. [98(104:116:122:128) sts.]

Shape Neckline
Next row: patt. 49(52:58:61:64) sts., turn work and leave rem. sts. on spare needle.
Dec. 1 st. at neck edge on next and every foll. 3rd row until 28(30:35:37:39) sts. rem.
Cont. straight in patt. until armhole measures same as back armhole, ending at side edge.

Shape Shoulder
Cast off 7(7:8:9:9) sts. at beg. of next row.
Work 1 row straight.
Cast off 7(8:9:9:10) sts. at beg. of next and foll. alt. row.
Work 1 row straight.
Cast off rem. 7(7:9:10:10) sts.
With right side of work facing, rejoin yarn to first of rem. 49(52:58:61:64) sts.
Work 1 row straight.
Dec. 1 st. at neck edge of next and every foll. 3rd row until 28(30:35:37:39) sts. rem.
Cont. straight in patt. until armhole measures same as back armhole, ending at side edge.
Shape shoulder as for first front shoulder.

NECKBAND

Sew up right shoulder seam.
With right side of work facing and 2¾mm. needles, pick up and k. 69(73:75:77:79) sts. down left front neck, 1 st. from centre front, 69(73:75:77:79) sts. up right front neck and 42(44:46:48:50) sts. from back neck. [181(191:197:203:209) sts.].
1st row: p.1, * k.1, p.1, rep. from * to 2 sts. before centre st., sl.1, k.1, p.s.s.o., p. centre st., k.2 sts. tog., p.1, ** k.1, p.1, rep. from ** to end.
2nd row: * k.1, p.1, rep. from * to 2 sts. before centre st., sl.1, k.1, p.s.s.o., k. centre st., k.2 sts. tog., **p.1, k.1, rep. from ** to end.
Rep. these 2 rows until band measures 3 cm. (1 in.).
Cast off in rib, still dec. at centre.

SLEEVE BANDS

Sew up left shoulder seam.
With right side of work facing and 2¾mm. needles, pick up 153(153:159:163:169) sts. evenly along armhole.
Work 3 cm. (1 in.) in k.1, p.1, rib, beg. and ending odd-numbered rows with p.1 and even-numbered rows with k.1.

MAKING UP

Press, very lightly so as not to stretch rib, according to the instructions on the ball bands.
Sew up side seams.

Popcorn Aran Sweater

Round-neck, thickly popcorn- and cable-patterned sports sweater, with ribbed welts and neckband

★★★ Suitable for experienced knitters

MATERIALS

Yarn
Sirdar Panorama DK
10(11:12:13) × 50g. balls

Needles
1 pair 3¼mm.
1 pair 4½mm.
1 cable needle
2 stitch holders

MEASUREMENTS

Bust
82(87:92:97) cm.
32(34:36:38) in.

Length
54(55:56:57) cm.
21¼(21½:22:22¼) in.

Sleeve Seam
42(43:44:45) cm.
16½(16¾:17¼:17¾) in.

TENSION

14 sts. and 14 rows = 10 cm. (4 in.) square over popcorn patt. on 4½mm. needles. If your tension square does not correspond to these measurements, see page 156 for adjustment instructions.

ABBREVIATIONS

k. = knit; p. = purl; st(s). = stitch(es); inc. = increas(ing) (see page 156); dec. = decreas-(ing) (see page 157); beg. = begin(ning); rem. = remain(ing); rep. = repeat; alt. = alternate; tog. = together; sl. = slip stitch (transfer one stitch from left needle, knit-wise unless otherwise stated, to right hand needle.); cont. = continue; patt. = pattern; foll. = following; folls. = follows; mm. = millimetres; cm. = centimetres; in. = inch(es); st.st. = stocking stitch; p.u. = pick up the loop before the next st. and k. or p. into the back of it.

BACK

Cast on 107(115:123:131) sts. with 3¼mm. needles. Work in k.1, p.1 rib for 7 cm. (2¾ in.), inc. on last row as folls.:
Rib 3(7:11:3), p.u., (rib 4(4:4:5), p.u.) 25 times, rib 4(8:12:3). [133(141:149:157) sts.]
Change to 4½mm. needles and patt.:
1st row: p.27(31:35:39), * k.9, p.26, rep. from * twice more, p.1(5:9:13).

2nd row: (p.3 tog., (k.1, p.1, k.1) into next st.) 6(7:8:9) times, * k.3, p.9, k.3, (p.3 tog., (k.1, p.1, k.1) into next st.) 5 times, rep. from * once, k.3, p.9, k.3, (p.3 tog., (k.1, p.1, k.1) into next st.) 6(7:8:9) times.
3rd row: as 1st row.
4th row: ((k.1, p.1, k.1) into next st., p.3 tog.) 6(7:8:9) times, * k.3, p.9, k.3, ((k.1, p.1, k.1) into next st., p.3 tog.) 5 times, rep. from * once, k.3, p.9, k.3, ((k.1, p.1, k.1) into next st., p.3 tog.) 6(7:8:9) times.
5th row: p.27(31:35:39), * sl. the next 3 sts. onto cable needle and leave at front of work, k. next 3 sts., then place the cable needle with the 3 sts. on it at back of work, k. the next 3 sts., then k. the 3 sts. from cable needle, p.26, rep. from * once more, p.1(5:9:13).
6th row: as 2nd row.
7th row: as 1st row.
8th row: as 4th row.
These 8 rows form the patt. and are repeated throughout.
Cont. straight in patt. until work measures 34 cm. (13¼ in.).

Shape Armholes
Cast off 6(7:8:9) sts. at beg. of next 2 rows, then dec. 1 st. at both ends of next 5 rows.
Dec. 1 st. at both ends of every alt. row 5(6:7:8) times. [101(105:109:113) sts.]
Cont. until armhole measures 18(20:22:23) cm. (7(7¾:8½:9) in.).

Shape Shoulders
Cast off 8 sts. at beg. of next 6 rows, 4(5:6:7) sts. at beg. of next 2 rows.
Leave rem. 45(47:49:51) sts. on a holder.

FRONT

Work as for back until armhole measures 14(15:17:18) cm. (5½(5¾:6½:7) in.), ending with a right side row.

Shape Neck
Patt. 34(35:36:37) sts., turn.
Leave rem. sts. on a spare needle.
** Dec. 1 st. at neck edge on the next and foll. 5 alt. rows. [28(29:30:31) sts.]
Work straight until length matches back to shoulder, ending at side edge.

Shape Shoulder
Cast off 8 sts. at beg. of next and 2 foll. alt. rows.
Work 1 row.
Cast off 4(5:6:7) sts.
Return to rem. sts., and with right side facing, sl. the next 33(35:37:39) sts. onto a

Shape Armholes

Cast off 5(5:6:6:7:7:8) sts. at beg. of next 2 rows.

Cast off 2 sts. at beg. of next 4 rows.

Dec. 1 st. at each end of next and foll. 3(4:4:5:5:6:6) alt. rows. [85(89:93:97:101: 105:109) sts.]

Cont. straight until armholes measure 19(20:21:22:23:24:25) cm. (7½(7¾:8¼:8½: 9:9½:9¾) in.), ending with a p. row.

Shape Shoulders

Cast off 4(5:5:5:6:6:6) sts. at beg. of next 8 rows.

Cast off 7(4:6:7:5:6:7) sts. at beg. of next 2 rows.

Cast off rem. 39(41:41:43:43:45:47) sts.

FRONT

Work as back until end of armhole shaping, ending with a p. row.
Work 2 more rows.

Shape Neckline

Next row: k.37(39:40:42:43:45:47), cast off 11(11:13:13:15:15:15), k. to end.

P. last group of sts. and place rem. sts. on spare needle.

Working only with sts. just purled, dec. 1 st. at neck edge on every alt. row 14(15:14:15:14:15:16) times. [23(24:26:27: 29:30:31) sts.]

Cont. straight until armhole measures the same as on back, ending with a k. row.

Shape Shoulder

Cast off 4(5:5:5:6:6:6) sts. at beg. of next and foll. 3 alt. rows.

Next row: k.

Cast off rem. 7(4:6:7:5:6:7) sts.

Return to sts. on spare needle and work to match 1st side, reversing all shapings.

SLEEVES

Cast on 65(67:69:71:73:75:77) sts. with 2¾mm. needles.

Work in k.1, p.1 rib as on back for 8 cm. (3¼ in.), ending with 2nd row.

Change to 3¾mm. needles.

Cont. in st.st.

AT THE SAME TIME, inc. 1 st. at each end of next and foll. 8th row 13(13:14:14:15: 15:15) times. [91(93:97:99:103:105:107) sts.]

Cont. straight until sleeve measures 43(44:45:46:47:48:49) cm. (16¾(17¼:17¾: 18:18½:18¾:19¼) in.), ending with a p. row.

Shape Top

Cast off 5(5:6:6:7:7:8) sts. at beg. of next 2 rows.

Cast off 2 sts. at beg. of next 4 rows.

Dec. 1 st. at each end of next and foll. 8(9:10:11:12:13:13) alt. rows. [55 sts.]

Next row: p.

Cast off 2 sts. at beg. of next 4 rows.

Cast off 3 sts. at beg. of foll. 4 rows.

Cast off 4 sts. at beg. of foll. 4 rows.

Cast off rem. 19 sts.

COLLAR

Cast on 251(257:261:267:271:277:281) sts. with 2¾mm. needles.

Work in k.1, p.1 rib as on back for 5(5:6: 6:7:7:7) cm. (2(2:2¼:2¼:2¾:2¾:2¾) in.).

Always in rib, cast off 4 sts. at beg. of next 8 rows.

Cast off 5 sts. at beg. of foll. 6 rows.

Cast off 6 sts. at beg. of foll. 20 rows.

Cast off 8 sts. at beg. of foll. 4 rows.

Cast off 6(7:9:10:12:13:15) sts. at beg. of foll. 2 rows.

Cast off rem. 25(29:29:33:33:37:37) sts.

MAKING UP

Do not press. Sew up shoulder seams.

Sew up side and sleeve seams.

Set in sleeves.

Sew up shaped edge of collar to neck edge, fixing the straight edge to cast off sts. at centre front so that they overlap right over left for woman and left over right for man.

Thick, Polo-neck Sports Sweater 1936

Simple sweater in allover cable pattern, with set-in sleeves, ribbed welts and polo collar

★★ Suitable for knitters with some previous experience

MATERIALS

Yarn
Phildar Shoot
15(16:17:18:19:20:21) × 50g. balls.

Needles
1 pair 4mm.
1 pair 5mm.
1 set of 4 double-pointed 4mm.
1 cable needle

MEASUREMENTS

Bust
82(87:92:97:102:107:112) cm.
32(34:36:38:40:42:44) in.

Length
64(65:66:67:68:69:70) cm.
25(25½:26:26¼:26¾:27:27½) in.

Sleeve Seam
48(48:48:50:50:51:51) cm.
18¾(18¾:18¾:19½:19½:20:20) in.

TENSION

24 sts. and 24 rows = 10 cm. (4 in.) square over cable patt. on 5mm. needles. If your tension square does not correspond to these measurements see page 156 for adjustment instructions.

ABBREVIATIONS

k. = knit; p. = purl; st(s). = stitch(es); inc. = increas(ing) (see page 156); dec. = decreas(ing) (see page 157); beg. = begin(ning); rem. = remain(ing); rep. = repeat; alt. = alternate; tog. = together; sl. = slip stitch (transfer one stitch from left needle, knitwise unless otherwise stated, to right hand needle.); cont. = continue; patt. = pattern; foll. = following; folls. = follows; mm. = millimetres; cm. = centimetres; in. = inch(es); st.st. = stocking stitch; C8F = cable 8 front: slip next 4 sts. onto cable needle, to front of work, k.4, k.4 sts. from cable needle.

BACK

Cast on 86(90:96:102:106:112:116) sts. with 4mm. needles.
Work 6 cm. (2¼ in.) in k.1, p.1 rib, ending with a right side row.
Inc. row: rib 5(7:0:3:0:3:0), * inc. 1 in next st., rib 3(3:4:4:4:4:4), rep. from * to last 5(7:1:4:1:4:1) sts., inc. 1, rib to end. [106(110:116:122:128:134:140) sts.]
Change to 5mm. needles and patt.
1st row: p.1(3:0:3:6:3:6) sts., * k.8, p.4, rep. from * to last 9(11:8:11:14:11:14) sts, k.8, p.1(3:0:3:6:3:6) sts.
2nd row: k.1(3:0:3:6:3:6) sts., * p.8, k.4, rep. from * to last 9(11:8:11:14:11:14) sts., p.8, k.1(3:0:3:6:3:6) sts.
3rd row: as 1st row.
4th, 6th, 8th and 10th rows: as 2nd row.
5th row: p.1(3:0:3:6:3:6) sts., * C8F, p.4, rep. from * to last 9(11:8:11:14:11:14) sts., C8F, p.1(3:0:3:6:3:6) sts.
7th and 9th rows: as 1st row.
These 10 rows form patt.
Cont. in patt. until work measures 42(42:42:42:43:43:43) cm. (16½(16½:16½:16½:16¾:16¾:16¾) in.).

Shape Armhole
Cast off 4(4:4:4:5:5:6) sts. at beg. of next 2 rows.
Cast off 3 sts. at beg. of next 2 rows.
Cast off 2 sts. at beg. of next 2(2:2:4:4:4:6) rows.
Cast off 1 st. at beg. of next 4(4:4:2:2:4:2) rows. [84(88:94:98:102:106:108) sts.] Work in patt. until armhole measures 19(20:21:22:22:23:24) cm. (7½(7¾:8¼:8½:8½:9:9½) in.) on the straight.

Shape Shoulder
Cast off 6(6:7:7:8:8:8) sts. at beg. of next 4(4:4:4:4:6:4) rows.
Cast off 6(7:7:8:8:9:9) sts. at beg. of next 4(4:4:4:4:2:4) rows.
Leave rem. 36(36:38:38:38:40:40) sts. on a spare needle.

FRONT

Work as for back until armhole measures 16(17:18:19:19:20:21) cm. (6¼(6½:7:7½:7½:7¾:8¼) in.) on the straight.

Shape Neck
Next row: patt. 35(37:39:41:43:44:45) sts., turn and leave rem. sts. on a spare needle.
Next row: cast off 3 sts., patt. to end.
Cast off 2 sts. at neck edge on alt. rows 3 times and 1 st. twice, then work until armhole matches back to shoulder, ending at armhole edge.

Shape Shoulder
Work as for back, then complete neck shaping:
Slip 14(14:16:16:16:18:18) sts. at centre neck onto holder.
Next row: rejoin yarn at neck edge of rem. 35(37:39:41:43:44:45) sts., cast off 3 sts., patt. to end.
Complete to match other side of neck, reversing shaping.

SLEEVES

Cast on 48(48:50:52:54:56:58) sts. with 4mm. needles.
Work 8 cm. (3 in.) in k.1, p.1 rib, ending with a right side row.
Inc. row (wrong side): rib 3(3:4:5:4:1:2) sts. * inc. 1 in next st., rib 5(5:5:5:4:5:5), rep. from * to last 3(3:4:5:5:1:2) sts., inc. 1, rib to end. [56(56:58:60:64:66:68) sts.]
Change to 5mm. needles and patt.
1st row: k.8(8:3:4:6:7:2) sts., p.4, k.8, rep. from * to last 12(12:7:8:10:11:6) sts., p.4, k.8(8:3:4:6:7:2) sts.
Cont. in patt. as for back working inc. sts. into patt. inc. 1 st. each end of 7th and every foll. 6th row. [80(76:74:76:80:86:88) sts.]
Now inc. 1 st. at each end of every foll. 4th row until there are 86(90:94:96:100:102:104) sts.
Cont. straight until work measures 48(48:48:50:51:51) cm. (18¾(18¾:18¾:19½:19½:20:20) in.).

Shape Top
Cast off 4(4:4:4:5:5:6) sts. at beg. of next 2 rows.
Dec. 1 st. at each end of every row until 50(46:42:44:42:40:40) sts. rem.
Dec. 1 st. at each end of every alt. row until 32 sts. rem.
Cast off 3 sts. at beg. of next 4 rows.
Cast off rem. 20 sts.

NECKBAND

Sew up shoulder seams.
With set of 4 double-pointed 4mm. needles and with right side of work facing, k.36(36:38:38:38:40:40) sts. from back neck, k. up 15 sts. down left front neck, k.14(14:16:16:16:18:18) sts. from centre neck, k. up 15 sts. up right side of neck. [80(80:84:84:84:88:88) sts.]
Work in rounds in k.1, p.1 rib until neckband measures 15 cm. (5¾ in.).
Cast off loosely in rib.

MAKING UP

Sew up side and sleeve seams.
Sew sleeves into armholes.
Press seams lightly on wrong side.

Cool, Cotton Singlet

Wide-rib singlet with low front neckline, grafted shoulder seam, shaped armholes, and neck and armhole welts in single rib

★ Suitable for beginners

MATERIALS

Yarn
Phildar Perle No. 5
7(8) × 40g. balls

Needles
1 pair 2mm.
1 pair 2½mm.
1 crochet hook 2½mm.

MEASUREMENTS

Bust
82–87(92–97) cm.
32–34(36–38) in.

Length
53(56) cm.
20¾(22) in.

TENSION

36 sts. and 45 rows = 10 cm. (4 in.) square over patt. on 2½mm. needles. If your tension square does not correspond to these measurements, see page 156 for adjustment instructions.

ABBREVIATIONS

k. = knit; p. = purl; st(s). = stitch(es); inc. = increas(ing) (see page 156); dec. = decreas(ing) (see page 157); beg. = begin(ning); rem. = remain(ing); rep. = repeat; alt. = alternate; tog. = together; sl. = slip stitch (transfer one stitch from left needle, knitwise unless otherwise stated, to right hand needle.); cont. = continue; patt. = pattern; foll. = following; folls. = follows; mm. = millimetres; cm. = centimetres; in. = inch(es); st.st. = stocking stitch.

BACK

Cast on 179(195) sts. with 2½mm. needles and work in patt. as folls.:
1st row: k.4(2), * p.1, k.4, rep. from * to last 5(3) sts., p.1, k.4(2).
2nd row: p.4(2), k.1, * p.4, k.1, rep. from * to last 4(2) sts., p.4(2). Rep. 1st and 2nd rows until work measures 3 cm. (1 in.).
Now patt. as folls.:
1st row: k.9(2), * p.1, k.9, rep. from * to last 10(3) sts., p.1, k.9(2).
2nd row: k. all k. sts., and p. all p. sts.
Rep. 1st and 2nd patt. rows until work measures 34(35) cm. (13¼(13¾) in.).

Shape Armholes

Keeping patt. straight, work as folls.:
Cast off 10(12) sts. at beg. of next 2 rows. Dec. 1 st. at each end of next 7(8) rows, then dec. 1 st. at each end of foll. 9(10) alt. rows. [127(135) sts.] **
Work straight for 10 cm. (4 in.).

Shape Neck

Keeping patt. straight, work as folls.:
Next row: work 40(43) sts., cast off centre 47(49) sts., work to end.
Work 1 row, leaving rem. set of sts. on a holder.
Cast off 8 sts. at neck edge, then cast off 6 sts. at neck edge on foll. 2 alt. rows, and 4 sts. on 3rd alt. row.
Now dec. 1 st. at neck edge on next 2(4) rows. Work straight for 3(5) rows.
Leave rem. 14(15) sts. on a st. holder.
Rejoin yarn to outside edge of rem. sts. and work other side to match, reversing shapings.

FRONT

Work as for back to **, ending with a wrong side row.

Shape Neck

Next row: work 49(52) sts., cast off centre 29(31) sts., work to end.
Dec. 1 st. at neck edge on the next 25(26) rows, then dec. 1 st. at neck edge on the foll. 10(11) alt. rows. Now work straight for 16(19) rows. Leave rem 14(15) sts. on a st. holder.
Rejoin yarn to shoulder edge of rem. sts., and work to match 1st side, reversing shapings.

MAKING UP AND BORDERS

Omitting ribbing, press pieces on wrong side.

Graft Right Shoulder Seam

Sl. the two sets of sts. onto two spare needles.
With right sides tog., hold needles parallel.
Starting at opposite edge to rem. tail of yarn, take off 1st st. at beg. of front needle with the crochet hook.
Now take off 1st st. from back needle and draw this through previous st. put onto crochet hook.
Take 2nd st. from front needle, draw this through the st. on the crochet hook.
Work in this way, taking sts. from front and back needles alternately, to end of seam.
Cast off by pulling yarn tail through last st.

Neck Rib

With 2mm. needles and right side facing, pick up and k.60(65) sts. down left side of front neck, 29(31) sts. across centre front neck, 92(102) sts. along right side of neck, 47(49) sts. across centre back neck, then 32(37) sts. up left side of back neck. [260(284) sts.]
Work in k.1, p.1 rib for 1 cm. (½ in.).
Cast off in rib.

Graft Left Shoulder Seam

Work as for right shoulder seam.

Armhole Rib

With 2mm. needles and right side facing, pick up and k.190(212) sts. around armhole.
Work in k.1, p.1 rib for 1 cm. (½ in.).
Cast off in rib.

MAKING UP

Sew up side and rib border seams.
Press lightly.

Snowflake Cardigan

Raglan-sleeved cardigan in two-colour pattern, with stand-up collar, ribbed welts and garter-stitch front bands

★★★ Suitable for experienced knitters only

MATERIALS

Yarn
Lister-Lee Motoravia DK
8(9) × 50g. balls (Main Col. A)
8(9) × 50g. balls (Contrast Col. B)

Needles
1 pair 3¼mm.
1 pair 4mm.

Buttons
10

MEASUREMENTS

Chest
92–97(102–107) cm.
36–38(40–42) in.

TENSION

22 sts. and 28 rows = 10 cm. (4 in.) square over patt. on 4mm. needles. If your tension square does not correspond to these measurements see page 156 for adjustment instructions.

ABBREVIATIONS

k. = knit; p. = purl; st(s). = stitch(es); inc. = increas(ing) (see page 156); dec. = decreas-(ing) (see page 157); beg. = begin(ning); rem. = remain(ing); rep. = repeat; alt. = alternate; tog. = together; sl. = slip stitch (transfer one stitch from left needle, knit-wise unless otherwise stated, to right hand needle.); cont. = continue; patt. = pattern; foll. = following; folls. = follows; mm. = millimetres; cm. = centimetres; in. = inch(es); st.st. = stocking stitch; g.st. = garter st.: every row k.

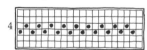

BACK

Cast on 120(128) sts. with 3¼mm. needles and B.
1st row: k.1, * p.1, k.1, rep. from * to end.
2nd row: p.1, * k.1, p.1, rep. from * to end.
Rep. these 2 rows for 7 cm. (2¾ in.) ending with 2nd row.
Next row: inc. 7 sts. evenly across the row. [127(135) sts.]
Change to 4mm. needles.
Joining in A and breaking off colours as required, cont. in st.st., working in patt. from charts 1, 2, 1, 3, 1, 2, 1.
Cont. repeating patt. in chart 4 as many times as required by raglan.

For right front start at * for all sizes
Rep. from start for back, sleeves and left front

□ A
▣ B

For back, sleeves and left front start here for

Medium

Large

Dec. 1 st. on every row at right edge 24 times.
Dec. 1 st. on alt. rows at right edge 21 times. Cast off on same row as back.

RIGHT FRONT

Work as for left, reversing design and shapings.

SLEEVES

Cast on 60(64) sts. with 3¼mm. needles and B.
Work in k.1, p.1 rib for 8 cm. (3¼ in.).
Next row: inc. 7(11) sts. evenly across the row. [67(75) sts.]
Change to 4mm. needles.
Work patt. in chart 4, 2(3) times.
Cont. in patt. as for back.
AT THE SAME TIME, inc. 1 st. at the beg. and end of every 5th row. [101(105) sts.]

Shape Top

Start on same row as back and front shapings.
Dec. 1 st. at beg. and end of next 16(17) rows.
Dec. 1 st. at beg. and end of alt. rows until only 19(21) sts. rem.
Cast off on same row as back and fronts.

FRONT BANDS

Right Band

Cast on 9 sts. with 3¼mm. needles and B.
Work in g.st. until band, slightly stretched, fits the front edge of the jacket.
Cast off.

Left Band

Mark off 10 buttonholes on right band starting at 3 cm. (1 in.) from lower edge and finishing at 1 cm. (½ in.) from top edge.
Work as for right band, incorporating buttonholes as appropriate: k.3, cast off 3, k.3, then cast on 3 sts. on next row.

COLLAR

Cast on 97(103) sts. with 4mm. needles and B.
Work in st.st. for 6 cm. (2½ in.).
Joining in A as required, work patt. in collar chart.
Break off A.
Work 4 more rows in B.
Cast off.

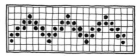

MAKING UP

Press each piece according to instructions on ball bands. Sew up raglan seams.
Fold collar wrong side out and sew up ends.
Turn collar and backstitch cast-off edge to neckline, keeping right side against right side.
Lift collar and slipstitch cast-on edge to wrong side of neckline.
Sew up front bands.
Sew side and sleeve seams.
Press seams if required. Sew on buttons.

AT THE SAME TIME, when work measures 40(41) cm. (15¾(16) in.), shape raglan.

Shape Raglan

Dec. 1 st. at beg. and end of next 25 rows.
Dec. 1 st. at beg. and end of alt. rows until 37(41) sts. rem.
Cast off.

LEFT FRONT

Cast on 60(64) sts. with 3¼mm. needles and B.
Work in k.1, p.1 rib for 7 cm. (2¾ in.) ending with 2nd row.
Next row: inc. 6 sts. evenly across the row. [66(70) sts.]
Change to 4mm. needles.
Work charts as for back until work measures 40(41) cm. (15¾(16) in.).

Shape Raglan

Start on same row as back shaping.

Feather-pattern, Cotton Sweater

Naturally dyed, feather-pattern, cotton sweater in eight toning pastel colours, with drop sleeves and ribbed cuffs

★ Suitable for adventurous beginners

MATERIALS

Yarn

Natural Dye Company Cotton

Naturally dyed cotton yarn in eight different colours sold as a pack including two handmade Dorset buttons, (mail order only, see page 167). Pack colours vary according to dye ingredients: here A = pale lilac, B = dark lilac, C = pale rose, D = medium rose, E = dark rose, F = white, G = cream, H = beige.

Needles

1 pair 2¾mm.
1 pair 3¼mm.

Buttons

included in pack: 3

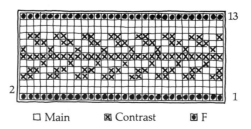

MEASUREMENTS

Bust

87(92:97) cm.
34(36:38) in.

Length

54 cm.
21¼ in.

TENSION

10 sts. and 12 rows = 5 cm. (2 in.) square over patt. with 3¼mm. needles. If your tension square does not correspond to these measurements, see page 156 for adjustment instructions.

ABBREVIATIONS

k. = knit; p. = purl; st(s). = stitch(es); inc. = increas(ing) (see page 156); dec. = decreas(ing) (see page 157); beg. = begin(ning); rem. = remain(ing); rep. = repeat; alt. = alternate; tog. = together; sl. = slip stitch (transfer one stitch from left needle, knitwise unless otherwise stated, to right hand needle.); cont. = continue; patt. = pattern; foll. = following; folls. = follows; mm. = millimetres; cm. = centimetres; in. = inch(es); st.st. = stocking stitch.

FRONT AND BACK PATTERN

	Main	Contrast
1st patt.	H	D
2nd patt.	E	G
3rd patt.	C	B
4th patt.	A	F
5th patt.	H	E
	armhole	
6th patt.	B	G
7th patt.	F	D
8th patt.	D	H
9th patt.	G	B

N.B. as marked on chart, 1st and 13th rows of each patt. are worked in F.

☐ Main   ☒ Contrast   ◖ F

BACK

Cast on 70(76:82) sts. with 3¼mm. needles and E.
Change to 2¾mm. needles.
Work 3 rows each of E, H, A, G, D, F, B in k.1 p.1 rib. (21 rows)
Change to 3¼mm. needles and H.
Work 5 patts. from chart, inc. 15(14:13) sts. evenly across 1st row of 1st patt., and working straight thereafter. [85(90:95) sts.]

Shape Armholes

Cast off 4 sts. at beg. of next 2 rows.
Dec. 1 st. at each end of next row and foll. 5(6:7) alt. rows. [65(68:71) sts.]
Cont. straight until 2nd patt. from beg. of armhole shaping has been worked.
Now inc. 1 st. at each end of next row and foll. 6th rows twice. [71(74:77) sts.]
Work straight until 4 patts. from beg. of armhole shaping have been worked, (i.e. 9 complete patts.).

Shape Shoulders

Cast off 10 sts. at beg. of next 2 rows, 10(11:12) sts. on foll. 2 rows.
Leave rem. 31(32:33) sts. on holder.

FRONT

Work as for back until 2nd patt. after the beg. of armhole shaping is worked, ending with a wrong side row.
Inc. 1 st. at both ends of next row. [67(70:73) sts.]
Next row: p.24(26:28) sts., p.2 tog., p.1, turn.
Dec. 1 st. at neck edge on next 9 rows and at the same time inc. 1 st. on 5th row of armhole edge.
Work 1 row. [18(20:22) sts.]
Inc. 1 st. at armhole edge on next and foll. 6th row. [20(22:24) sts.]
Work 4 rows.

Shape Shoulder

Cast off 10(11:12) sts.
Work 1 row.
Cast off rem 10(11:12) sts., leaving centre 13(12:11) sts. on st. holder.
Work the other front, reversing shapings.

SLEEVES

Cast on 40 sts. with 3¼mm. needles and yarn E.
Change to 2¾mm. needles and work in k.1, p.1 rib as for back and in same col. sequence.

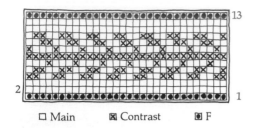

□ Main ⊠ Contrast ◨ F

Change to 3¼mm. needles.
Now work 8 patts., inc. 18 sts. evenly across 1st row, and working straight thereafter. [58 sts.]

Shape Top
Cast off 4 sts. at beg. of next 2 rows.
Dec. 1 st. at each end of next and every foll. 3rd row until 24 sts. rem.
Cont. straight until 4th patt. from beg. of top shaping has been worked, (i.e. 12 complete patts.).
Next row: * p.3 tog., rep. from * to end. [8 sts.]
Cast off.

SLEEVE PATTERN

	Main	Contrast
1st patt.	D	F
2nd patt.	F	E
3rd patt.	B	C
4th patt.	H	D
5th patt.	E	G
6th patt.	C	B
7th patt.	A	F
8th patt.	H	E
	armhole	
9th patt.	B	G
10th patt.	F	D
11th patt.	D	H
12th patt.	G	B

N.B. as marked on chart, 1st and 13th rows of each patt. are worked in F.

SHOULDER RIB

With 2¾mm. needles and F, with right side of work facing, pick up and k.24(26:28) sts. on left back shoulder.
Work 2 rows in k.1, p.1 rib.
Next row: rib 4(6:8) sts., cast off 2 sts., rib 6, cast off 2 sts., rib 10.
Next row: rib across, casting on 2 sts. over those cast off on previous row.
Rib 2 rows.
Cast off.

NECK WELT

Sew up right shoulder seam.
With right side facing and F, pick up and k. approx 86 sts. around neck, using 2¾mm. needles.
Work 5 rows in k.1, p.1 rib.
Cast off.

MAKING UP

Set in sleeves.
Sew up sleeve and side seams.
Very lightly, press seams on wrong side.
Sew buttons on left front shoulder.

Cricket Sweater in Basket Pattern   1937

Patterned, V-neck cricket sweater in extra-soft yarn, with ribbed hem and cuff welts, garter-stitch neck border

★★ Suitable for knitters with some previous experience

MATERIALS

Yarn
Jaeger Luxury Spun DK
13(13:14) × 50g. balls

Needles
1 pair 3¼mm.
1 pair 4mm.

MEASUREMENTS

Bust/Chest
87(97:107) cm.
34(38:42) in.

Length
53(55:56) cm.
20¾(21½:22) in.

Sleeve Seam
46(47:48) cm.
18(18½:18¾) in.

TENSION

26 sts. and 32 rows = 10 cm. (4 in.) square over patt. with 4mm. needles. If your tension square does not correspond to these measurements see page 156 for adjustment instructions.

ABBREVIATIONS

k. = knit; p. = purl; st(s). = stitch(es); inc. = increas(ing) (see page 156); dec. = decreas-(ing) (see page 157); beg. = begin(ning); rem. = remain(ing); rep. = repeat; alt. = alternate; tog. = together; sl. = slip stitch (transfer one stitch from left needle, knit-wise unless otherwise stated, to right hand needle.); cont. = continue; patt. = pattern; foll. = following; folls. = follows; mm. = millimetres; cm. = centimetres; in. = inch(es); st.st. = stocking stitch; m.1 = make 1 st.: pick up loop from between needles and work into the back of it.

BACK

Cast on 106(118:130) sts. with 3¼mm. needles.
1st row: k.2, * p.2, k.2, rep. from * to end.
2nd row: p.2, * k.2, p.2, rep. from * to end.
Rep. 1st and 2nd row for 6 cm. (2¼ in.) ending with a 1st row.
Next row: inc. 1 st. at each end of row. [108(120:132) sts.]
AT THE SAME TIME, make a loop with contrasting yarn and place between 54th and 55th (60th and 61st/66th and 67th) sts. to mark centre of work.

Change to 4mm. needles and work as folls.:

87(107) cm. (34(42) in.) sizes only:

1st row (right side): p.6, (k.6, p.6) 4(5) times, (p.6, k.6) 4(5) times, p.6.
2nd and every alt. row: k. all k. sts. and p. all p. sts.
3rd row: as 1st row.
5th row: as 1st row.
7th row: p.1, m.1, p.2, (k.6, p.6) 8(10) times, k.6, p.2, m.1, p.1. [110(134) sts.]
9th row: p.4, (k.6, p.6) 8(10) times, k.6, p.4.
11th row: as 9th row.
13th row: p.1, m.1, (k.6, p.6) 4(5) times, k.12, (p.6, k.6) 4(5) times, m.1, p.1. [112(136) sts.]
15th row: p.2, (k.6, p.6) 4(5) times, k.12, (p.6, k.6) 4(5) times, p.2.
17th row: as 15th row.
19th row: k.1, m.1, k.4, (p.6, k.6) 8(10) times, p.6, k.4, m.1, k.1. [114(138) sts.]
21st row: k.6, (p.6, k.6) 9(11) times.
23rd row: as 21st row.
24th row: k. all k. sts. and p. all p. sts.
These 24 rows set the patt.

97cm. (38 in.) size only:

1st row (right side): (k.6, p.6) 5 times, (p.6, k.6) 5 times.
2nd and every alt. row: k. all k. sts. and p. all p. sts.
3rd row: as 1st row.
5th row: as 1st row.
7th row: k.1, m.1, k.2, (p.6, k.6) 9 times, p.6, k.2, m.1, k.1.
9th row: k.4, (p.6, k.6) 9 times, p.6, k.4.
11th row: as 9th row.
13th row: k.1, m.1, p.6, (k.6, p.6) 4 times, k.12, (p.6, k.6) 4 times, p.6, m.1, k.1. [124 sts.]

15th row: k.2, p.6, (k.6, p.6) 4 times, k.12, (p.6, k.6) 4 times, p.6, k.2.
17th row: as 15th row.
19th row: p.1, m.1, p.4, (k.6, p.6) 9 times, k.6, p.4, m.1, p.1. [126 sts.]
21st row: p.6, (k.6, p.6) 10 times.
23rd row: as 21st row.
24th row: k. all k. sts. and p. all p. sts.
These 24 rows set the patt.
All sizes:
Cont. in patt., moving patt. outwards from centre marker by 3 sts. on next and every foll. 6th row.
AT THE SAME TIME, inc. 1 st. at each end of next and every foll. 6th row to obtain 118(132:146) sts.
Cont. straight, but still moving patt. outwards from centre, until back measures 33 cm. (13 in.), ending with a wrong side row.

Shape Armholes

Keeping patt. correct, cast off 4 sts. at beg. of next 2 rows.
Dec. 1 st. at each end of next 3(5:7) rows.
Work 1 row.
Dec. 1 st. at each end of next and every foll. alt. row until 96(104:112) sts. rem.
Work straight until back measures 53(55: 56) cm. (20¾(21½:22) in.), ending with a wrong side row.

Shape Shoulders

Cast off 9(10:10) sts. at beg. of next 4 rows.
Cast off 9(9:11) sts. at beg. of foll. 2 rows.
Cast off rem. 42(46:50) sts.

FRONT

Work as back until only 32 rows rem. to start of shoulder shaping, ending with a wrong side row.

Shape Neck

Keeping patt. correct, divide for neck as folls.:
Next row: patt. 46(50:54), work 2 sts. tog., turn and leave rem. sts. on spare needle.
Dec. 1 st. at neck edge on every row until 37 sts. rem.
Work 1 row.
Dec. 1 st. at neck edge on next and every foll. alt. row until 27(29:31) sts. rem.
Work 1 row.

Shape Shoulder

Work as on back.
Return to sts. on spare needle, rejoin yarn, work 2 sts. tog., patt. to end.
Finish to match 1st side reversing all shapings.

RIGHT SLEEVE

** Cast on 50(54:58) sts. with 3¼mm. needles.
Work in k.2, p.2, rib as on back, ending with 1st row.
Next row: rib 3(5:3), * m.1, rib 5(9:4), rep. from * to last 2(4:3) sts., m.1, rib to end. [60(60:72) sts.]
Change to 4mm. needles and work in patt. as folls.: **
1st row (right side): (k.6, p.6) 5(5:6) times.
2nd and every alt. row: k. all k. sts. and p. all p. sts.

3rd and 5th rows: as 1st row.
7th row: p.3, (k.6, p.6) 4(4:5) times, k.6, p.3.
9th and 11th rows: as 7th row.
13th row: p.1, m.1, p.5, (k.6, p.6) 4(4:5) times, k.5, m.1, k.1.
Cont. in patt., moving patt. 3 sts. to the *left* on every foll. 6th row.
AT THE SAME TIME, inc. 1 st. at each end of every foll. 6th(6th:7th) row to obtain 92(98:104) sts.
Work straight, still moving patt., until sleeve measures 46(47:48) cm. (18(18½:18¾) in.), ending with a wrong side row.

Shape Top

Keeping patt. correct, cast off 4 sts. at beg. of next 2 rows.
Dec. 1 st. at each end of next and every foll. alt. row until 50(50:54) sts. rem.
Work 1 row.
Dec. 1 st. at each end of next and every foll. row until only 26 sts. rem.
Cast off.

LEFT SLEEVE

Work as right sleeve from ** to **.
1st row (right side): (p.6, k.6) 5(5:6) times.
2nd and every alt. row: k. all k. sts. and p. all p. sts.
3rd and 5th rows: as 1st row.
7th row: p.3, (k.6, p.6) 4(4:5) times, k.6, p.3.
9th and 11th rows: as 7th row.
13th row: k.1, m.1, k.5, (p.6, k.6) 4(4:5) times, p.5, m.1, p.1.
Cont. in patt., moving patt. 3 sts. to the *right* on every foll. 6th row.
AT THE SAME TIME, inc. for sides to match right sleeve.
Finish to match first sleeve.

NECKBAND

Cast on 2 sts. with 3¼mm. needles.
Work in garter st. (every row k.).
AT THE SAME TIME, inc. 1 st. at beg. of next and every foll. alt. row to obtain 8 sts.
Cont. as folls.:
1st row: k.
2nd row: k.1, m.1, k. to last 2 sts., k.2 sts. tog. (8 sts. left).
Rep. 1st and 2nd rows until shorter side is long enough to fit round neck edge *on top of work*, ending with 1st row.
Dec. 1 st. at beg. of next and every foll. alt. row until 2 sts. rem.
Work 1 row.
K.2 sts. tog. and fasten off.

MAKING UP

Press every piece following instructions on ball bands.
Sew up shoulder seams.
Sew up side and sleeve seams.
Set in sleeves.
Sew up short slanted ends of neckband, thus forming a point.
Position neckband on top of work and sew up inner edge to neckline edge.
Sew up outer edge of neckline loosely.
Press seams if required.

Leafy, Openwork Cardigan

Lightweight cardigan in openwork design, with set-in sleeves, ribbed round neck, hem and cuffs, moss-stitch front bands

★★ Suitable for knitters with some previous experience

MATERIALS

Yarn
Pingouin Pingolaine
6(7:7:8) × 50g. balls

Needles
1 pair 2¾mm.
1 pair 3¼mm.

Buttons
7

MEASUREMENTS

Bust
79–84(87–92:94–99:102–107) cm.
31–33(34–36:37–39:40–42) in.

Length
56(56:57:57) cm.
22(22:22¼:22¼) in.

Sleeve Seam
45 cm.
17¾ in.

TENSION

26 sts. and 38 rows = 10 cm. (4 in.) square over patt. with 3¼mm. needles. If your tension square does not correspond to these measurements, see page 156 for adjustment instructions.

ABBREVIATIONS

k. = knit; p. = purl; st(s). = stitch(es); inc. = increas(ing) (see page 156); dec. = decreas-(ing) (see page 157); beg. = begin(ning); rem. = remain(ing); rep. = repeat; alt. = alternate; tog. = together; sl. = slip stitch (transfer one stitch from left needle, knit-wise unless otherwise stated, to right hand needle.); cont. = continue; patt. = pattern; foll. = following; folls. = follows; mm. = millimetres; cm. = centimetres; in. = inch(es); st.st. = stocking stitch; m.st. = moss stitch; y.fwd. = yarn forward; tog. = together; t.b.l. through back of loops.

BACK

Cast on 105(115:125:135) sts. with 2¾mm. needles and work in k.1, p.1 rib, beg. and ending right side rows with p.1, and wrong side rows with k.1.

Cont. until work measures 5 cm. (2 in.) from beg., ending with a right side row. Change to 3¼mm. needles and p.1 row on wrong side, working 7 incs. evenly, spaced across it.
Cont. on these 112(122:132:142) sts. in patt.
1st row: k.2, * y.fwd., k.2, k.2 tog., k.2 tog., t.b.l., k.2, y.fwd., k.2, rep. from * to end.
2nd and alt. rows: p.
3rd row: k.3, * y.fwd., k.1, k.2 tog., k.2 tog. t.b.l., k.1, y.fwd., k.4, rep. from * ending last rep. k.3.
5th row: k.4, * y.fwd., k.2 tog., k.2 tog. t.b.l., y.fwd., k.6, rep. from * ending last rep. k.4.
7th row: k.1, * k.2 tog. t.b.l., k.2, (y.fwd., k.2) twice, k.2 tog., rep. from * to last st., k.1.
9th row: k.1, * k.2 tog. t.b.l., k.1, y.fwd., k.4, y.fwd., k.1, k.2 tog., rep. from * to last st., k.1.
11th row: k.1, * k.2 tog. t.b.l., y.fwd., k.6, y.fwd., k.2 tog., rep. from * to last st., k.1.
12th row: p.
These 12 rows form one patt.
Cont. in patt. until work measures 37 cm. (14½ in.) from beg., ending with a p. row.

Shape Armholes
Cast off 3 sts. at beg. of next 2 rows, 2 sts. at beg. of next 4 rows and 1 st. at beg. of next 6 rows. [92(102:112:122) sts.]
Cont. without shaping until work measures 56(56:57:57) cm. (22(22:22¼:22¼) in.) from beg., ending with a p. row.

Shape Shoulder
Cast off 8(10:10:12) sts. at beg. of next 4 rows and 11(11:15:15) sts. at beg. of next 2 rows.
Cast off rem. 38(40:42:44) sts. for back neck.

RIGHT FRONT

Cast on 53(59:63:69) sts. with 2¾mm. needles and work in rib with m.st. border:
1st row (right side): k.1, * p.1, k.1, rep. from * to end.
2nd row: * p.1, k.1, rep. from * to last 11 sts., (k.1, p.1) 5 times, k.1.
Cont. in this way until you have worked 8(8:10:10) rows then make buttonhole.
Next row: m.st. 4, cast off 3, work to end.

Next row: cast on 3 sts. over buttonhole.
Make 5 more buttonholes at intervals of 9 cm. (3½ in.), throughout work. At same time cont. until work measures 5 cm. (2 in.) from beg., ending with a 1st row.
Change to 3¼mm. needles.
Next row: p.42(48:52:58) sts., working 5(4:5:4) incs. evenly spaced during this section, then m.st rem. 11 sts.
Cont. on these 58(63:68:73) sts., working in patt. with m.st. border.
First and Third sizes:
1st row: m.st.11, k.1, k.2 tog. t.b.l., k.2, y.fwd., k.2, then rep. from * in 1st patt. row above, to end.
2nd and alt. rows: p. to last 11 sts., m.st.11.
Second and Fourth sizes:
1st row: m.st.11, k.2, then rep. from * in 1st patt. row (after right front) to end.
2nd and alt. rows: p. to last 11 sts., m.st.11.
All sizes:
Cont. in patt. as now set noting that for first and third sizes you have a half-patt. at front edge after the m.st. border.

Cont. until you have worked 1 more row than on back to armhole, thus ending at side edge.

Shape Armhole

Cast off 3 sts. at beg. of next row, 2 sts. at same edge on next 2 alt. rows and 1 st. on next 3 alt. rows.

Cont. on rem. 48(53:58:63) sts. until work measures 52(52:53:53) cm. (20½(20½:20¾:20¾) in.) from beg., ending at front edge.

Shape Neck and Shouler

Next row: m.st.11 and place these sts. on a safety pin, cast off 3(3:4:4) sts., patt. to end.

Cont. in patt. and cast off at neck edge on alt. rows 2 sts. 2(3:3:4) times and 1 st. 3(2:2:1) times.

Cont. on rem. 27(31:35:39) sts. until work matches back to shoulder, ending at armhole edge.

Cast off 8(10:10:12) sts. at beg. of next row and next alt. row.

Work 1 row, then cast off rem. 11(11:15:15) sts.

LEFT FRONT

Cast on 53(59:63:69) sts. with 2¾mm. needles and work in rib with m.st. border.

1st row: * k.1, p.1, rep. from * to last st., k.1.

2nd row: k.1, (p.1, k.1) 5 times, * k.1, p.1, rep. from * to end.

Rep. these 2 rows until work measures 5 cm. (2 in.), ending with a first row.

Change to 3¼mm. needles.

Next row: m.st.11, then p. to end, working 5(4:5:4) incs. evenly spaced.

Cont. on these 58(63:68:73) sts. in patt. with m.st. border.

1st row: k.2, then rep. from * in first patt. row 4(5:5:6) times in all, then for first and third sizes only, y.fwd., k.2, k.2 tog., k.1, then for all sizes m.st.11.

Cont. in patt. as now set keeping m.st. border at front edge and noting that for first and third sizes you have an extra half-patt. at front edge inside this border. Complete as for right front, reversing all shapings, and omitting buttonholes.

SLEEVES

Cast on 63(63:71:71) sts. with 2¾mm. needles and work in k.1, p.1, rib for 5 cm. (2 in.), ending with a right side row.

Change to 3¼mm. needles and p.1 row working 19(19:21:21) incs. evenly spaced across it. [82(82:92:92) sts.]

Now work in patt. as for back but inc. 1 st. at both ends of every foll. 16th(16th:20th:20th) row 8(8:6:6) times, working extra sts. into patt. where pos-

sible, or keeping them in st.st. if they cannot be worked into patt.

Cont. on 98(98:104:104) sts. until work measures 45 cm. (17¾ in.) from beg.

Shape Top

Cast off 3 sts. at beg. of next 2 rows, 2 sts. at beg. of next 4 rows, 1 st. at beg. of next 20(20:22:22) rows and 2 sts. at beg. of next 20(20:22:22) rows. Cast off rem. 24 sts.

NECKBAND

Sew up shoulder seams.

Place sts. of right front border onto a 2¾mm. needle so that point is at inner edge, rejoin yarn, and with right side facing pick up and k.81(83:87:89) sts. evenly round neck edge, then work in m.st. on the 11 sts. of left front border.

Next row: m.st.11, * k.1, p.1, rep. from * to last 12 sts., k.1, m.st.11.

Cont. thus in rib with m.st. borders, work 4 more rows then make buttonhole at right front edge on next 2 rows.

Work 5 more rows. Cast off.

MAKING UP

Sew in sleeves matching centre of sleeve head to shoulder seam.

Sew up side and sleeve seams.

Sew on buttons. Press as instructions on ball band.

Classic Mohair Cardigan 1965

Simple, hip-length cardigan with long sleeves, hemmed lower edge and wide neck welt

★ Suitable for beginners

MATERIALS

Yarn
Emu Filigree
10(11:11:12:12) × 25g. balls

Needles
1 pair 5mm.
1 pair 5½mm.

Buttons
5

Facing Ribbon
1½ metres (1¾ yards)

MEASUREMENTS

Bust
82(87:92:97:102) cm.
32(34:36:38:40) in.

Centre Back
61(62:63:64:64) cm.
24(24½:24¾:25¼:25¼) in.

Sleeve Seam
45(46:46:47:47) cm.
17¾(18:18:18½:18½) in.

TENSION

14 sts. and 20 rows = 10 cm. (4 in.) square

over st.st. on 5½mm. needles. If your tension square does not correspond to these measurements see page 156 for adjustment instructions.

ABBREVIATIONS

k. = knit; p. = purl; st(s). = stitch(es); inc. = increas(ing) (see page 156); dec. = decreas-(ing) (see page 157); beg. = begin(ning); rem. = remain(ing); rep. = repeat; alt. = alternate; tog. = together; sl. = slip stitch (transfer one stitch from left needle, knitwise unless otherwise stated, to right hand needle.); cont. = continue; patt. = pattern; foll. = following; folls. = follows;

mm. = millimetres; cm. = centimetres; in. = inch(es); st.st. = stocking stitch.

BACK

Cast on 63(67:71:75:79) sts. loosely with 5mm. needles.
Work in st.st., starting with a p. row, for 6 rows.
Next row: k., using a 5½mm. needle, working into the back of the stitch.
Change back to 5mm. needles and work a further 5 rows in st.st., starting with a k. row.
Next row: fold up cast off edge to inside and p. the next st. tog. with 1st st. of cast on edge: work in this manner across row, thus forming the hem.
Change to 5½mm. needles.
Now, starting with a k. row, cont. straight in st.st. until the work measures 40 cm. (15¾ in.) from the cast on edge, ending with a p. row.

Shape Armholes
Cast off 3 sts. at beg. of next 2 rows.
Dec. 1 st. at each end of every foll. alt. row 5(6:7:8:8) times in all. [47(49:51:53:57) sts.]
Cont. in st.st. on these sts. until work measures 20(21:22:23:23) cm. (7¾(8¼:8½: 9:9) in.) from beg. of armhole shaping, ending with a p. row.

Shape Shoulders
Cast 4(4:5:5:6) sts. at beg. of next 2 rows.
Cast off 5 sts. at beg. of foll. 2 rows.
Cast off 29(31:31:33:35) sts. loosely for back neck.

LEFT FRONT

Cast on 37(39:41:43:45) sts. loosely with 5mm. needles.
Work in st.st, starting with a p. row, for 6 rows.
Next row: k., using a 5½mm. needle, and working into back of st.
Change back to 5mm. needles and cont. in st.st. with rib at centre front edge as folls.:
1st row (right side): k. to last 6 sts., * p.1, k.1, rep. from * to end.
2nd row: * p.1, k.1, rep. from * twice more, p. to end.
Rep. these 2 rows once more, then work the 1st row again.
Next row: work row to fold up hem as given for the back, but working the 1st 6 sts. ribwise.
Change to 5½mm. needles and, starting with a 1st row, work the 2 row patt. as given until work measures 40 cm. (15¾ in.) ending with a 2nd row, at the armhole edge.

Shape Armholes
Cast off 5 sts. at beg. of next row, work to end.
Work 1 row.
Dec. 1 st. at beg. of next and every foll. alt. row, 4(5:6:7:8) times in all. [28(29:30:31:32) sts.]
Cont. in patt. on these sts. until work measures 15(16:17:18:18) cm. (6(6¼:6½:

7:7) in.) from beg. of armhole shaping, ending at armhole edge.

Shape Neckline
Next row: work in patt. to last 13 sts., place these 13 sts. on safety pin, turn.
Work 1 row.
Dec. 1 st. at neck edge of next 6(7:7:8:8) rows.
Cont. in st.st. until work measures 20(21:22:23:23) cm. (7¾(8¼:8½:9:9) in.) from beg. of armhole shaping, ending at armhole edge.

Shape Shoulders
Cast off 4(4:5:5:6) sts. at beg. of next row.
Work 1 row.
Cast off rem. 5 sts.
Mark position of buttons as folls.: the 1st is 9 cm. (3½ in.) from hemline edge, the last is 7·5 cm. (3 in.) below centre front neck point (the 5th buttonhole is on the neckline), the rem. 2 are evenly spaced between these 2.

RIGHT FRONT

Work as given for the left front, reversing shapings, and working buttonholes to correspond to markings on left front.

Work each buttonhole as folls.:
1st row: cast off the 2 centre sts. of the 6 st. rib section.
2nd row: cast on 2 sts. over those cast off on previous row.

SLEEVES

Cast on 35(37:39:41:43) sts. with 5mm. needles.
Work in single rib as folls.:
1st row: k.2, * p.1, k.1, rep. from * to last st., k.1.
2nd row: k.1, * p.1, k.1, rep. from * to end.
Rep. these 2 rows until work measures 5 cm. (2 in.), ending with a 2nd row.
Change to 5½mm. needles and cont. in st.st., inc. 1 st. at each end of every foll. 8th row until there are 51(53:55:57:59) sts., then cont. without shaping until work measures 45(46:46:47:47) cm. 17¾(18:18: 18½:18½) in.) from cast on edge, ending with a p. row.

Shape Top Sleeve
Cast off 4 sts. at beg. of next 2 rows.
Dec. 1 st. at each end of every foll. alt. row, 8 times.
Dec. 1 st. at each end of every row, 4(5:6:7:8) times in all.
Cast off 5 sts. at beg. of next 3 rows.
Cast off rem. 4 sts.

COLLAR

Using small backstitch, sew up both shoulder seams.
Using 5½mm. needles, and working from the right side, pick up 13 sts. from safety pin at righthand front edge, 13(15:17: 17:19) sts. from neck edge, 31(33:35:35:37) sts. from back neck, 13(15: 17:17:19) sts. from neck edge and rem. 13 sts. from safety pin. [83:(89:95:95:101) sts.]
1st row (wrong side): p.1 * k.1, p.1, rep. from * to end.
2nd row: k.1, * p.1, k.1, rep. from * to end.
Rep. these 2 rows until 12 rows have been worked.
AT THE SAME TIME make buttonhole above previous buttonholes, on the 6th and 7th rows.
When 12 rows have been worked, mark this row with a thread, then change to 5mm. needles and work a further 13 rows, making a buttonhole, as before, on the 6th and 7th rows of this section.
Cast off loosely in rib.

MAKING UP

Sew collar to inside, and hem down loosely.
Neatly oversew two sides of buttonhole on collar together.
Sew sleeve seams and side seams, using small backstitch.
Pin sleeves into place and sew.
Sew facing ribbon to front edges.
Make buttonholes in ribbon and oversew edges of them.
Sew buttons into place.

Sleeveless, Cabled Sweater

V-neck, sleeveless, lambswool sweater in cable, reversed stocking- and garter-stitch stripes, with ribbed welts

★★ Suitable for knitters with some previous experience

MATERIALS

Yarn
George Picaud Feuvert
6(6:7:7) × 50g. balls

Needles
1 pair 3¼mm.
1 pair 4mm.
1 cable needle

MEASUREMENTS

Bust/Chest
92(97:102:107) cm.
36(38:40:42) in.

Length
59(62:65:66) cm.
23¾(24½:25½:26) in.

TENSION

14 sts. and 19 rows = 5 cm. (2 in.) square over stocking stitch on 4mm. needles. If your tension square does not correspond to these measurements see page 156 for adjustment instructions.

ABBREVIATIONS

k. = knit; p. = purl; st(s). = stitch(es); inc. = increas(ing) (see page 156); dec. = decreas-(ing) (see page 157); beg. = begin(ning); rem. = remain(ing); rep. = repeat; alt. = alternate; tog. = together; sl. = slip stitch (transfer one stitch from left needle, knit-wise unless otherwise stated, to right hand needle.); cont. = continue; patt. = pattern; foll. = following; folls. = follows; mm. = millimetres; cm. = centimetres; in. = inch(es); st.st. = stocking stitch; C8 = cable 8: slip next 4 sts. onto cable needle and leave at back of work, k.4, then k.4 from cable needle.

BACK

Cast on 132(138:144:154) sts. with 3¼mm. needles.
Work in k.1, p.1 rib for 7 cm. (2¾ in.), inc. 13 sts. evenly across last row. [145(151: 157:167) sts.]
Change to 4mm. needles and cont. in patt.
1st row: (p.1, k.8, p.3(0:p.3:k.5, p.3)), *k.1, p.3, k.8, p.3, rep. from * to last 13(1:4:9) sts., (k.1, p.3, k.8, p.1(k.1:k.1, p.3:k.1, p.3, k.5)).
2nd row: k.1(k.4:k.7:p.5, k.7), *p.8, k.7, rep. from * to last 9(12:0:5) sts., (p.8, k.1(p.8, k.4:0:p.5)).
3rd row: as 1st row.
4th row: as 2nd row.
5th row: (p.1, k.8, p.3(0:p.3:k.5, p.3)), *k.1, p.3, C8, p.3, rep. from * to last 13(1:4:9) sts., (k.1, p.3, k.8, p.1(k.1:k.1, p.3:k.1, p.3, k.5)).
6th row: as 2nd row.
7th and 8th rows: as 1st and 2nd rows.
These 8 rows form the patt.
Cont. in patt. until back measures 37(38: 40:41) cm. (14½(15:15½:16) in.), ending with wrong side row.

Shape Armhole
Keeping patt. correct, cast off 4(4:5:5) sts. at beg. of next 2 rows.
Cast off 3(3:3:4) sts. at beg. of next 2 rows.
Cast off 2(3:2:2) sts. at beg. of next 2 rows.
Cast off 1(3:2:2) sts. at beg. of next 2 rows.
Cast off 0(1:1:1) st. at beg. of next 2 rows. [124(122:130:138) sts.]
Cont. without shaping until back measures 59(62:65:68) cm. (23¼(24½: 25½:26½) in.), ending with wrong side row.

Shape Shoulders
1st row: cast off 8(9:9:9) sts., patt. 38(36:40:44), cast off 32 sts. for centre neck, patt. to end.
Complete this side first.
2nd row: cast off 8(9:9:9) sts., patt. to end.
3rd row: cast off 5 sts., patt. to end.
4th row: cast off 8(8:9:9) sts., patt. to end.
5th row: work without shaping.
6th row: cast off 8(8:8:9) sts., patt. to end.
Cast off rem. sts.
Rejoin yarn to sts. on st. holder, slipping first st. onto a safety pin for neckband. Work to match first side, reversing all shapings.

FRONT

Work as back until front measures 38(40: 43:46) cm. (15(15¾:17:18) in.) from cast on edge, ending with wrong side row. (All armhole shaping should be complete.)

Shape Neck
Patt. 62(61:65:69), turn and leave rem. sts. on st. holder.
Dec. 1 st. at neck edge on next and every foll. 3rd. row until 46(45:49:53) sts. rem.
Cont. without shaping until front measures same as back to shoulder shaping, ending with wrong side row.

Shape Shoulders
Cast off 8(9:9:9) sts. at beg. of next row.
Cast off 5 sts. at beg. of next row (neck edge).
Cast off 8(9:9:9) sts. at beg. of next row.
Work one row straight.
Cast off 8(8:9:9) sts. at beg. of next row.
Work one row straight.
Cast off 8(8:8:9) sts. at beg. of next row.
Work one row straight.
Cast off rem. sts.
Rejoin yarn to sts. on st. holder and work to match, reversing all shapings.
Sew up right shoulder seam.

NECKBAND

With 3¼mm. needles and right side of work facing, pick up and k.70(72:74:77) sts. down left side of neck, k. centre st. from safety pin (leave a marker on this st.), pick up and k.70(72:74:77) sts. up right side of neck and 44(46:48:48) sts. across centre back.
Work in k.1, p.1 rib for 2·5 cm. (1 in.), dec. 1 st. on either side of centre st. on every row.
Cast off in rib.
Sew up left shoulder seam.

ARMHOLE BORDER

With 3¼mm. needles and right side of work facing, pick up and k.160(168:172:176) sts. evenly around armhole.
Work in k.1, p.1 rib for 2·5 cm. (1 in.).
Cast off in rib.

MAKING UP

Sew up side seams.
Press through damp cloth.

Shetland Sports Sweater

Lightweight yet warm shetland sweater in easy, textured pattern, with set-in sleeves, ribbed welts and narrow roll-collar

★ Suitable for beginners

MATERIALS

Yarn
Pingouin Pingolaine
8(9:9:10) × 50g. balls

Needles
1 pair 3mm.
1 pair 3¾mm.
1 set of 4 double-pointed 3mm.
1 cable needle

MEASUREMENTS

Chest
95(100:105:110) cm.
37½(39½:41½:43½) in.

Length
66(68:70:72) cm.
26(26¾:27½:28¼) in.

Sleeve Seam
48(49:50:51) cm.
18¾(19¼:19½:20) in.

TENSION

27 sts. = 10 cm. (4 in.) over patt. on 3¾mm. needles. If your tension does not correspond to this measurement, see page 156 for adjustment instructions.

ABBREVIATIONS

k. = knit; p. = purl; st(s). = stitch(es); inc. = increas(ing) (see page 156); dec. = decreas-(ing) (see page 157); beg. = begin(ning); rem. = remain(ing); rep. = repeat; alt. = alternate; tog. = together; sl. = slip stitch (transfer one stitch from left needle, knit-wise unless otherwise stated, to right hand needle.); cont. = continue; patt. = pattern; foll. = following; folls. = follows; mm. = millimetres; cm. = centimetres; in. = inch(es); st.st. = stocking stitch; c.4 = cable 4: sl. next 2 sts. onto cable needle, hold at back of work, k. next 2 sts., k.2 sts. from cable needle.

BACK

Cast on 130(138:146:154) sts. with 3mm. needles.
Work in k.2, p.2 rib for 8 cm. (3¼ in.), inc. 10 sts. evenly across last row. [140(148: 156:164) sts.]
Change to 3¾mm. needles and patt.:
1st row: p.4, * k.4, p.4, rep. from * to end.
2nd row: k.4, * p.4, k.4, rep. from * to end.
3rd row: p.4, * c.4, p.4, rep. from * to end.
4th row: as 2nd.
5th row: as 2nd.

6th row: as 1st.
7th row: c.4, * p.4, c.4, rep. from * to end.
8th row: as 1st.
These 8 rows form the patt. and are rep. throughout.
Cont. in patt. until work measures 45(46:47:48) cm. 17¾(18:18½:18¾) in.), ending with a wrong side row.

Shape Armholes
Cast off 8 sts. at beg. of next 2 rows.
Dec. 1 st. at each end of next and every alt. row until there are 108(116:124:132) sts.
Work without shaping until armholes measure 21(22:23:24) cm. (8¼(8½:9:9½) in.), ending with a wrong side row.

Shape Shoulders
Cast off 11(12:13:14) sts. at beg. of next 6 rows.
Sl. rem. 42(44:46:48) sts. onto holder.

FRONT

Work as for back until armholes measure

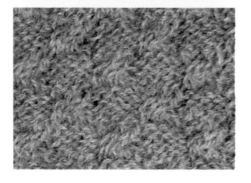

13(14:15:16) cm. (5(5½:5¾:6¼) in.), end-ing with a wrong side row.

Shape Neck
Patt. across 67(72:77:82) sts. and place these on holder, patt. across rem. 41(44: 47:50) sts. for 1st side of neck and shoulder.
Dec. 1 st. at neck edge on next and every row until there are 33(36:39:42) sts.
Cont. in patt. until armhole measures same as back to shoulder, ending at arm-hole edge.

Shape Shoulder
Cast off 11(12:13:14) sts. at beg. of next and foll. 2 alt. rows.
Leave centre 26(28:30:32) sts. on holder, rejoin yarn at centre front and work 2nd side to correspond with 1st side, reversing shaping.

SLEEVES

Cast on 64(64:72:72) sts. with 3mm. needles.
Work in k.2, p.2 rib for 8 cm. (3¼ in.), inc. 4 sts. evenly across last row. [68(68:76:76) sts.]
Change to 3¾mm. needles and patt. as given for back, inc. 1 st. at each end of 5th and every foll. 6th row until there are 100(104:108:112) sts.
Work without shaping until sleeve measures 48(49:50:51) cm. (18¾(19¼: 19½:20) in.).

Shape Top
Cast off 8 sts. at beg. of next 2 rows.
Keeping patt. correct, dec. 1 st. at each end of next and every alt. row until 44 sts. rem.
Cast off 2 sts. at beg. of next 6 rows.
Cast off rem. 32 sts.

NECKBAND

Sew up shoulder seams.
With right side of work facing, and using set of 3mm. needles, pick up and k.40 sts. down left side of neck, k. across 26(28: 30:32) sts. from centre front, pick up and k.40 sts. up right side of neck and k. across rem. 42(44:46:48) sts. from back. [148(152: 156:160) sts.]
Work in k.2, p.2 rib for 8 cm. (3¼ in.).
Cast off loosely, in rib.

MAKING UP

Set in sleeves, matching centre of sleeve head to shoulder seam.
Sew up side and sleeve seams.
Press, using damp cloth and warm iron.

Scandinavian Patterned Sweater

Fitted, waist-length sweater in allover two-tone diamond pattern with set-in sleeves, ribbed welts, doubled-over and hemmed neckband

★★ Suitable for knitters with some previous experience

MATERIALS

Yarn
Hayfield Grampian 4 ply
5(5:6) × 50g. balls (Main Col. A)
2(2:3) × 50g. balls (Contrast Col. B)

Needles
1 pair 2¾mm.
1 pair 3¼mm.
1 set of 4 double-pointed 2¾mm.

MEASUREMENTS

Bust
82(87:92) cm.
32(34:36) in.

Length
51(52:53) cm.
20(20½:20¾) in.

Sleeve Seam
46 cm.
18 in.

TENSION

28 sts. = 10 cm. (4 in.) over patt. on 3¼mm. needles. If your tension does not correspond to this measurement, see page 156 for adjustment instructions.

ABBREVIATIONS

k. = knit; p. = purl; st(s). = stitch(es); inc. = increas(ing) (see page 156); dec. = decreas-(ing) (see page 157); beg. = begin(ning); rem. = remain(ing); rep. = repeat; alt. = alternate; tog. = together; sl. = slip stitch (transfer one stitch from left needle, knit-wise unless otherwise stated, to right hand needle.); cont. = continue; patt. = pattern; foll. = following; folls. = follows; mm. = millimetres; cm. = centimetres; in. = inch(es); st.st. = stocking stitch.

BACK

Cast on 101(121:121) sts. with 2¾mm. needles and A.
1st row: k.1, * p.1, k.1, rep. from * to end.
2nd row: p.1, * k.1, p.1, rep. from * to end.
Rep. 1st and 2nd rows for 9 cm. (3½ in.) ending with 1st row.
Next row: inc. 11(13:13) sts. evenly across row. [112(134:134) sts.]
Change to 3¼mm. needles.
Joining in and breaking off colours as required, cont. in st.st. working in patt. from chart.
Cont. until work measures 32 cm. (12½ in.) from beg., ending with a p. row.

Shape Armholes

Keeping patt. correct, cast off 1(7:3) sts. at beg. of next 2 rows, then 2 sts. at beg. of next 2(4:2) rows.
Dec. 1 st. at each end of next and foll. 4(5:8) alt. rows. [96(102:108) sts.]
Cont. straight in patt. until armholes measure 19(20:21) cm. (7½(7¾:8¼) in.) ending with a p. row.

Shape Shoulders

Cast off 6(7:7) sts. at beg. of next 4 rows.
Cast off 7(7:8) sts. at beg. of foll. 4 rows.
Leave rem. 44(46:48) sts. on a holder.

FRONT

Cast on 121(121:141) sts. with 2¾mm. needles and A.
Work in k.1, p.1 rib for 9 cm. (3½ in.) ending with 1st row.
Next row: inc. 13(13:15) sts. evenly across

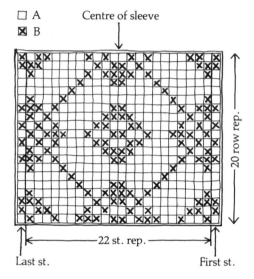

□ A   Centre of sleeve
☒ B

— 20 row rep. —
— 22 st. rep. —
Last st.   First st.

row. [134(134:156) sts.]
Change to 3¼mm. needles.
Work as for back to beg. of armholes.

Shape Armholes

Keeping patt. correct, cast off 12(7:15) sts. at beg. of next 2 rows.
Cast off 2 sts. at beg. of foll. 2(4:2) rows.
Dec. 1 st. at each end of next and foll. 5(5:7) rows. [96(102:108) sts.]
Cont. straight in patt. until armholes measure 13(14:15) cm. (5(5½:5¾) in.) end-ing with a p. row.

Shape Neck and Shoulders

Next row: k.41(43:45) sts., turn work and leave rem. sts. onto spare needle.
Cont. in patt., dec. at the beg. of next row and foll. alt. rows:
5 sts. once, 3 sts. once, 2 sts. twice and 1 st. 3 times. [26(28:30) sts.]
Cont. straight until armhole measures the same as on back.
Shape shoulder as for back.
Return to sts. on spare needle.
Sl.14(16:18) sts. onto a holder.
Rejoin yarn and cont. to match first side.

SLEEVES

Cast on 55(57:59) sts. with 2¾mm. needles and A.
Work in k.1, p.1 rib for 9 cm. (3½ in.) end-ing with 1st row.
Next row: inc. 9 sts. evenly across row. [64(68:72) sts.]
Change to 3¼mm. needles.

Cont. in st.st., working in patt. from chart.
AT THE SAME TIME, inc. 1 st. at each end of 5th and every foll. 8th row to obtain 90(96:102) sts.
Cont. straight until sleeve measures 46 cm. (18 in.) from beg., ending with a p. row.

Shape Top
Keeping patt. correct, cast off 6(7:8) sts. at beg. of next 2 rows.
Dec. 1 st. at each end of next and foll. 11(13:15) rows. [54 sts.]

Dec. at beg. of next row and all foll. rows: 2 sts. 8 times, 3 sts. 4 times, 4 sts. twice [18 sts.]
Cast off.

NECKBAND
Sew up shoulder seams.
With right side facing and double-pointed 2¾mm. needles, pick up and k.29 sts. down left front neck, k.14(16:18) sts. from front holder, pick up and k.29 sts. up right front neck and k.44(46:48) sts. from back holder. [116(120:124) sts.]

Work in rounds of k.1, p.1 rib for 5 cm. (2 in.).
Cast off loosely in rib.

MAKING UP
Press each piece according to instructions on ball band.
Sew up side and sleeve seams.
Set in sleeves.
Fold neckband in half to inside and slip-stitch.
Press seams.

Overchecked Husky Sweater

V-neck, unisex sweater with raglan sleeves and ribbed welts, in two-tone slipped-stitch overcheck pattern

★★ Suitable for knitters with some previous experience

MATERIALS

Yarn
Hayfield Grampian Chunky
11(11:12:13:13) × 50g. balls (Main Col. A)
5(6:6:7:7) × 50g. balls (Contrast Col. B)

Needles
1 pair 5½mm.
1 pair 6½mm.
1 set of 4 double-pointed 5½mm.
Stitch holder.

MEASUREMENTS

Chest
92(97:102:107:112) cm.
36(38:40:42:44) in.

Length
66(67:68:69:70) cm.
26(26¼:26¾:27:27½) in.

Sleeve Seam
46(47:48:49:50) cm.
18(18½:18¾:19¼:19½) in.

TENSION

14 sts. and 24 rows = 10 cm. (4 in.) square over patt. on 6½mm. needles. If your tension square does not correspond to these measurements see page 156 for adjustment instructions.

ABBREVIATIONS

k. = knit; p. = purl; st(s). = stitch(es); inc. = increas(ing) (see page 156); dec. = decreas(ing) (see page 157); beg. = begin(ning);
rem. = remain(ing); rep. = repeat; alt. = alternate; tog. = together; sl. = slip stitch (transfer one stitch from left needle, knit-wise unless otherwise stated, to right hand needle.); cont. = continue; patt. = pattern; foll. = following; folls. = follows; mm. = millimetres; cm. = centimetres; in. = inch(es); st.st. = stocking stitch; sl.1P = slip stitch purlwise; p.s.s.o. = pass the sl. st. over.

BACK

Cast on 71(75:79:83:87) sts. with 5½mm. needles and A.
1st row: k.1, * p.1, k.1, rep. from * to end.
2nd row: p.1, * k.1, p,1, rep. from * to end.

Rep. these 2 rows for 9 cm. (3½ in.) ending with 2nd row. Change to 6½mm. needles and cont. in patt. as folls.:
1st row: with A, k. to end.
2nd row: with A, k.3, * p.1, k.3, rep. from * to end.
3rd row: with B, k.1, * sl.1P, k.1, rep. from * to end, keeping yarn at back of work when slipping sts.
4th row: with B, p.1, * sl.1P, p.1, rep. from * to end, keeping yarn at front (wrong side) of work when slipping sts.
These 4 rows form the patt. and are rep. throughout.
Cont. in patt. until work measures 43 cm. (16¾ in.) from beg., ending with 4th row.

Shape Raglan
Keeping patt. correct, cast off 3 sts. at beg. of next 2 rows, then work 2 rows.
Dec. 1 st. at each end of next row, then work 3 rows.
Rep. the last 4 rows 4(3:3:2:2) times more. [55(61:65:71:75) sts.]
Dec. 1 st. at each end of next and every alt. row until 21(21:23:23:25) sts. rem. ending with a wrong side row.
Leave sts. on holder.

FRONT

Work as for back as far as armholes, ending with 4th row.

Shape Raglan and Divide for Neck
Cast off 3 sts. at beg. of next 2 rows.
Next row: patt. 32(34:36:38:40), turn and leave rem. sts. on spare needle.
Next row: patt. to end.
Dec. 1 st. at each end of next row, then work 3 rows.

Cont. to dec. at neck edge on every 6th row until 8(8:9:9:10) sts. in all have been dec. at this edge.

AT THE SAME TIME cont. to dec. at armhole edge on next row and on every foll. 4th row 3(2:2:1:1) times more, then on every alt. row until 2 sts. rem. ending with a wrong side row.

Cast off.

Return to sts. on spare needle.

Sl. 1st st. onto a safety pin for neck, rejoin yarn and patt. to end.

Cont. to match first side, reversing all shapings.

SLEEVES

Cast on 35(35:35:39:39) sts. with 5½mm. needles and A, and work in rib as for back for 7 cm. (2¾ in.) ending with 2nd row.

Change to 6½mm. needles and cont. in patt. as on back, inc. 1 st. at each end of 5th and every foll. 8th row until there are only 51(53:55:57:59) sts., then at each end of every 6th row until there are 55(57:59:61:63) sts.

Cont. without shaping until sleeve measures 46(47:48:49:50) cm. (18(18½: 18¾:19¼:19½) in.) from beg. ending with 4th row.

Shape Top

Cast off 3 sts. at beg. of next 2 rows, then work 2 rows.

Dec. 1 st. at each end of next row, then work 3 rows.

Rep. the last 4 rows 5 times more.

Dec. 1 st. at each end of next and every alt. row until 9 sts. rem., ending with a wrong side row.

Leave sts. on holder.

NECKBAND

Sew up raglan seams.

With set of 4 5½mm. needles and A, k. sts. of back neck and left sleeve, knitting 2 tog. at seam, pick up 25(27:29:31:33) sts. down left front neck, k. centre front st. from safety pin, pick up 25(27:29:31:33) sts. up right front neck, then k. sts. of right sleeve, knitting last st. of sleeve tog. with first st. of back neck.

[88(92:98:102:108) sts.]

Next round: work in k.1, p.1 rib to 2 sts. before centre front, k.2 tog., p.1, sl.1, k.1, p.s.s.o., rib to end.

Rep. this round for 3 cm. (1 in.).

Cast off in rib, still dec. at centre front.

MAKING UP

Press according to instructions on ball band.

Sew up side and sleeve seams.

Press seams.

Finely Cabled Sweater

Lightweight, round-necked sweater with allover fine cable pattern, ribbed welts and hemmed neck border

1957

★★ Suitable for knitters with some previous experience

MATERIALS

Yarn
Rowan Botany 3 ply
9(9:10:10) × 50g. balls

Needles
1 pair 2¼mm.
1 pair 3mm.
1 cable needle

MEASUREMENTS

Chest
92(97:102:107) cm.
36(38:40:42) in.

Length
64(65:67:68) cm.
25(25½:26¼:26¾) in.

Sleeve Seam
46(46:47:47) cm.
18(18:18½:18½) in.

TENSION

40 sts. and 48 rows = 10 cm. (4 in.) square over patt. on 3mm. needles. If your tension square does not correspond to these measurements see page 156 for adjustment instructions.

ABBREVIATIONS

k. = knit; p. = purl; st(s). = stitch(es); inc. = increas(ing) (see page 156); dec. = decreas-(ing) (see page 157); beg. = begin(ning); rem. = remain(ing); rep. = repeat; alt. = alternate; tog. = together; sl. = slip stitch (transfer one stitch from left needle, knit-wise unless otherwise stated, to right hand needle.); cont. = continue; patt. = pattern; foll. = following; folls. = follows; mm. = millimetres; cm. = centimetres; in. = inch(es); st.st. = stocking stitch; m.1 = make 1 st. by picking up horizontal loop lying before next st. and working into back of it; C6B = cable 6 back: slip next 3 sts. onto cable needle and leave at back of work, k.3, then k.3 from cable needle.

BACK

** Cast on 146(154:164:172) sts. with 2¼mm. needles and work in k.1, p.1 rib for 8 cm. (3¼ in.).
Next row: rib 5(8:14:17), m.1, (rib 3, m.1) 45(46:45:46) times, rib to end. [192(201: 210:219) sts.]
Change to 3mm. needles and work in patt. as folls.:
1st and 3rd rows: p.1, k.1, p.1, * k.6, p.1, k.1, p.1, rep. from * to end.
2nd and 4th rows: k.3, * p.6, k.3, rep. from * to end.
5th row: p.1, k.1, p.1, * C6B, p.1, k.1, p.1, rep. from * to end.
6th row: as 2nd.
7th row: as 1st.
8th row: as 2nd.
These 8 rows form patt.
Work in patt. until back measures 42 cm. (16½ in.), ending with right side facing.

Shape Armholes

Cast off 7(8:9:10) sts. at beg. of next 2 rows. Dec. 1 st. at each end of next and every foll. alt. row until 154(159:160:165) sts. rem. **
Work straight until armholes measure 22(23:25:26) cm. (8½(9:9¾:10¼) in.) ending with right side facing.

Shape Shoulders

Cast off 9 sts. at beg. of next 8 rows, then 9(9:9:10) sts. at beg. of foll. 2 rows. Leave rem. 64(69:70:73) sts. on a spare needle.

FRONT

Work as for back from ** to **.
Work straight until armholes measure 15(16:18:18) cm. (5¾(6¼:7:7) in.), ending with right side facing.

Shape Front Neck

Next row: patt. 59(61:61:63) sts., k.2 tog., turn and leave rem. sts. on a spare needle.

Cont. on these sts. for first side, dec. 1 st. at neck edge on every row until 45(45: 45:46) sts. rem.
Work straight until armhole matches back to shoulder, ending with right side facing.

Shape Shoulder

Cast off 9 sts. at beg. of next and foll. 3 alt. rows. Work 1 row.
Cast off rem. 9(9:9:10) sts.
With right side facing, slip centre 32(33: 34:35) sts. onto a length of yarn, rejoin yarn to neck edge of rem. sts., k.2 tog., patt. to end.
Work to match first side, reversing shapings.

SLEEVES

Cast on 78(82:86:90) sts. with 2¼mm. needles and work in k.1, p.1, rib for 9 cm. (3¼ in.).
Next row: rib 4(3:7:5), m.1, (rib 3(4:3:4), m.1) 23(19:24:20) times, rib to end. [102(102:111:111) sts.]
Change to 3mm. needles and work in patt. as given for back, *shaping sides* by inc. 1 st. at each end of 5th and every foll. 6th row until there are 156(156:165:165) sts. taking inc. sts. into patt.
Work straight until sleeve measures 46(46: 47:47) cm. (18(18:18½:18½) in.), ending with same row of patt. as on back and front.

Shape Top

Cast off 7(8:9:10) sts. at beg. of next 2 rows.
Dec. 1 st. at each end of next and every alt. row until 84(72:69:53) sts. rem.
Work 1 row.
Dec. 1 st. at each end of every row until 40(40:41:41) sts. rem.
Cast off rem. sts.

MAKING UP AND NECK BORDER

Sew up right shoulder seam.
With right side facing, using 2¼mm. needles, k. up 28(28:28:32) sts. down left side of neck, k.32(33:34:35) sts. from front, k. up 28(28:28:32) sts. up right side of neck, k.64(69:70:73) sts. from back. [152(158:160:172) sts.]
Work in k.1, p.1, rib for 7 cm. (2¾ in.).
Using a 3mm. needle, cast off loosely in rib.
Sew up left shoulder and neck border.
Fold neck border in half to wrong side and slip-hem loosely in position.
Sew up side and sleeve seams.
Sew in sleeves.

MAKING UP AND BORDERS

Sew up shoulder seams, matching patt.
Sew in sleeves, placing markers level with beg. of armhole shapings.
Sew up side and sleeve seams.

Borders

These are all worked with 2¾mm. needles.
For lower border, cast on 11 sts. and work in g.st. until this strip is long enough to fit around lower edge of jacket.
Cast off and backstitch in place.
For front border cast on 11 sts. and work 10 rows in g.st. then make buttonhole as folls.:
Next row: k.4, cast off 3, k. to end.
On foll. row cast on 3 sts. over cast off sts.
Cont. in g.st., making 4 more buttonholes each 5 cm. (2 in.) above cast-off edge of previous one.
Now cont. in g.st. until border fits all round entire front and neck edges from lower edge of hem border, stretching it slightly around neck edge, to lower edge of other hem border.
Cast off and sew in place.
Make 2 similar strips each long enough to fit around lower edge of sleeve. Sew them in place, joining ends level with sleeve seams.
For pocket borders cast on 7 sts. and work in g.st. until strip fits along cast-off edge of pocket openings.
Cast off, backstitch strips into place.
Slipstitch pocket lining in place on wrong side and neatly sew across ends of borders on right side. Sew on buttons.

Chunky Aran Cardigan 1956

Quickly-knitted, thick wool Aran cardigan, with single-thickness patterned shawl collar, set-in sleeves, ribbed welts

★★★ Suitable for experienced knitters only

MATERIALS

Yarn
Yarn Store Natural British Wool
8(9:9) × 100g. hanks

Needles
1 pair 4½mm. 6
1 pair 6mm. 9
Cable needle.

Buttons
5

MEASUREMENTS

Bust
82–27(92–97:102–107) cm.
32–34(36–38:40–42) in.

Length
67(68:69) cm.
26¼(26¾:27) in.

Sleeve Seam
46 cm.
18 in.

TENSION

18 sts. and 22 rows = 10 cm. (4 in.) square over st. 2 on 6mm. needles. If your tension square does not correspond to these measurements, see page 156 for adjustment instructions.

ABBREVIATIONS

k. = knit; p. = purl; st(s). = stitch(es); inc. = increas(ing) (see page 156); dec. = decreas(ing) (see page 157); beg. = begin(ning); rem. = remain(ing); rep. = repeat; alt. = alternate; tog. = together; sl. = slip stitch (transfer one stitch from left needle, knitwise unless otherwise stated, to right hand needle.); cont. = continue; patt. = pattern; foll. = following; folls. = follows; mm. = millimetres; cm. = centimetres; in. = inch(es); st.st. = stocking stitch; y.fwd. = yarn forward; y.bk. = yarn back; cross 2 = miss next st., k. into front of second st., k. the missed st.

St. 1 = k.1, p.1 rib, beg. and ending right side rows with k.1, wrong side rows with p.1.
St. 2 = Aran patt.:
1st row: p.1(3:5), (y.bk., sl.1, y.fwd., p.1) 1(3:5) times, cross 2, * (p.1, y.bk., sl.1, y.fwd.) twice, p.1, (cross 2, p.2) 3 times, cross 2, rep. from * to last 10(16:22) sts., (p.1, y.bk, sl.1, y.fwd.,) twice, p.1, cross 2, (p.1, y.bk, sl.1, y.fwd.) 1(3:5) times, p.1(3:5).
2nd row: k.1(3:5), (p.1, k.1) 1(3:5) times, p.2, * (k.1, p.1) twice, k.1, (p.2, k.2) 3 times, p.2, rep. from * to last 10(16:22) sts., (k.1, p.1) twice, k.1, p.2, (k.1, p.1) 1(3:5) times, k.1(3:5).
3rd row: p.1(3:5), (y.bk., sl.1, y.fwd., p.1) 1(3:5) times, cross 2, * (p.1, y.bk., sl.1, y.fwd.) twice, p.1, cross 2, p.1, (k. into front of second st., p. first st., sl. next st. onto spare needle and hold at front of work, p. next st., k.1 from spare needle) twice, p.1, cross 2, rep. from * to last 10(16:22) sts., (p.1, y.bk., sl.1, y.fwd.) twice, p.1, cross 2, (p.1, y.bk., sl.1, y.fwd.) 1(3:5) times, p.1(3:5).
4th row: k.1(3:5), (p.1, k.1) 1(3:5) times, p.2, * (k.1, p.1) twice, k.1, p.2, k.1, p.1, k.2, p.2, k.2, p.1, k.1, p.2, rep. from * to last 10(16:22) sts., (k.1, p.1) twice, k.1, p.2, (k.1, p.1) 1(3:5) times, k.1(3:5).
5th row: p.1(3:5), (y.bk., sl.1, y.fwd., p.1) 1(3:5) times, cross 2, * (p.1, y.bk., sl.1, y.fwd.) twice, p.1, cross 2, p.1, k.2, cross 2, p.2, k.1, p.1, cross 2, rep. from * to last 10(16:22) sts., (p.1, y.bk., sl.1, y.fwd.) twice, p.1, cross 2, (p.1, y.bk., sl.1, y.fwd.) 1(3:5) times, p.1(3:5).
6th row: as 4th row.
7th row: p.1(3:5), (y.bk., sl.1, y.fwd., p.1) 1(3:5) times, cross 2, * (p.1, y.bk., sl.1, y.fwd.) twice, p.1, cross 2, p.1, (sl. next st. onto spare needle and hold at front of work, p. next st., k.1 from spare needle, miss next st., k. second st., p. missed st.) twice, p.1, cross 2, rep. from * to last

10(16:22) sts. (p.1, y.bk., sl.1, y.fwd.) twice, p.1, cross 2, (p.1, y.bk., sl.1, y.fwd.) 1(3:5) times, p.1(3:5).
8th row: as 2nd row.
These 8 rows form patt.

BACK

Cast on 91(103:115) sts. with 4½mm. needles.
Work in st. 1 for 6 cm. (2¼ in.), ending with a wrong side row.
Change to 6mm. needles and st. 2.
Cont. until back measures 46 cm. (18 in.).

Shape Armholes

Cast off 3(5:7) sts. at beg. of next 2 rows.
Dec. 1 st. at each end of next 3 rows, then on every alt. row until 73(77:81) sts. rem.
Work straight until armholes measure 19(20:21) cm. (7½(7¾:8¼) in.), measured on the straight.

Shape Shoulders

Cast off 6 sts. at beg. of next 6 rows and 6(7:8) sts. at beg. of foll. 2 rows.
Cast off rem. 25(27:29) sts. for neck.

LEFT FRONT

Cast on 49(55:61) sts. with 4½mm. needles.
Work in st. 1 for 6 cm. (2¼ in.), ending with a wrong side row, and inc. 1 st. at end of last row. [50(56:62) sts.]
Change to 6mm. needles and st. 2 as folls.:
1st row: p.1(3:5), (y.bk., sl.1, y.fwd., p.1) 1(3:5) times, cross 2, * (p.1, y.bk., sl.1, y.fwd.) twice, p.1, (cross 2, p.2) 3 times, cross 2, rep. from * to last 7 sts., (y.fwd., p.1, y.bk., sl.1) 3 times, p.1.
2nd row: (k.1, p.1) 3 times, k.1, * (p.2, k.2) 3 times, p.2, (k.1, p.1) twice, k.1, rep. from * to last 5(11:17) sts., p.2, (k.1, p.1) 1(3:5) times, k.1(3:5).
Keeping patt. in this order, work until front measures same as back to armholes, ending at side edge with same patt. row.

Shape Armhole and Neck

1st row: cast off 3(5:7) sts., work to last 2 sts., work 2 tog.
2nd row: work to end.
3rd row: k.2 tog., work to end.
4th row: p.2 tog., work to last 2 sts., p.2 tog.
5th row: as 3rd row.
6th row: work to end.
Dec. 1 st. at armhole edge on next and alt. rows 3(5:7) times in all, *at same time* dec. 1 st. at neck edge on next and every foll. 3rd row. [37(38:38) sts.]
Cont. to dec. at neck edge only on every 3rd row until 25(26:27) sts. rem.
Work 0(1:0) rows, ending at armhole edge.

Shape Shoulder

Still dec. at neck edge once more, cast off at armhole edge on next and alt. rows, 6 sts. 3 times.
Work 1 row.
Cast off rem. 6(7:8) sts.

RIGHT FRONT

Mark positions for 5 buttons on left front, first to be 1 cm. (½ in.) above lower edge and 5th 1 cm. (½ in.) below first neck dec.
Follow instructions for left front, reversing front border, patt. and shapings, and working buttonholes to match markers as folls.: from centre front edge work 2, cast off 3, work to end.
In next row cast on 3 sts. above cast off sts.

SLEEVES

Cast on 41(43:45) sts. with 4½mm. needles.
Work in st. 1 for 6 cm. (2¼ in.), ending with a right side row.
Next row: p.2(3:4), * p. twice into next st., p.4, rep. from * to last 4(5:6) sts., p. twice into next st., p.3(4:5). [49(51:53) sts.]
Change to 6mm. needles and st. 2.

1st row: p.1(2:3), cross 2 * (p.1, y.bk., sl.1, y.fwd.) twice, p.1, (cross 2, p.2) 3 times, cross 2, rep. from * to last 8(9:10) sts., (p.1, y.bk., sl.1, y.fwd.) twice, p.1, cross 2, p.1(2:3).
Work 9(7:5) rows in this way.
Working all inc. sts. into patt., inc. 1 st. at each end of next and every foll. 10th(7th:6th) row until there are 65(73:81) sts.
Work straight until sleeve measures 46 cm. (18 in.).

Shape Top

Cast off 3(5:7) sts. at beg. of next 2 rows.
Dec. 1 st. at each end of next 3 rows, then on every alt. row until 35 sts. rem.
Dec. 1 st. at each end of next 5 rows.
Cast off 3 sts. at beg. of next 4 rows.
Cast off.

COLLAR

Cast on 129(131:133) sts. with 4½mm. needles.
P.1 row, k.1 row, p.1 row.
Change to 6mm. needles and st. 2.
1st row: p.1(2:3), y.bk., sl.1, y.fwd., p.1, cross 2, rep. from * of first row of patt. to last 10(11:12) sts., (p.1, y.bk., sl.1, y.fwd.) twice, p.1, cross 2, p.1, y.bk., sl.1, y.fwd., p.1(2:3)
Keeping patt. in this order, work 2 rows.
Dec. 1 st. at each end of next 38 rows.
Cast off.

MAKING UP

Sew up shoulder seams.
Set in sleeves.
Sew up side and sleeve seams.
Turn under first 3 rows at edge of collar and slipstitch neatly down.
Pin collar to neck, taking care to balance patt. at each side. Sew with a flat edge-to-edge seam.
Press. Sew on buttons.

Cotton Tennis Sweater

1949

Stocking stitch, V-neck sweater with front and back double cable panels, ribbed welts, and two contrast-coloured stripes in neck welt

★ Suitable for beginners

MATERIALS

Yarn
Phildar Perle 5
10(10:11:11:12) × 40g. balls Col. A
1(1:1:1:1) × 40g. ball Col. B
1(1:1:1:1) × 40g. ball Col. C

Needles
1 pair 2mm.
1 pair 2¾mm.
1 cable needle

MEASUREMENTS

Bust
92(97:102:107:112) cm.
36(38:40:42:44) in.

Length
66(67:68:69:70) cm.
26(26¼:26¾:27:27½) in.

Sleeve
56 cm.
22 in.

TENSION

30 sts. and 40 rows = 10 cm. (4 in.) square over st.st. on 2¾mm. needles. If your tension square does not correspond to these measurements, see page 156 for adjustment instructions.

ABBREVIATIONS

k. = knit; p. = purl; st(s). = stitch(es); inc. = increas(ing) (see page 156); dec. = decreas-(ing) (see page 157); beg. = begin(ning); rem. = remain(ing); rep. = repeat; alt. = alternate; tog. = together; sl. = slip stitch (transfer one stitch from left needle, knit-wise unless otherwise stated, to right hand needle.); cont. = continue; patt. = pattern; foll. = following; folls. = follows; mm. = millimetres; cm. = centimetres; in. = inch(es); st.st. = stocking stitch; C6F = cable 6 forward: slip next 3 sts. onto cable needle, leave at front of work, k.3, k.3 sts. from cable needle; C6B = cable 6 back: slip next 3 sts. onto cable needle, leave at back of work, k.3, k.3 sts. from cable needle; t.b.l. = through back of loop.

BACK

Cast on 146(154:162:170:178) sts. with 2mm. needles and A, using thumb method.
1st row (wrong side): p.2, * k.2, p.2, rep. from * to end.
Work 8 cm. (3 in.) in k.2, p.2, rib, ending with a right side row.
Inc. row (wrong side): rib 31(34:37:40:43), (inc. 1 in next st., rib 2) 4 times, rib 60(62:64:66:68), (inc. 1, rib 2) 4 times, rib 31(34:37:40:43). [154(162:170:178:186) sts.]
Change to 2¾mm. needles and patt.
1st row: k.31(34:37:40:43), p.2, k.12, p.2, k.60(62:64:66:68), p.2, k.12, p.2, k.31(34:37:40:43).
2nd row: p.31(34:37:40:43), k.2, p.12, k.2, p.60(62:64:66:68), k.2, p.12, k.2, p.31(34:37:40:43).
3rd row: k.31(34:37:40:43), p.2, C6B, C6F, p.2, k.60(62:64:66:68), p.2, C6B, C6F, p.2, k.31(34:37:40:43) sts.
4th row: as 2nd row.
5th row: as 1st row.
6th row: as 2nd row.
These 6 rows form patt.
Cont. in patt. until work measures 44 cm. (17¼ in.).

Shape Armhole
Cast off 8(9:10:11:12) sts. at beg. of next 2 rows.
Dec. 1 st. at each end of every alt. row until 122(126:130:134:138) sts. rem.
Work straight until armhole measures 20(21:22:23:24) cm. (7¾(8¼:8½:9:9½) in.) on the straight.

Shape Shoulders
Cast off 8(8:9:9:9) sts. at beg. of next 4(2:4:6:4) rows.
Cast off 9(9:9:10:10) sts. at beg. of next 4(6:4:2:4) rows.
Work neckband on rem. 54(56:58:60:62) sts.
Change to 2mm. needles and k.2, p.2 rib.
1st row: k.2(3:2:3:2), * p.2, k.2, rep. from *, ending last rep. k.2(3:2:3:2).
Work 2 more rows in A. Break A.
With B, p.1 row.
Work 2 rows in rib. Break B.
With A, k.1 row.
Work 3 rows in rib. Break A.
With C, k.1 row.
Work 2 rows in rib. Break C.
With A, p.1 row.
Cont. in rib until neckband measures 4 cm. (1½ in.).
Cast off in rib.

FRONT

Cast on 146(154:162:170:178) sts. with 2mm. needles and A.
Work 8 cm. (3¼ in.) in k.2, p.2, rib as for back.
Inc. row: rib 58(62:66:70:74), (inc. 1 in next st., rib 2) 4 times, rib 6,(inc. 1, rib 2) 4 times, rib 58(62:66:70:74). [154(162:170:178:186) sts.].
Change to 2¾mm. needles and patt.
1st row: k.58(62:66:70:74), p.2, k.12, p.2, k.6, p.2, k.12, p.2, k.58(62:66:70:74).
2nd row: p.58(62:66:70:74), k.2, p.12, k.2, p.6, k.2, p.12, k.2, p.58(62:66:70:74).
3rd row: k.58(62:66:70:74), p.2, C6B, C6F, p.2, k.6, p.2, C6B, C6F, p.2, k.58(62:66:70:74).
4th row: as 2nd row.
5th row: as 1st row.
6th row: as 2nd row.
These 6 rows form patt.
Cont. in patt. until work measures 44 cm. (17¼ in.).

Shape Armhole
Cast off 8(9:10:11:12) sts. at beg. of next 2 rows.
Dec. 1 st. at each end of every alt. row until 122(126:130:134:138) sts. rem.
P.1 row.

Shape Neck
1st row: k.40(42:44:46:48), sl.1, k.1, p.s.s.o., patt. 16 sts., k.3, turn and leave

rem. 61(63:65:67:69) sts. on a spare needle.

2nd row: p.3, k.2, p.12, k.2, p. to end.

3rd row: k.39(41:43:45:47), sl.1, k.1, p.s.s.o., patt. 16 sts., k.3.

4th row: as 2nd row.

Rep. 3rd and 4th rows, dec. 1 st. every alt. row as set, at edge of cable panel, until a total of 34(35:36:37:38) sts. rem.

Cont. without further shaping until armhole measures the same as back to shoulder, ending at armhole edge.

Shape Shoulder

Cast off 8(8:9:9:9) sts. at beg. of next and foll. alt. rows 2(1:2:3:2) times.

Cast off 9(9:9:10:10) sts. at beg. of alt. rows 2(3:2:1:2) times.

Rejoin yarn at centre front to rem. 61(63:65:67:69) sts.

Next row: k.3, patt. 16 sts., k.2 tog., k. to end.

Next row: p.41(43:45:47:49), k.2, p.12, k.2, p.3.

Complete to match other side of neck, reversing shaping.

SLEEVES

Cast on 70(74:78:82:86) sts. with 2mm. needles and A.

1st row (wrong side): p.2 * k.2, p.2, rep. from * to end.

Work 10 cm. (4 in.) in k.2, p.2, rib, ending with a wrong side row.

Change to 2¾mm. needles and beg. with a k. row, cont. in st.st.

Inc. 1 st. at each end of 5th and every foll. 8th row until there are 114(118:122:126:130) sts.

Work straight until sleeve measures 56 cm. (22 in.).

Shape Top

Cast off 8(9:10:11:12) sts. at beg. of next 2 rows.

Dec. 1 st. at each end of every row until 78(80:82:84:86) sts. rem.

Dec. 1 st. at each end of every alt. row until 38(38:38:40:40) sts. rem.

Cast off 3 sts. at beg. of next 6 rows.

Cast off rem. 20(20:20:22:22) sts.

NECKBAND

With 2mm. needles and A, with right side of work facing, pick up 68(70:72:74:76) sts. down left side of neck to centre, pick up 68(70:72:74:76) sts. up right side of neck. [136(140:144:148:152) sts.]

1st row (wrong side): k.0(2:0:2:0), (p.2, k.2) 16(16:17:17:18) times, (p.2, k.1) twice, (p.2, k.2) 16(16:17:17:18) times, p.2, k.0(2:0:2:0).

2nd row: rib 65(67:69:71:73), p.2 tog. t.b.l., k.2, p.2 tog., rib 65(67:69:71:73).

3rd row: break A. With B, p. to end. Cont. in stripes as for back neckband and dec. 1 st. on each side of centre 2 sts. on next and every foll. alt. row as set in 2nd row.

Work until front neckband matches back neckband. Cast off in rib.

MAKING UP

Sew up shoulder and neckband seams.
Sew up side and sleeve seams.
Sew sleeve top into armhole.
Press on wrong side.

Diamond-patterned, Aran Cardigan 1981

Waist-length, round-neck cardigan in reversed stocking stitch, with diamond and cable pattern on fronts and back, and ribbed welts

★★★ Suitable for experienced knitters

MATERIALS

Yarn
Pingouin Comfortable Sport
14(15:16) × 50g. balls

Needles
1 pair 3¾mm.
1 pair 4½mm.
Cable needle

Buttons
7

MEASUREMENTS

Bust
87(92:97) cm.
34(36:38) in.

Length
51(54:57) cm.
20(21¼:22¼) in.

Sleeve Seam
42 cm.
16½ in.

TENSION

14 sts. and 18 rows = 7 cm. (2¾ in.) square over st.st. on 4½mm. needles. If your tension square does not correspond to these measurements, see page 156 for adjustment instructions.

ABBREVIATIONS

k. = knit; p. = purl; st(s). = stitch(es); inc. = increas(ing) (see page 156); dec. = decreas(ing) (see page 157); beg. = begin(ning); rem. = remain(ing); rep. = repeat; alt. = alternate; tog. = together; sl. = slip stitch (transfer one stitch from left needle, knitwise unless otherwise stated, to right hand needle.); cont. = continue; patt. = pattern; foll. = following; folls. = follows; mm. = millimetres; cm. = centimetres; in. = inch(es); st.st. = stocking stitch; Cb3 = sl. next st. onto cable needle and hold at back of work, k.2, then k.1 from cable needle; Cf3 = sl. next 2 sts. onto cable needle and hold at front of work, k.1, then k.2 from cable needle; Bc3 = sl. next st. onto cable needle and hold at back of work, k.2, then p.1 from cable needle; Fc3 = sl. next 2 sts. onto cable needle and hold at front of work, p.1, then k.2 from cable needle; Cb4 = sl. next 2 sts. onto cable needle and hold at front of work, k.2, then k.2 from cable needle; y.o.n. = yarn over needle.

BACK

Cast on 100(104:108) sts. with 3¾mm. needles.

Work 20 rows in k.1, p.1 rib.

Change to 4½mm. needles and work in patt. as folls.:

1st row (wrong side): k.24(26:28), p.4, k.44, p.4, k.24(26:28).

2nd row: p.23(25:27), Cb3, Cf3, p.42, Cb3, Cf3, p.23(25:27).

3rd row: k. the k. sts. and p. the p. sts. as they face you.

4th row: p.22(24:26), Cb3, k.2, Cf3, p.40, Cb3, k.2, Cf3, p.22(24:26).

5th and alt. rows: as 3rd row.

6th row: p.21(23:25), Bc3, Cb4, Fc3, p.38, Bc3, Cb4, Fc3, p.21(23:25).

8th row: p.20(22:24), Bc3, p.1, k.4, p.1, Fc3, p.36, Bc3, p.1, k.4, p.1, Fc3, p.20(22:24).

10th row: p.19(21:23), Bc3, p.2, Cb4, p.2, Fc3, p.34, Bc3, p.2, Cb4, p.2, Fc3, p.19(21:23).

12th row: p.18(20:22), Bc3, p.3, k.4, p.3, Fc3, p.32, Bc3, p.3, k.4, p.3, Fc3, p.18(20:22).

14th row: p.18(20:22), k.2, p.4, Cb4, p.4, k.2, p.32, k.2, p.4, Cb4, p.4, k.2, p.18(20:22).

16th row: p.18(20:22), Fc3, p.3, k.4, p.3, Bc3, p.32, Fc3, p.3, k.4, p.3, Bc3, p.18(20:22).

18th row: p.19(21:23), Fc3, p.2, Cb4, p.2, Bc3, p.34, Fc3, p.2, Cb4, p.2, Bc3, p.19(21:23).

20th row: p.20(22:24), Fc3, p.1, k.4, p.1, Bc3, p.36, Fc3, p.1, k.4, p.1, Bc3, p.20(22:24).

22nd row: p.21(23:25), Fc3, Cb4, Bc3, p.38, Fc3, Cb4, Bc3, p.21(23:25).

24th row: p.22(24:26), Fc3, k.2, Bc3, p.40, Fc3, k.2, Bc3, p.22(24:26).

26th row: p.23(25:27), Fc3, Bc3, p.42, Fc3, Bc3, p.23(25:27).

28th row: p.24(26:28), sl. next 2 sts. onto cable needle and hold at front of work. k.2, then k.2 from cable needle, p.44, sl. next 2 sts. onto cable needle and hold at front of work, k.2, then k.2 from cable needle, p.24(26:28).

These 28 rows form patt.

When 8th(12th:16th) row of 3rd patt. rep. has been worked, shape armholes.

Shape Armholes

Cast off 5 sts. at beg. of next 2 rows, 2 sts. at beg. of foll. 2 rows, then dec. 1 st. at each end of the next 3 alt. rows. [80(84: 88) sts.

Cont. straight in patt. until 22nd(2nd: 10th) rows of 4th(5th:5th) patt. rep. have been completed.

Shape Neck

Work 25(27:29), k.2 tog., turn.

Work on these sts. only.

Dec. 1 st. at neck edge on every row until 22(24:26) sts. rem.

Cast off.

Sl. centre 26 sts. onto a st. holder to be worked later as neckband.

Rejoin yarn and complete other side of neck, reversing shapings.

RIGHT FRONT

Cast on 58(60:62) sts. with 3¾mm. needles and work in k.1, p.1 rib for 7 rows.

Buttonhole row: rib 5, cast off next st., rib to end.

Next row: rib to last 5 sts., y.o.n., rib to end.

When 20 rib rows have been completed, change to 4½mm. needles, sl. the 10 sts. of inside edge onto a safety pin to be worked later as front band, and work the foll. patt. over rem. 48(50:52) sts.

1st row (wrong side): k.24(26:28) sts., p.4, k.20.

2nd row: p.19, Cb3, Cf3, p.23(25:27).

3rd and alt. rows: k. the k. sts. and p. the p. sts. as they face you.

4th row: p.18, Cb3, k.2, Cf3, p.22(24:26).

6th row: p.17, Bc3, Cb4, Fc3, p.21(23:25).

8th row: p.16, Bc3, p.1, k.4, p.1, Fc3, p.20(22:24).

10th row: p.15, Bc3, p.2, Cb4, p.2, Fc3, p.19(21:23).

12th row: p.14, Bc3, p.3, k.4, p.3, Fc3, p.18(20:22).

14th row: p.14, k.2, p.4, Cb4, p.4, k.2, p.18(20:22).

16th row: p.14, Fc3, p.3, k.4, p.3, Bc3, p.18(20:22).

18th row: p.15, Fc3, p.2, Cb4, p.2, Bc3, p.19(21:23).

20th row: p.16, Fc3, p.1, k.4, p.1, Bc3, p.20(22:24).

22nd row: p.17, Fc3, Cb4, Bc3, p.21(23:25).

24th row: p.18, Fc3, k.2, Bc3, p.22(24:26).

26th row: p.19, Fc3, Bc3, p.23(25:27).

28th row: p.20, sl. next 2 sts. onto cable needle and hold at front of work, k.2, then k.2 from cable needle, p.24(26:28).

These 28 rows form patt.

When 8th (12th:16th) rows of 3rd patt. rep. have been completed, shape armhole.

Shape Armhole

On outside edge, cast off 5 sts., then 2 sts. on foll. alt. row.

Now dec. 1 st. at same edge on next 2 alt. rows. [39(41:43) sts.

When 5th(13th:21st) rows of 4th patt. rep. have been completed, shape neck.

Shape Neck

At inside edge, cast off 6 sts. on next row, then 3 sts. on foll. alt. row.

Now dec. 1 st. at same edge on every alt. row until 22(24:26) sts. rem.

Complete patt. to match back, then cast off.

LEFT FRONT

Work as for right front, reversing all shapings, and omitting buttonholes.

SLEEVES

Cast on 50(54:58) sts. with 3¾mm. needles and work in k.1, p.1 rib for 14 rows, working 4 incs. evenly along last rib row. [54(58:62) sts.

Change to 4½mm. needles and work a diamond patt. in centre of row as set for back, e.g.

1st row (wrong side): k.25(27:29), p.4, k.25(27:29) etc.

Cont. to work in patt., inc. 1 st. at each end of every foll. 8th row until there are 76(80:84) sts.

Work straight until sleeve measures 42 cm. (16½ in.) from beg.

Shape Top

Cast off 5 sts. at beg. of next 2 rows, then dec. 1 st. at each end of every alt. row until 24 sts. rem.

Cast off 4 sts. at beg. of next 2 rows.

Cast off rem. sts.

FRONT BANDS

Return to band of left front and work in k.1, p.1 rib until length reaches beg. of neck shaping.

Sl. sts. onto a safety pin.

Work band for right front, and cont. to work six buttonholes as set, spaced 14 rows apart.

Do not cast off.

Sew up shoulder seams.

NECKBAND

With 3¾mm. needles and right side facing, work across 10 sts. of right front band, pick up and k. 32 sts. up right front neck, 40 sts. at back neck and 32 sts. down left front neck, then work 10 sts. of left front band. [124 sts.

Work in k.1, p.1 rib for 7 rows, working the 7th buttonhole as set on 4th and 5th rows.

Cast off ribwise.

MAKING UP

Set in sleeves.

Sew up sleeve and side seams.

Stitch on front bands.

Sew on buttons.

Fine-knit Classic Sweater

Loose, hip-length, round-neck, unisex sweater in stocking stitch, with ribbed hem, cuffs and doubled-over neckband

★ Suitable for beginners

MATERIALS

Yarn
Sirdar Country Style 4 ply
6(7:8:8:9:10:10) × 50g. balls

Needles
1 pair 2¾mm.
1 pair 3¼mm.
2 stitch holders

MEASUREMENTS

Bust/Chest
82(87:92:97:102:107:112) cm.
32(34:36:38:40:42:44) in.

Length
54(55:56:60:61:62:64) cm.
21¼(21½:22:23½:24:24¼:25) in.

Sleeve Seam
42(43:45:46:47:49:49) cm.
16½(16¾:17¾:18:18½:19¼:19¼) in.

TENSION

14 sts. and 18 rows = 5 cm. (2 in.) square over patt. on 3¼mm. needles. If your tension square does not correspond to these measurements, see page 156 for adjustment instructions.

ABBREVIATIONS

k. = knit; p. = purl; st(s). = stitch(es); inc. = increas(ing) (see page 156); dec. = decreas-(ing) (see page 157); beg. = begin(ning); rem. = remain(ing); rep. = repeat; alt. = alternate; tog. = together; sl. = slip stitch (transfer one stitch from left needle, knit-wise unless otherwise stated, to right hand needle.); cont. = continue; patt. = pattern; foll. = following; folls. = follows; mm. = millimetres; cm. = centimetres; in. = inch(es); st.st. = stocking stitch; m.1 = make 1 st.: pick up horizontal loop lying before next st. and k. or p. into back of it.

BACK

Cast on 113(121:127:135:141:149:155) sts. with 2¾mm. needles.
Work in k.1, p.1 rib for 8 cm. (3¼ in), inc. on last row as folls.:
Rib 6(10:14:8:11:10:13), m.1, (rib 10(10:10: 12:12:13:13), m.1) 10 times, rib 7(11:13:7: 10:9:12). [124(132:138:146:152:160:166) sts.]
Change to 3¼mm. needles and, starting with a k. row, work in st.st.

Cont. straight until work measures 36(36:36:37:37:37:37) cm. (14(14:14:14½: 14½:14½:14½) in.) from beg.

Shape Armholes
Cast off 6(7:8:8:8:9:9) sts. at beg. of next 2 rows.
Dec. 1 st. at both ends of the next 3 rows.
Dec. 1 st. at both ends of the foll. 8(9:9:7:8: 9:10)alt. rows. [90(94:98:110:114:118:122) sts.]
Work straight until armhole measures 18(19:21:23:24:26:27) cm. (7(7½:8¼:9:9½: 10¼:10½) in.)

Shape Shoulders
Cast off 5(5:5:7:7:7:7) sts. at beg. of next 8 rows, and 5(6:7:4:5:6:7) sts. at beg. of next 2 rows.
Leave rem. 40(42:44:46:48:50:52) sts. on a holder.

FRONT

Work as given for back until armhole measures 13(14:15:18:19:21:22) cm. (5(5½: 5¾:7:7½:8¼:8½) in.)

Shape Neck
K.33(34:35:40:41:42:43) sts., turn, leave rem. sts. on a spare needle.
* Dec. 1 st. at neck edge on the next and foll. 7 alt. rows. [25(26:27:32:33:34:35) sts.]
Work straight until length matches back to shoulder, ending at side edge.

Shape Shoulder
Cast off 5(5:5:7:7:7:7) sts. at beg. of next and foll. 3 alt. rows.
Work 1 row.
Cast off 5(6:7:4:5:6:7) sts.
Return to rem. sts., right side facing.
Sl. the next 24(26:28:30:32:34:36) sts. onto a holder, rejoin yarn to next st. and k. to end of row.
Complete to match first side from * to end.

SLEEVES

Cast on 51(55:59:63:67:71:75) sts. with 2¾mm. needles.
Work in k.1, p.1 rib for 8 cm. (3 in.), inc. 1 st. on the last row. [52(56:60:64:68:72: 76) sts.]
Change to 3¼mm. needles and, starting with a k. row, work in st.st.
Inc. 1 st. at both ends of the next and every foll. 6th row until there are 92(96:100:106:110:114:118) sts.
Work straight until sleeve measures 42(43:45:46:47:49:49) cm. (16½(16¾:17¼: 18:18½:19¼:19¼) in.)

Shape Top
Cast off 6(7:8:8:8:9:9) sts. at beg. of next 2 rows.
Dec. 1 st. at both sides of the next 3 rows.
Dec. 1 st. at both ends of every foll. alt. row until there are 42(42:42:42:44:44:46) sts. Work 1 row.
Cast off 4 sts. at beg. of next 8 rows.
Cast off rem. 10(10:10:10:12:12:14) sts.

NECKBAND

Sew up left shoulder seam.
With 2¾mm. needles, and right side facing, pick up and k.40(42:44:46:48:50:52) sts. from back neck, 24 sts. from left side front neck, 24(26:28:30:32:34:36) sts. from centre front neck, and 24 sts. from right side front neck. [112(116:120:124: 128:132:136) sts.]
Work in k.1, p.1 rib for 5 cm. (2 in.).
Cast off fairly loosely in rib.

MAKING UP

Press work on the wrong side under a damp cloth, omitting ribbing.
Sew up right shoulder and neckband.
Fold neckband onto wrong side and sew down.
Set in sleeves, matching centre of sleeve head to shoulder seam.
Sew up side and sleeve seams.

V-neck Golfing Cardigan

Stocking-stitch cardigan with knitted horizontal check line, crochet vertical line, hemmed cuffs and lower edge and set-in sleeves

★★ Suitable for knitters with some previous experience

MATERIALS

Yarn
Patons Clansman DK
9(10:11) × 50g. balls Main Col. A
2(2:2) × 50g. balls Contrast Col. B

Needles
1 pair 3¼mm.
1 pair 3¾mm.
1 3mm. crochet hook

Buttons
6 leather

MEASUREMENTS

Bust
87(92:97) cm.
34(36:38) in.

Length
54(58:64) cm.
21¼(22¾:25) in.

Sleeve Seam
42 cm.
16½ in.

TENSION

24 sts. and 34 rows = 10 cm. (4 in.) square over patt. on 3¾mm. needles. If your tension square does not correspond to these measurements see page 156 for adjustment instructions.

ABBREVIATIONS

k. = knit; p. = purl; st(s). = stitch(es); inc. = increas(ing) (see page 156); dec. = decreas-(ing) (see page 157); beg. = begin(ning); rem. = remain(ing); rep. = repeat; rep(s). = repeat(s); alt. = alternate; tog. = together; sl. = slip stitch (transfer one stitch from left needle, knitwise unless otherwise stated, to right hand needle.); cont. = continue; patt. = pattern; foll. = following; folls. = follows; mm. = millimetres; cm. = centimetres; in. = inch(es); st.st. = stocking stitch.

BACK

Cast on 112(123:134) sts. with 3¼mm. needles and A.
Starting with a k. row, work 7 rows in st.st.

Next row: k. into back of each st. to end to form hemline ridge.
Change to 3¾mm. needles and work in patt., joining in and breaking off colours as required. **
1st row (right side): k.6, * p.1, k.10, rep. from * to last 7 sts., p.1, k.6.
2nd row: p.6, * k.1, p.10, rep. from * to last 7 sts., k.1, p.6.
3rd to 12th row: as 1st and 2nd row, 5 times.
13th row: in B, as 1st.

14th row: in A, as 2nd.
These 14 rows form patt.
Work a further 7(8:9) patt. reps. ***

Shape Armholes
Keeping patt. correct, cast off 7 sts. at beg. of next 2 rows, then 4 sts. at beg. of foll. 2 rows.
Now dec. 1 st. at each end of next and every alt. row until 84(95:106) sts. rem.
Cont. in patt. until armhole measures 18(19:20) cm. (7(7½:7¾) in.), ending with a wrong side row.

Shape Neck
Next row: patt. 29(33:37), turn and leave rem. sts. on spare needle.
Dec. 1 st. at neck edge on every row until 25(29:33) sts. rem.
Work straight until armhole measures 20(21:22) cm. (7¾(8¼:8½) in.), ending with a wrong side row.
Cast off.
With right side facing, rejoin appropriate yarn to rem. sts.
Cast off centre 26(29:32) sts., work to end.
Work to match first side, reversing shapings.

RIGHT FRONT

Cast on 57(62:68) sts. with 3¼mm. needles and A, and work as back to ***, noting that patt. on 2nd size will read:
1st row: * p.1, k.10, rep. from * to last 7 sts., p.1, k.6.
2nd row: p.6, * k.1, p.10, rep. from * to last st., k.1.

Shape Armhole and Neck
Work as folls., keeping patt. correct throughout:
Next row: k.2 tog., patt. to end.
Cast off 7 sts. at beg. of next row.
Work 1 row.
Next row: cast off 4 sts., work to last 2 sts., dec. 1 st.
Now dec. 1 st. at armhole edge on next and foll. 2 alt. rows, at the same time dec. 1 st. at front edge on every foll. 3rd row from previous dec. until 40(45:51) sts. rem.
Now dec. 1 st. on every 3rd row at front edge only until 25(29:33) sts. rem.
Work straight until front matches back at armhole edge, ending with a wrong side row.
Cast off.

LEFT FRONT

Work as for right front, reversing shapings and reversing patt. for 2nd size.

SLEEVES

Cast on 57(68:79) sts. with 3¼mm. needles and A and work as for back to **. Now work in patt. as on back, shaping sides by inc. 1 st. at each end of 7th and every foll. 9th row until there are 81(92:103) sts., taking inc. sts. into patt. Work straight until 10 patt. reps. in all have been completed.

Shape Armholes

Cast off 7 sts. at beg. of next 2 rows, then dec. 1 st. at each end of next and every alt. row until 23(24:25) sts. rem.
Work 1 row.
Cast off 4 sts. at beg. of next 2 rows.
Cast off rem. sts.

FRONT BAND

Cast on 14 sts. with 3¼mm. needles and A and work 8 rows in k.1, p.1 rib.
1st buttonhole row: rib 6, cast off 2 sts., rib to end.
2nd buttonhole row: rib, casting on 2 sts. over those cast off on previous row.
Work 16 rows in k.1, p.1 rib.
Work a further buttonhole as before.
Cont. thus until 6(7:8) buttonholes in all have been worked.
Now work in rib until band fits from ridge up right front, round back of neck and down left front to ridge, when very slightly stretched.
Cast off in rib.

MAKING UP

Omitting ribbing, press lightly on wrong side following instructions on the ball band.
With 3mm. crochet hook and B, work a chain up each p. row on right side to complete the black squares.
Sew up shoulder seams.
Insert sleeves.
Sew up side and sleeve seams, matching patt.
Fold hem at ridge to wrong side and sl.-hem loosely in position.
Sew on front band.
Press seams.
Sew on buttons.

Luxurious Fair Isle Cardigan

Round-neck silky cardigan, with seven-colour Fair Isle pattern on yoke and cuffs, and ribbed welts

★★ Suitable for knitters with some previous experience

MATERIALS

Yarn
Maxwell Cartlidge Pure Silk
7(7:7:7:7:7) × 50g. balls (Main Col A)
1(1:1:1:1:1) × 50g. ball each of Contrast
Cols. B, C, D, E, F, G, H.

Needles
1 pair 3mm.
1 pair 3¼mm.
1 pair 3½mm.

Buttons
6

MEASUREMENTS

Bust
82(87:92:97:102:107) cm.
32(34:36:38:40:42) in.

Length
55(55:57:57:58:60) cm.
21½(21½:22¼:22¼:22¾:23½) in.

Sleeve Seam
44 cm.
17¼ in.

TENSION

30 sts. and 36 rows = 10 cm. (4 in.) square over st.st. on 3¼mm. needles. If your tension square does not correspond to these measurements, see page 156 for adjustment instructions.

ABBREVIATIONS

k. = knit; p. = purl; st(s). = stitch(es); inc. = increas(ing) (see page 156); dec. = decreas-(ing) (see page 157); beg. = begin(ning); rem. = remain(ing); rep. = repeat; alt. = alternate; tog. = together; sl. = slip stitch (transfer one stitch from left needle, knit-wise unless otherwise stated, to right hand needle.); cont. = continue; patt. = pattern; foll. = following; folls. = follows; mm. = millimetres; cm. = centimetres; in. = inch(es); st.st. = stocking stitch.

BACK

Cast on 129(137:143:151:159:167) sts. with 3mm. needles and A.
1st row: k.1, * p.1, k.1, rep. from * to end.
2nd row: p.1, * k.1, p.1, rep. from * to end.
Rep. these 2 rows for 6 cm. (2¼ in.).
Change to 3¼mm. needles and st.st.
Work until back measures 36(36:37:37:38:38) cm. (14(14:14½:14½:15:15) in.)

Shape Armholes
Cast off 8 sts. at beg. of next 2 rows.
Dec. 1 st. at each end of every row 9(13:14:18:22:22) times. [95(95:99:99:99:107) sts.]
Cont. in st.st. until armhole measures 19(19:20:20:20:21) cm. (7½(7½:7¾:7¾:7¾:8¼) in.)

Shape Shoulders
Cast off 10(10:10:10:10:13) sts. at beg. of next 4(4:2:2:2:2) rows.
Cast off 11 sts. at beg. of next 2(2:4:4:4:4) rows.
Leave rem. 33(33:35:35:35:37) sts. on spare needle or st. holder for neckband.

RIGHT FRONT

Cast on 59(63:67:71:75:79) sts. with 3mm. needles and A.
Work in rib as for back for 6 cm. (2¼ in.).
Change to 3¼mm. needles and work in st.st. until front measures same as back to armhole shaping, ending at armhole edge.

Shape Armhole
Next row: cast off 8 sts., p. to end.
Dec. 1 st. at armhole edge on every row 9(13:

13:17:21:25) times. [42(42:44:44:44:48) sts.]
1st and 2nd sizes only: p.1 row.
Change to 3½mm. needles.
All sizes now have right side facing.
Work 27 rows from chart, working the 12 st. rep. 3(3:3:3:3:4) times across row and odd sts. as marked on chart.
Change to 3¼mm. needles.
Cont. in st.st. until armhole measures 11(11:13:13:13:14) cm. (4¼(4¼:5:5:5:5½) in.), ending at neck edge.

Shape Neck
Next row: cast off 2(2:1:1:1:3) sts., k. to end.
Dec. 1 st. at neck edge on every row 10(10:11:11:11:11) times.
Cont. without shaping until armhole measures same as back to shoulder shaping, ending at armhole edge.

Shape Shoulder
1st row: cast off 10(10:10:10:10:11) sts., p. to end.
2nd row: k.
3rd row: cast off 10(10:11:11:11:11) sts., p. to end.
4th row: k.
Cast off rem. sts.

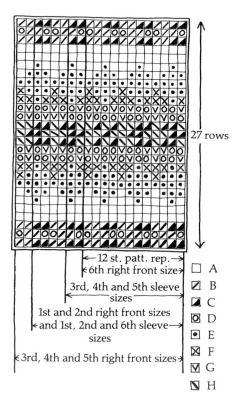

27 rows

← 12 st. patt. rep. →
← 6th right front size →
← 3rd, 4th and 5th sleeve sizes →
← 1st and 2nd right front sizes and 1st, 2nd and 6th sleeve sizes →
← 3rd, 4th and 5th right front sizes →

☐ A
◩ B
◪ C
⊡ D
⊡ E
⊠ F
☑ G
◪ H

LEFT FRONT

Work as for right front, reversing shapings.

SLEEVES

Cast on 64(64:68:68:68:70) sts. with 3mm. needles and A.
Work in rib as for back for 5 cm. (2 in.), increasing 14(14:18:18:18:20) sts. evenly across last row. [78(78:86:86:86:90) sts.]
Change to 3¼mm. needles.
Work in st.st. for 2 cm. (¾ in.).
Change to 3½mm. needles and work 27 rows from chart as marked on chart for sleeves, working 12 st. rep. 6(6:7:7:7:7) times across row and odd sts. as marked on chart.
Change to 3¼mm. needles and inc. 1 st. at each end of next and every foll. 6th row until there are 92(92:96:96:96:98) sts.

Cont. without shaping until sleeve measures 44 cm. (17¼ in.).

Shape Top
Dec. 1 st. at each end of every alt. row 18(18:21:21:21:22) times.
Cast off 2 sts. at beg. of next 12(12:10:10:10:10) rows. Cast off rem. 32(32:34:34:34:34) sts.

NECKBAND

Sew up shoulder seams.
With right side facing, 3mm. needles and A, pick up and k.31 sts. from right neck, k.33(33:35:35:35:37) sts. from back holder or spare needle, pick up and k.31 sts. from left front. [95(95:97:97:97:99) sts.]
Work 8 rows in k.1, p.1 rib.
Cast off in rib.

LEFT BORDER

With 3mm. needles and A, pick up and k.164 sts. evenly along left front.
Work 7 rows in k.1, p.1 rib.
Cast off in rib.

RIGHT BORDER

With 3mm. needles and A, pick up and k.164 sts. evenly along right front.
Work 3 rows in k.1, p.1 rib.
Next row: rib 4 sts., * cast off 3 sts., rib 22, rep. from * to last 4 sts., rib 4.
Next row: rib 4 sts., * cast on 3 sts., rib 23, rep. from * to last 4 sts., rib 4.
Work 2 rows in rib.
Cast off in rib.

MAKING UP

Sew up side and sleeve seams.
Set in sleeves.
Sew on buttons opposite buttonholes.
Press lightly with a damp cloth.

V-neck, sleeveless slipover in fine yarn, with shaped armholes and double-rib-pattern welts

★★ Suitable for knitters with some previous experience

MATERIALS

Yarn
Lister-Lee Motoravia 4 ply
4(4:5:5:6) × 50g. balls

Needles
1 pair 2¾mm.
1 pair 3¼mm.

MEASUREMENTS

Chest
92(97:102:107:112) cm.
36(38:40:42:44) in.

Length
61(61:64:64:65) cm.
24(24:25:25:25½) in.

TENSION

14 sts. and 18 rows = 5 cm. (2 in.) square over patt. on 3¼mm. needles. If your tension square does not correspond to these measurements see page 156 for adjustment instructions.

ABBREVIATIONS

k. = knit; p. = purl; st(s). = stitch(es); inc. = increas(ing) (see page 157); dec. = decreas-(ing) (see page 157); beg. = begin(ning); rem. = remain(ing); rep. = repeat; alt. = alternate; tog. = together; sl. = slip stitch (transfer one stitch from left needle, knitwise unless otherwise stated, to right hand needle.); cont. = continue; patt. = pattern; foll. = following; folls. = follows; mm. = millimetres; cm. = centimetres; in. = inch(es); st.st. = stocking stitch; sl.1K. = slip one stitch knitwise; sl.1P. = slip one stitch purlwise; y.fwd. = yarn forward; y.bk. = yarn back.

BACK

** Cast on 128(136:144:152:160) sts. with 2¾mm. needles and work in rib as folls.:
1st row (right side): * k.2, p.2, rep. from * to end.
2nd row: as 1st row.
Rep. these two rows until work measures 10 cm. (4 in.). Change to 3¼mm. needles and work in patt. throughout as folls.:
1st row: k.1, * sl.1K., k.7, rep. from * to last 7 sts., sl.1K., k.6.
2nd row: p.6, * y.bk., sl.1P., y.fwd., p.7, rep. from * to last 2 sts., y.bk., sl.1P., y.fwd., p.1.
3rd row: k.2, * sl.1K., k.7, rep. from * to last 6 sts., sl.1K., k.5.
4th row: p.5, * y.bk., sl.1P., y.fwd., p.7, rep. from * to last 3 sts., y.bk., sl.1P., y.fwd., p.2.

5th row: k.3, * sl.1K., k.7, rep. from * to last 5 sts., sl.1K., k.4.

6th row: p.4, * y.bk., sl.1P., y.fwd., p.7, rep. from * to last 4 sts., y.bk., sl.1P., y.fwd., p.3.

7th row: k.4, * sl.1K., k.7, rep. from * to last 4 sts., sl.1K., k.3.

8th row: p.3, * y.bk., sl.1P., y.fwd., p.7, rep. from * to last 5 sts., y.bk., sl.1P., y.fwd., p.4.

9th row: k.5, * sl.1K., k.7., rep. from * to last 3 sts., sl.1K., k.2.

10th row: p.2., * y.bk., sl.1P., y.fwd., p.7, rep. from * to last 6 sts., y.bk., sl.1P., y.fwd., p.5.

11th row: k.6, * sl.1K., k.7, rep. from * to last 2 sts., sl.1K., k.1.

12th row: p.1, y.bk., sl.1P., y.fwd., p.7, rep. from * to last 7 sts., y.bk., sl.1P., y.fwd., p.6.

13th row: * k.7., sl.1K., rep from * to end.

14th row: * y.bk., sl.1P., y.fwd., p.7, rep. from * to end.

15th row: * sl.1K., k.7, rep. from * to end.

16th row: * p.7., y.bk., sl.1P., y.fwd., rep. from * to end.

These 16 rows form the patt.

Cont. until back measures 33(33:36:36:36) cm. (13(13:14:14:14) in.) from beg., ending with a wrong side row.

Shape Armholes

Cast off 10 sts. at beg. of next 2 rows, dec. 1 st. at both ends of next and every foll. alt. row 7(7:7:9:9) times.

[92(100:108:114:120) sts.] **

Work straight until back measures 60(60:62:62:63) cm. (23½(23½:24¼:24¼: 24¾) in.), ending with a wrong side row.

Shape Shoulders

Cast off 6(7:8:9:10) sts. at beg. of next 4 rows.

Cast off 8(9:10:10:10) sts. at beg. of next 2 rows.

Put rem. 52(54:56:58:60) sts. onto a st. holder or a spare needle.

FRONT

Work as for back from ** to **.
Work 4(4:4:0:0) rows straight.

Shape Neck

Work 45(49:53:55:59) sts., turn, leaving rem. sts. on a spare needle.

Dec. 1 st. at neck edge on next and every foll. alt. row until 20(23:26:28:30) sts. rem. Cont. straight until front measures same as back to shoulder shaping, ending with a wrong side row.

Shape Shoulder

Cast off 6(7:8:9:10) sts. at beg. of next 2 alt. rows.

Cast off 8(9:10:10:10) sts. at beg. of next row.

Slip centre 2 sts. onto a safety pin for neckband, rejoin yarn to rem. sts. and work other half of front to match, reversing shapings.

NECKBAND

Join right shoulder seam.

With 2¾mm. needles and right side facing, pick up and k. 62(62:62:62:66) sts. down left front, k. across 2 sts. left on pin, k. 64(62:64:66:68) sts. up right front and k. across 52(54:56:58:60) sts. at back. [180(180:184:188:196) sts.]

1st row: (k.2, p.2) 28(28:29:30:31) times, * k.2, p.2 tog., p.2 (centre sts.), p.2 tog., * k.2, p.2, rep. from * 14(14:14:14:15) more times. Work 11 more rows in rib, dec. each side of centre 2 sts. on every row.
Cast off loosely in rib.

ARMHOLE BAND

Sew up left shoulder seam.
With 2¾mm. needles, and right side facing, pick up and k.152(152:152:152:158) sts. around armhole and work in k.2., p.2 rib for 12 rows.
Cast off loosely in rib.

MAKING UP

Press as advised on ball band.
Sew up neckband seam and side seams.

Cowl-necked Seaman's Sweater

Comfortable, unisex, long and roomy stocking-stitch sweater in Aran yarn, with huge cowl neck, deep cuffs and hem welt in double rib

★ Suitable for beginners

MATERIALS

Yarn
Sunbeam Aran or Bainin
17(18:19) × 50g. balls

Needles
1 pair 5mm.
1 set of 4 double-pointed 4½mm.

MEASUREMENTS

Bust/Chest
Small (Medium : Large)
Length
69(71:72) cm.
27(27¾:28¼) in.

Sleeve Seam (including cuff)
58 cm.
22¾ in.

TENSION

9 sts. and 12 rows = 5 cm. (2 in.) square over st.st. on 5mm. needles. If your tension square does not correspond to these measurements, see page 156 for adjustment instructions.

ABBREVIATIONS

k. = knit; p. = purl; st(s). = stitch(es); inc. = increas(ing) (see page 156); dec. = decreas-(ing) (see page 157); beg. = begin(ning); rem. = remain(ing); rep. = repeat; alt. = alternate; tog. = together; sl. = slip stitch (transfer one stitch from left needle, knit-wise unless otherwise stated, to right hand needle.); cont. = continue; patt. = pattern; foll. = following; folls. = follows; mm. = millimetres; cm. = centimetres; in. = inch(es); st.st. = stocking stitch; m.1 = make 1 st.: pick up horizontal loop lying before next st. and k. into the back of it.

BACK

** Cast on 86(90:94) sts. with 5mm. needles.
1st row: sl.1, k.1, * p.2, k.2, rep. from * to end.
2nd row: sl.1, k.3, p.2, * k.2, p.2, rep. from * to last 4 sts., k.4.

Rep. 1st and 2nd rows for 9 cm. (3½ in.), ending with a 2nd row.
Next row: sl.1, k. to end.
Foll row: sl.1, k.1, p. to last 2 sts., k.2. **
Rep. last 2 rows until back measures 69(71:72) cm. (27(27¾:28¼) in.) from beg., ending with a wrong side row.
Next row: cast off 26(28:30) sts. knitwise for shoulder, k.34 sts., including st. on needle, and sl. onto st. holder for collar, cast off 26(28:30) rem. sts. for 2nd shoulder.

FRONT

Work as for back from ** to **.
Cont. until front is 10 rows less than back to shoulders.

Shape Neck
Next row: k.35(37:39) sts., turn, leaving rem. sts. on spare needle, to be worked later.
Dec. 1 st. at neck edge on the next 9 rows.
Cast off 26(28:30) rem. sts. knitwise.
Leave centre 16 sts. on a st. holder, rejoin yarn to rem. sts. and complete to match 1st side.

SLEEVES

Cast on 66(66:70) sts. with 5mm. needles.
1st row: sl.1, k.1, * p.2, k.2, rep. from * to end.
2nd row: sl.1, k.3, p.2, * k.2, p.2, rep. from * to the last 4 sts., k.4.
Rep. 1st and 2nd rows for 13 cm. (5 in.), ending with a 2nd row.
Next row: sl.1, k. to end.
Foll. row: sl.1, k.1, p. to last 2 sts., k.2.
Rep. 1st and 2nd rows twice more.
Next row: k.2, m.1, k. to last 2 sts., m.1, k.2.
Cont. to inc. in this way at each end of every 6th row until there are 78(78:82) sts. Work straight until sleeve measures 58 cm. (22¾ in.) from beg., ending with a wrong side row.
Cast off knitwise.

MAKING UP AND COLLAR

Press each piece lightly with warm iron and damp cloth.
Sew up shoulder seams.

Collar

With set of 4½mm. needles, pick up and k.18 sts. down left side of front neck edge, (k.1, p.1) into each st. on front st. holder, pick up and k.18 sts. up right side of neck, and (k.1, p.1) into each st. on back st. holder.
Work 15 cm. (5¾ in.) in rounds of k.2, p.2, rib.
Cast off in rib.
Sew up side seams, leaving 22 cm. (8½ in.) open for armholes.
Sew up sleeve seams, set in sleeves.
Press seams lightly.

Traditional, Shaped Waistcoat

Firmly shadow-ribbed waistcoat with pockets and shaped hemline has mitred front border, sleeve and pocket borders in tubular rib

★★ Suitable for knitters with some previous experience

MATERIALS

Yarn
Patons Clansman 4 ply
7(7:8:9) × 50g. balls.

Needles
1 pair 3¼mm.

Buttons
5

MEASUREMENTS

Chest
97(102:107:112) cm.
38(40:42:44) in.

Length
54(56:57:58) cm.
21¼(22:22¼:22¾) in.

TENSION

30 sts. and 40 rows = 10 cm. (4 in.) square over patt. on 3¼mm. needles. If your tension square does not correspond to these measurements, see page 156 for adjustment instructions.

ABBREVIATIONS

k. = knit; p. = purl; st(s). = stitch(es); inc. = increas(ing) (see page 156); dec. = decreas-(ing) (see page 157); beg. = begin(ning); rem. = remain(ing); rep. = repeat; alt. = alternate; tog. = together; sl. = slip stitch (transfer one stitch from left needle, knit-wise unless otherwise stated, to right hand needle.); cont. = continue; patt. = pattern; foll. = following; folls. = follows; mm. = millimetres; cm. = centimetres; in. = inch(es); st.st. = stocking stitch; tw.2 = twist 2: k. into front of 2nd st., then front of first st. on left-hand needle, and sl. 2 sts. off needle tog.; y.fwd. = yarn forward; y.bk. = yarn back; sl.1P = sl. 1 st. purlwise.
N.B. The stitch used for the main part has a tendency to pull sideways and must be pressed straight when the garment is finished.

BACK

Cast on 121(127:133:139) sts. and work in patt. as folls.:
1st row: k.1, * (tw.2) twice, p.1, k.1, rep. from * to end.

2nd row: p.
These 2 rows form patt.
Work straight in patt. for 8 rows.

Shape Sides
Inc. 1 st. at each end of next and every foll. 4th row until there are 145(153:161:169) sts., taking inc. sts. into patt.
Work straight in patt. until back measures 30 cm. (11¾ in.), ending with right side facing.

Shape Armholes
Cast off 6(7:8:9) sts. at beg. of next 2 rows.
Dec. 1 st. at each end of next and every foll. alt. row until 115(121:123:129) sts. rem.
Work straight until armhole measures 24(26:27:28) cm. (9½(10¼:10½:11) in.), ending with right side facing.

Shape Shoulders
Cast off 6 sts. at beg. of next 10(6:4:2) rows, then 7 sts. at beg. of foll. 0(4:6:8) rows.
Cast off rem. 55(57:57:61) sts.

POCKET LININGS (2)

Cast on 45 sts. and work in st.st. for 9 cm. (3½ in.), ending with a k. row.
Leave sts. on a spare needle.

RIGHT FRONT

Cast on 7 sts. and work 2 rows in patt. as for back.
3rd row: k. twice into first st., work to last st., k. twice into last st.
4th row: p. twice into first st., work to end.

Rep. last 2 rows until there are 40 sts., taking inc. sts. into patt.
Next row: k. twice into first st., work to end.
Next row: cast on 6 sts., p. to end.
Rep. last 2 rows 3 times more. [68 sts.]
Next row: work to end.
Next row: cast on 5(11:17:23) sts., p. to end. [73(79:85:91) sts.]
Place marker at end of last row.
Work straight in patt. until front measures 9 cm. (3½ in.) from marker, ending with a wrong side row.

Place Pocket Lining
Next row: patt. 14(17:20:23), cast off next 45 sts., patt to end.
Next row: work to cast off sts., in place of these p. across sts. of pocket lining, p. to end.
Work straight in patt. until side front from marker upwards, matches back to arm-hole, ending with a right side row.

Shape Armhole and Front Slope
Next row: cast off 6(7:8:9), work to end.
Dec. 1 st. at each end of next and every foll. alt. row until 47(52:53:58) sts. rem.
Work 1 row.
Cont. dec. 1 st. at front slope on every alt. row until 46(49:50:49) sts. rem.
Work 1 row.
Dec. 1 st. at front slope on next and every foll. 4th row until 30(32:33:34) sts. rem.
Work straight until armhole matches back to shoulder, ending with a right side row.

Shape Shoulder
Cast off 6 sts. at beg. of next and foll. 3(2:1:0) alt. rows. Work 1 row.
Cast off 7 sts. at beg. of foll. 0(1:2:3) alt. rows. Work 1 row.
Cast off rem. 6(7:7:7) sts.

LEFT FRONT

Work as for right front, reversing shapings.

MAKING UP AND BORDERS

Block and press, following instructions on ball band.
Sew up shoulder seams.
Sew up side seams.

Front Border
Cast on 16 sts. and work as folls.:
1st row: * k.1, y.fwd., sl.1P, y.bk., rep. from * to end.
Rep. this row throughout.

Work straight until border, starting at right side seam, fits along right front edge from side to point.

Work mitre
1st row: work to last 2 sts., turn.
2nd and every alt. row: work to end.
3rd row: work to last 4 sts., turn.
5th row: work to last 6 sts., turn.
Cont. in this way, working 2 sts. less on every alt. row until 2 sts. rem.
Now work 2 sts. more on every alt. row until all sts. are worked.
Work straight until strip fits up to marker.

Work half mitre
1st row: work to last 6 sts., turn.
2nd row: work to end.
3rd row: work to last 12 sts., turn.
4th row: work to end.
5th row: work to last 6 sts., turn.
6th row: work to end.
Work straight until strip fits up front to start of front slope shaping.
Work half mitre again.
Work straight until strip fits around to centre back of neck.
Cast off.
Work 2nd front border to match, beg. at right side seam and working across lower edge of back, before working around front. Mark the positions of 5 buttons between half mitres on right front, with lowest button 3 cm. (1¼ in.) above lower half mitre, and work buttonholes as folls.:
1st row: work 6, cast off 4 sts., work to end.
Next row: patt. to cast off sts., cast on 4, patt. to end.
Complete to match first border.

Armhole Border
Cast on 14 sts. and work in patt. as for front border until border fits around armhole when very slightly stretched. Cast off.

Pocket Edge and Finishing
Cast on 16 sts. and work in patt. as given for front border until strip fits along pocket cast off sts. when slightly stretched. Cast off.
Stitch sides of pocket edges neatly to right side of work, and pocket linings to wrong side.
Sew armhole borders around armholes.
Sew front borders to waistcoat, allowing them to overlap main work slightly to give a neat finish.
Sew on buttons.

Stripy Cotton Sweater

Easy sweater in stocking-stitch stripes, with set-in, full-length sleeves, a narrow roll neck and single-ribbed welts

★ Suitable for beginners

MATERIALS

Yarn
Yarn Store Cable Cotton
11(11:11:12) × 50g. balls (Main Col. A)
2(2:2:3) × 50g. balls (Contrast Col. B)

Needles
1 pair 3mm.
1 pair 3¾mm.

MEASUREMENTS

Bust
82(87:92:97) cm.
32(34:36:38) in.

Length
54(54:60:60) cm.
21¼(21¼:23½:23½) in.

Sleeve Seam
40 cm.
15¾ in.

TENSION

23 sts. and 32 rows = 10 cm. (4 in.) square over st.st. on 3¾mm. needles. If your tension square does not correspond to these measurements, see page 156 for adjustment instructions.

ABBREVIATIONS

k. = knit; p. = purl; st(s). = stitch(es); inc. = increas(ing) (see page 156); dec. = decreas-(ing) (see page 157); beg. = begin(ning); rem. = remain(ing); rep. = repeat; alt. = alternate; tog. = together; sl. = slip stitch (transfer one stitch from left needle, knit-wise unless otherwise stated, to right hand needle.); cont. = continue; patt. = pattern; foll. = following; folls. = follows; mm. = millimetres; cm. = centimetres; in. = inch(es); st.st. = stocking stitch; m.1 = make 1 st.: pick up horizontal loop lying before next st. and work into back of it.

BACK

Cast on 92(96:100:104) sts. with 3mm. needles and A.
Next row: * k.1, p.1, rep. from * to end.
Rep. this row until work measures 4 cm. (1½ in.).
Next row: k.6(6:5:5), m.1, * k.16(17:18:19), m.1, rep. from * to last 6(5:5:4) sts., k.6(5:5:4). [98(102:106:110) sts.]

Change to 3¾mm. needles. P.1 row.
Work in st. st. in stripe patt. as folls.:
Work 2 rows in B, work 12 rows in A.
Cont. straight until the 6th(6th:7th:7th) stripe patt. has been completed. [Work should measure approx. 30(30:36:36) cm. (11¾(11¾:14:14) in.) from beg.]

Shape Armhole
Cast off 3(4:5:6) sts. at beg. of next 2 rows. [92(94:96:98) sts.]
Cast off 3 sts. at beg. of next 2 rows. [86(88:90:92) sts.]
K.2 tog. at beg. of next 4 rows. [82(84:86:88) sts.] **
Cont. in stripe patt. until armhole measures 20 cm. (8 in.).
Cast off 24(25:26:27) sts., sl. centre 34 sts. onto a holder, cast off rem. 24(25:26:27) sts.

FRONT

Work as for back to **.

Cont. in stripe patt. until armhole measures 16 cm. (6¼ in.).

Shape Neck
Next row: k.29(30:31:32), sl. centre 24 sts. onto a holder, k.29(30:31:32).
Cont. on first group of sts.
Dec. 1 st. at neck edge on every row for 5 rows. [24(25:26:27) sts.]
Work straight in stripe patt. until front measures same as back.
Cast off rem sts.
Rejoin yarn to other set of sts. and complete as first group, reversing shapings.

SLEEVES

Cast on 48 sts. with 3mm. needles and A.
Work in k.1, p.1 rib as on back for 4 cm. (1½in.).
Next row: k.4, m.1, * k.8, m.1, rep. from * to last 4 sts., k.4. [54 sts.].
Change to 3¾mm. needles, p. 1 row.
Working in stripe patt. as for front and back, inc. 1 st. at each end of every 5th row, until there are 92 sts. Cont. working straight until the end of the 8th stripe. [Work measures approx. 40 cm. (15¾ in.) from beg.]

Shape Top
Cast off 5 sts. at beg. of next 2 rows. [82 sts.]
K.2 tog. at beg. of every row until 46 sts. rem.
Cast off 5 sts. at beg. of next 2 rows. [36 sts.]
K.3 tog. across next row. [12 sts.]
Cast off rem. 12 sts.

NECKBAND

With 3mm. needles and A, k.34 sts. from back stitch holder, pick up and k.16 sts. from first side of front neck, 24 sts. from front stitch holder, then pick up and k.16 sts. from other side of front neck. [90 sts.]
Work in k.1, p.1 rib for 20 rows.
Cast off loosely.

MAKING UP

Pin out pieces, with right side down, to correct measurement and press gently. Darn in and secure all ends of stripe threads neatly.
Sew up shoulder seams and set in sleeves.
Sew up side and sleeve seams.
Join up neck rib neatly.
Press seams.

Moss-stitch Woolly Tunic

1982

Long-sleeved, ample tunic in moss stitch throughout, with unshaped armholes, dropped shoulder line, and moss-stitch, shirt-style collar

★ Suitable for beginners

MATERIALS

Yarn
Rowan Classic Tweed DK
12(13) × 50g. balls

Needles
1 pair 3¾mm.
1 pair 4mm.

MEASUREMENTS

Bust
82–87(92–97) cm.
32–34(36–38) in.

Length
69(71) cm.
27(27¾) in.

Sleeve Seam
46(48) cm.
18(18¾) in.

TENSION

21 sts. and 32 rows = 10 cm. (4 in.) square over patt. on 4mm. needles. If your tension square does not correspond to these measurements see page 156 for adjustment instructions.

ABBREVIATIONS

k. = knit; p. = purl; st(s). = stitch(es); inc. = increas(ing) (see page 156); dec. = decreas-(ing) (see page 157); beg. = begin(ning); rem. = remain(ing); rep. = repeat; alt. = alternate; tog. = together; sl. = slip stitch (transfer one stitch from left needle, knit-wise unless otherwise stated, to right hand needle.); cont. = continue; patt. = pattern; foll. = following; folls. = follows; mm. = millimetres; cm. = centimetres; in. = inch(es); st.st. = stocking stitch; m.1 = make one st. purlwise by picking up horizontal loop lying before next st. and working into the back of it.

BACK

Cast on 134(146) sts. with 3¾mm. needles and work in k.1, p.1 rib for 12 cm. (4¾ in.). Change to 4mm. needles and dec. as folls.:
1st size: k.1, * p.2 tog., k.1, p.1, k.2 tog., p.1, k.1, rep. from * to last 5 sts., p.2 tog., k.1, p.1, k.1. 2nd size: k.1, p.1, k.1, * p.2 tog., k.1, p.1, k.2 tog., p.1, k.1, rep. from * to last 7 sts., p.2 tog., (k.1, p.1) twice, k.1. [101(111) sts.]

Now work in patt.:
1st row: * k.1, p.1, rep. from * to last st., k.1.
2nd row: as 1st row.
Rep. these 2 rows until work measures 46(50) cm. (18(19½) in.) from cast-on edge.

Shape Armholes

Keeping patt. correct, shape armhole as folls.:
Dec. 1 st. at each end of foll. 10(12) alt. rows. [81(87) sts.]
Now cont. straight in patt. with border as folls.:
1st row: k.9, * p.1, k.1, rep. from * to last 10 sts., p.1, k.9.
2nd row: as 1st row.
Rep. these 2 rows until work measures 18(19) cm. (7(7½) in.) from beg. of arm-hole shaping.

Shape Neck

Keeping patt. correct, shape neck as folls.:
k.31(34), cast off centre 19 sts., k. to end.
Dec. 1 st. at neck edge on foll. 4 rows. [27(30) sts.]
Cast off. Rejoin yarn to rem. 31(34) sts. and complete to match first side.

FRONT

Work as for back until armhole measures 12(13) cm. (4¾(5¼) in.).

Shape Neck

Keeping patt. and border correct, shape neck as folls.:
k.35(38), cast off centre 11 sts., k. to end.
Dec. 1 st. at neck edge on foll. 4 rows, then dec. 1 st. at neck edge on foll. 4 alt. rows. [27(30) sts.]
Cont. straight for 10 rows.
Cast off.
Rejoin yarn to rem. 35(38) sts. and complete to match first side.

SLEEVES

Cast on 48(50) sts. with 3¾mm. needles and work in k.1, p.1 rib for 12 cm. (4¾ in.).
Change to 4mm. needles.
Inc. row: k.1, (p.1, k.1) 3(4) times, * m.1, k.1, p.1, k.1, rep. from * to last 8 sts., m.1, (k.1, p.1) 4 times. [60(62) sts.]
Work in patt. as for back, inc. 1 st. at each end of every 6th row 13(14) times. [86(90) sts.]
Cont. straight until work measures 46(48) cm. (18(18¾) in.).

Shape Armhole

Dec. 1 st. at each end of foll. 10(12) alt. rows. [66(66) sts.]
Cast off.

COLLAR

Cast on 115(119) sts. with 3¾mm. needles and work collar as folls.:
1st row (right side): k.3, * p.1, k.1, rep. from * to last 4 sts., p.1, k.3.
2nd row: as 1st row.
Rep. 1st and 2nd rows 10 more times.
K. 4 rows.
Cast off.

MAKING UP

Press pieces on wrong side omitting rib-bing. Sew up shoulder seams, carefully matching garter st. edges.
Set in sleeve by sewing cast-off edge of sleeve to straight edge of armhole and dec. shaping of sleeve to dec. shaping of body.
Sew up sleeve and side seams, reversing sleeve seam for 6 cm. (2¼ in.) from lower edge for turn back cuff.
Sew collar to neckline: place edges of collar to centre front neck and check that centre back of collar corresponds to centre back neck. Sew seam on right side of back and front, to be hidden when collar is tur-ned down in wear.
Press seams.

V-neck, Pattern-striped Sweater

1950

Hip-length, V-neck sweater in panels of stocking-stitch and twisted-stitch patterns, with set-in sleeves and ribbed welts

★★ Suitable for knitters with some previous experience

MATERIALS

Yarn
3 Suisses Super Lana
10(11:11:12:12) × 50g. balls

Needles
1 pair 3mm.
1 pair 3¾mm.

MEASUREMENTS

Chest
92(97:102:107:112) cm.
36(38:40:42:44) in.

Length
66(67:68:69:70) cm.
26(26¼:26¾:27:27½) in.

Sleeve Seam
48(48:49:49:50) cm.
18¾(18¾:19¼:19¼:19½) in.

TENSION

28 sts. and 28 rows = 10 cm. (4 in.) square over pattern on 3¾mm. needles. If your tension square does not correspond to these measurements, see page 156 for adjustment instructions.

ABBREVIATIONS

k. = knit; p. = purl; st(s). = stitch(es); inc. = increas(ing) (see page 156); dec. = decreas-(ing) (see page 157); beg. = begin(ning); rem. = remain(ing); rep. = repeat; alt. = alternate; tog. = together; sl. = slip stitch (transfer one stitch from left needle, knit-wise unless otherwise stated, to right hand needle.); cont. = continue; patt. = pattern; foll. = following; folls. = follows; mm. = millimetres; cm. = centimetres; in. = inch(es); st.st. = stocking stitch; p.f.b. = p. into front and back of next st.; T.2 L. = twist 2 left, thus: pass needle behind 1st st., k. into back of 2nd st., then k. 1st st. and slip both off needle; T.2 R. = twist 2 right, thus: pass needle in front of 1st st., lift up 2nd st. and k. it, then k. 1st st. and slip both off needle; t.b.l. = through back of loops.

BACK

Cast on 123(129:133:139:143) sts. with 3mm. needles and work in single rib, beg. and ending right side rows with k.1 and wrong side rows with p.1.
Cont. until work measures 9 cm. (3½ in.), ending with a right side row.
Inc. row: p.2(0:2:0:2), p.f.b., * k.1, p.5, k.1, p.1, p.f.b., p.1, rep. from * to last 10(8:10:8:10) sts., k.1, p.5, k.1, p.f.b., p.2(0:2:0:2). [136(143:147:154:158) sts.]
Change to 3¾mm. needles and patt.
1st row: k.4(2:4:2:4), * p.1, T.2 L., k.1, T.2 R., p.1, k.4, rep. from * ending last rep. k.2 for 2nd and 4th sizes.
2nd row: p.4(2:4:2:4), * k.1, p.5, k.1, p.4, rep. from * ending last rep. with p.2 for 2nd and 4th sizes.
3rd row: k.4(2:4:2:4), * p.1, T.2 R., k.1, T.2 L., p.1, k.4, rep. from * ending last rep. k.2 for 2nd and 4th sizes.
4th row: as 2nd.
These 4 rows form the patt. Cont. in patt. until work measures 44(45:45:46:46) cm. (17¼(17¾:17¾:18:18) in.) from beg., ending with a wrong side row.

Shape Armholes

Cast off 3 sts. at beg. of next 2 rows.
Cast off 2 sts. at beg. of next 4(6:6:8:8) rows.
Cast off 1 st. at beg. of next 6(6:8:8:10) rows.
Cont. on rem. 116(119:121:124:126) sts. until armholes measure 22(22:23:23:24) cm. (8½(8½:9:9:9½) in.) on the straight, ending with a wrong side row.

Shape Shoulders and Neck

Cast off 9 sts. at beg. of next 4 rows.
Next row: cast off 9 sts., patt. until there are 19(20:21:22:23) sts. on right needle, leave these for right back, cast off next 24(25:25:26:26) sts., patt. to end.
Cont. on 28(29:30:31:32) sts. now rem. on needle for left back. Cast off 9 sts. at beg. of next row and 11 sts. at neck edge on foll. row. Cast off rem. 8(9:10:11:12) sts. to complete shoulder slope.
Rejoin yarn to neck edge of right back sts., cast off 11 sts., patt. to end. Cast off rem. 8(9:10:11:12) sts.

FRONT

Work as for back until you have worked 4 rows fewer than on back to start of arm-hole shaping.

Shape Neck and Armholes

Next row: work 68(71:73:77:79), turn and cont. on these sts. for left front, leaving rem. sts. on a holder.
For neck shaping dec. 1 st. at neck edge on every alt. row 16(16:15:16:16) times, then on every foll. 4th row 7(7:8:8:8) times. AT SAME TIME keep side edge straight for 3 more rows then cast off 3 sts. at beg. of next row, 2 sts. at same edge on next 2(3:3:4:4) alt. rows and 1 st on next 3(3:4:4:5) alt. rows.
Cont. until armhole matches back, ending at side.

Shape Shoulder

Cast off 9 sts. at beg. of next row and next 2 alt. rows.
Work 1 row, then cast off rem. 8(9:10:11:12) sts.
Return to sts. left unworked: for 1st, 4th and 5th sizes, patt. to end; for 2nd and 3rd sizes cast off 1 st., patt. to end.
Complete as for left front with all shapings at opposite edges, beg. armhole 1 row after that of left front.

SLEEVES

Cast on 59(59:63:63:63) sts. with 3mm. needles.

Work in rib as on back welt for 9 cm. (3½ in.), ending with a right side row.

Inc. row: p.0(0:2:2:2), p.f.b., * k.1, p.5, k.1, p.1, p.f.b., p.1, rep. from * to last 8(8:10: 10:10) sts., k.1, p.5, k.1, p.f.b., p.0(0:2: 2:2). [66(66:70:70:70) sts.]

Change to 3¾mm. needles and patt.

1st row: k.2(2:4:4:4), rep. from * in 1st patt. row of back, ending last rep. k.2 for 1st and 2nd sizes.

Cont. in patt. as now set for 3 more rows, then inc. 1 st. at both ends of next row, then every foll. 6th row 7(7:8:8:5) times, then at both ends of every foll. 4th row 14(14:13:13:18) times, working extra sts. into patt. [110(110:114:114:118) sts.]. Cont. until sleeve measures 48(48:49: 49:50) cm. (18¾(18¾:19¼:19¼:19½) in.) from beg.

Shape Top

Cast off 3 sts. at beg. of next 2 rows, 2 sts. at beg. of next 4(6:6:8:8) rows, 1 st. at beg. of next 6(6:8:8:10) rows, 2 sts. at beg. of next 14(12:14:12:12) rows and 4 sts. at beg. of next 8 rows.

Cast off rem. 30(30:28:28:30) sts.

NECKBAND

With right side of work facing you and using 3mm. needles, pick up and k.64(64: 66:66:68) sts. down left front neck edge, 1 st. at centre and 64(64:66:66:68) sts. up right front neck.

1st row (wrong side): p.1, * k.1, p.1, rep. from * to end. The centre front st. is a k. rib on right side.

2nd row: rib until 2 sts. before centre front st., p.2 tog. t.b.l., k.1, p.2 tog., rib to end.

3rd row: rib until 2 sts. before centre front st., k.2 tog., p.1, k.2 tog. t.b.l., rib to end.

Cont. to dec. thus on next 7 rows.

Cast off ribwise.

With right side of work facing, using 3mm. needles, pick up and k.47(49:49: 51:51) sts. across back neck edge.

Work 10 rows in rib without shaping.

Cast off ribwise

MAKING UP

Sew up shoulder seams and ends of neck-bands. Sew up sleeves.

Sew up side and sleeve seams.

Wave-stitch,V-neck Sweater

Decorative, yet very simple, unisex V-neck sweater in wave stitch, with set-in sleeves and firmly ribbed welts

★★ Suitable for knitters with some previous experience

MATERIALS

Yarn
Patons Clansman 4 ply
9(9:10:10:11:11) × 50g. balls

Needles
1 pair 2¾mm.
1 pair 3¼mm.

MEASUREMENTS

Bust/Chest
82(87:92:97:102:107) cm.
32(34:36:38:40:42) in.

Length
61(62:63:65:66:67) cm.
24(24¼:24¾:25½:26:26¼) in.

Sleeve Seam
42(43:44:46:47:47) cm.
16½(16¾:17¼:18:18½:18½) in.

TENSION

28 sts. and 40 rows = 10 cm. (4 in.) square over patt. on 3¼mm. needles. If your tension square does not correspond to these measurements, see page 156 for adjustment instructions.

ABBREVIATIONS

k. = knit; p. = purl; st(s). = stitch(es); inc. = increas(ing) (see page 156); dec. = decreas-(ing) (see page 157); beg. = begin(ning); rem. = remain(ing); rep. = repeat; alt. = alternate; tog. = together; sl. = slip stitch (transfer one stitch from left needle, knit-wise unless otherwise stated, to right hand needle.); cont. = continue; patt. = pattern; foll. = following; folls. = follows; mm. = millimetres; cm. = centimetres; in. = inch(es); st.st. = stocking stitch.

BACK

Cast on 105(113:121:129:137:145) sts. with 2¾mm. needles.
1st row: k.2, * p.1, k.1, rep. from * to last st., k.1.
2nd row: k.1, * p.1, k.1, rep. from * to end.
These 2 rows form rib.
Cont. until work measures 7 cm. (2¾ in.), dec. 3 sts. during last row. [102(110:118:126:134:142) sts.]
Change to 3¼mm. needles.
1st row: k.
2nd row: p.
3rd row: k.
4th row: k.6, * p.2, k.6, rep. from * to end.
5th row: p.6, * k.2, p.6, rep. from * to end.
6th and 7th rows: as 4th and 5th.
8th row: as 4th.
9th row: k.

10th row: p.
11th row: k.
12th row: k.2, * p.2, k.6, rep. from * to last 4 sts., p.2, k.2.
13th row: p.2, * k.2, p.6, rep. from * to last 4 sts., k.2, p.2.
14th and 15th rows: as 12th and 13th.
16th row: as 12th.
These 16 rows form the patt.
Cont. in patt. and shape sides by inc. 1 st. at each end of next row, then on every foll. 14th row until there are 118(126:134:142:150:158) sts., incorporating extra sts. into patt.
Cont. straight until work measures 43 cm. (16¾ in.), not stretched, ending after a row worked on wrong side.

Shape Armholes
Cast off 5(6:7:8:9:10) sts. at beg. of next 2 rows. **
Dec. 1 st. at each end of next 3(3:5:5:5:5) rows, then on every alt. row until 96(100:106:110:116:120) sts. rem.
Cont. without shaping until work measures 61(62:63:65:66:67) cm., 24(24¼:24¾:25½:26:26¼) in. at centre, not stretched, ending after a row worked on wrong side.

Shape Shoulders
Cast off 10(10:11:11:12:12) sts. at beg. of next 4 rows, then 10(11:11:12:12:13) sts. at beg. of next 2 rows.
Cast off rem. sts.

FRONT

Work as for back to **
Dec. 1 st. at each end of next 2(2:4:4:4:4) rows.

Shape Neck
Next row: work 2 tog., patt. 50(53:54:57:60:63), turn.
Cont. on this group.
Dec. 1 st. at both edges on every right-side row until 45(46:51:52:55:56) sts. rem.
Cont. dec. at neck edge only on every right-side row until 40(42:45:47:50:52) sts. rem., then on every foll. 4th row until 30(31:33:34:36:37) sts. rem.
Cont. straight until front measures same as back to shoulder shaping, ending at armhole edge.

Shape Shoulder

Cast off 10(10:11:11:12:12) sts. at beg. of next and foll. alt. row.

Work 1 row. Cast off.

Rejoin yarn to sts. left for other side and work to match first side, reversing all shapings.

SLEEVES

Cast on 55(57:59:61:63:65) sts. with 2¾mm. needles and work 7 cm. (2¾ in.) in rib as on back, ending after a 1st row.

Next row: rib 3(4:4:2:10:2), * inc. in next st., rib 7(11:4:6:2:4), rep. from * to last 4(5:5:3:11:3) sts., inc. in next st., rib to end. [62(62:70:70:78:78) sts.]

Change to 3¼mm. needles and patt. as on front, inc. 1 st. at each end of 17th row, then on every foll. 6th row until there are 74(92:88:106:102:118) sts., then on every foll. 8th row until there are 92(98:104:110:116:122) sts., incorporating extra sts. into patt.

Cont. straight until work measures approx. 42(43:44:46:47:47) cm., 16½(16¾:17¼:18:18½:18½) in., ending after similar patt. row as on back before armhole shaping.

Shape Sleeve Top

Cast off 5(6:7:8:9:10) sts. at beg. of next 2 rows.

Work 4 rows straight.

Dec. 1 st. at each end of every right-side row until 44 sts. rem., then on every row until 30 sts. rem.

Cast off.

NECKBAND

Sew up shoulder seams.

Cast on 2 sts. with 2¾mm. needles.

1st row: p.2.

2nd row: (k.1, p.1) into first st., then (p.1, k.1) into next st.

3rd row: p.1, k.2, p.1.

4th row: k.1, (p.1, k.1) into next st., (k.1, p.1) into next st., k.1.

5th row: p.1, k.1, p.2, k.1, p.1.

6th row: k.1, p.1, (k.1, p.1) into next st., (p.1, k.1) into next st., p.1, k.1.

Cont. in this way working 2 into each of the 2 centre sts. of every even row, and working all sts. into rib, until there are 24 sts.

Next row: rib.

Next row: rib 12, turn and leave rem. sts. on a spare needle.

Cont. on these 12 sts. until strip fits up front edge and round to centre back of neck, allowing for rib to be a little stretched.

Cast off in rib.

Rejoin yarn to centre edge of rem. sts. and work 2nd strip as first.

MAKING UP

Omitting welt and cuffs, press lightly using a warm iron and damp cloth.

Sew up side and sleeve seams.

Set in sleeves.

Sew neckband in position, slightly overlapping edge of neckband over main part and joining ends at back of neck.

Press seams.

Moroccan, Multicoloured Waistcoat

Sleeveless waistcoat in ten-colour allover pattern incorporating Moroccan motifs, with front and armhole borders in striped rib

★★★ Suitable for experienced knitters only

MATERIALS

Yarn

Natural Dye Company Wool

Naturally dyed woollen yarn sold as pack including 5 handmade Dorset buttons (not photographed). Pack contains 75g. in col. A, 50g. each in cols. F and M, 25g. each in cols. B, C, D, E, G, H, J. Cols. vary according to dye ingredients: here A = grey, B = white, C = gold, D = biscuit, E = salmon pink, F = purple, G = rust, H = mauve, M = marled green, J = wine.

Needles

1 pair 2¼mm.

1 pair 3mm.

Buttons

included in pack: 5

MEASUREMENTS

Chest

92(97:102:107:112) cm.

36(38:40:42:44) in.

Length

62(63:65:66:67) cm.

24¼(24¾:25½:26:26¼ in.)

TENSION

20 sts. = 7 cm. (2¾ in.) over st.st. on 3mm. needles. If your tension does not correspond to these measurements, see page 156 for adjustment instructions.

ABBREVIATIONS

k. = knit; p. = purl; st(s). = stitch(es); inc. = increas(ing) (see page 156); dec. = decreas-(ing) (see page 157); beg. = begin(ning); rem. = remain(ing); rep. = repeat; alt. = alternate; tog. = together; sl. = slip stitch (transfer one stitch from left needle, knit-wise unless otherwise stated, to right hand needle.); cont. = continue; patt. = pattern; foll. = following; folls. = follows; mm. = millimetres; cm. = centimetres; in. = inch(es); st.st. = stocking stitch.

BACK

Beg. striped patt.

Cast on 127(135:143:151:159) sts., with 3mm. needles and H.

1st row: with H, k. to end.

2nd row: with A, p. to end.

3rd row: with A, k. to end.

4th row: as 2nd.

5th row: as 3rd.

6th row: with F, p. to end.

7th row: with G, k. to end.

8th row: with D, p. to end.

9th row: with M, k. to end.

10th row: with M, p. to end.

11th row: as 9th.

12th row: as 10th.

13th row: with J, k. to end.

14th row: with D, p. to end.

These 14 rows form patt.

Cont. in patt. until work measures 39 cm. (15¼ in.) from beg., ending with a p. row.

Shape Armholes

Keeping patt. correct, cast off at beg. of next and every row 5 sts. twice and 4 sts. twice.

Dec. 1 st. at each end of next and every alt. row until 97(103:109:115:121) sts. rem.

Cont. without shaping until armholes measure 23(24:26:27:28) cm. (9(9½:10¼:10½:11) in.) from beg., ending with a p. row.

Shape Shoulders

Cast off at beg. of next and every row 7(8:8:9:9) sts. 6 times and 7(6:8:7:9) sts. twice.

Cast off rem. 41(43:45:47:49) sts.

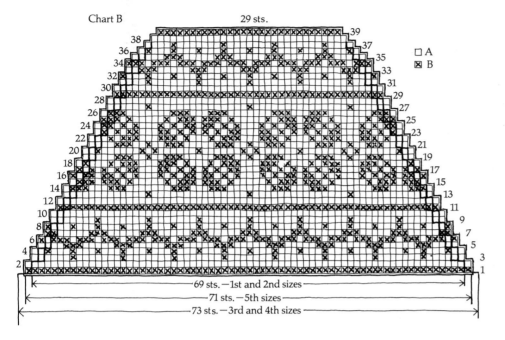

Chart B   29 sts.

☐ A
☒ B

← 69 sts. —1st and 2nd sizes →
← 71 sts. —5th sizes →
← 73 sts. —3rd and 4th sizes →

[105(109:113:123:127) sts.]

2nd, 3rd, 4th and 5th sizes: dec. 1 st. at each end of foll. 1(1:4:5) alt. rows. [107 (111:115:117) sts.]

All sizes: work 1 row, thus ending with a wrong side row.

Now work 39 rows from Chart A, repeating the 16 patt. sts. 6(6:6:7:7) times across, working the first 5(6:8:2:3) sts. and last 4(5:7:1:2) sts. on k. rows, and first 4(5:7:1:2) sts. and last 5(6:8:2:3) sts. on p. rows as indicated.

Next row: in A, p.

Work in patt. as folls.:

1st row: k.2(3:3:3:2)A, * k.1B, k.3A, rep. from * to last 3(4:4:4:3) sts., k.1B, k.2(3:3:3:2)A.

2nd row: in A, p.

3rd row: in A, k.

4th row: p.4(1:1:1:4)A, * p.1B, p.3A, rep. from * to last 5(2:2:2:5) sts., p.1B, p.4(1:1:1:4)A.

5th row: as 3rd row.

6th row: as 2nd row.

Rep. these 6 rows until back measures 51(53:57:58:60) cm. (20(20¾:22¼:22¾: 23½) in.), ending with a wrong side row.

Shape Shoulders

Keeping patt. straight, cast off 10(10:10: 11:11) sts. at beg. of the next 4 rows, then 10(11:11:10:10) sts. at beg. of the foll. 2 rows.

Leave rem. 45(45:49:51:53) sts. on a spare needle.

FRONT

Work as for back from ** until 30th row from Chart A has been worked.

Divide for Neck

Keeping patt. straight, work as folls.:

Next row: patt. 42(43:44:45:45), turn and leave rem. sts. on a spare needle.

Dec. 1 st. at neck edge on every row until 30(31:31:32:32) sts. rem.

Cont. in patt. until front matches back to start of shoulder shaping, ending with a

wrong side row.

Shape Shoulder

Cast off 10(10:10:11:11) sts. at beg. of next and foll. alt. row.

Work 1 row.

Cast off rem. 10(11:11:10:10) sts.

With right side facing, sl. centre 21(21:23:25:27) sts. onto a length of yarn. Rejoin appropriate col. yarn to rem. sts., patt. to end.

Finish to match first side, reversing shapings.

SLEEVES

Cast on 54(54:56:58:58) sts. with 2¾mm. needles and A, and work in k.1, p.1 rib for 5 cm. (2 in.).

Next row: rib 3(3:7:5:5), * m.1, rib 4(4:3:3:3), rep. from * to last 3(3:7:5:5) sts., m.1, rib to end. [67(67:71:75:75) sts.]

Change to 3¼mm. needles, join in B and work in patt. as given for the back from *** to ***.

Cont. in patt. as given for back, shaping

sides by inc. 1 st. at each end of next and every foll. 8th(7th:6th:6th:6th) row until there are 91(95:101:107:109) sts., taking inc. sts. into patt.

Work straight until sleeve seam measures approx. 43(43:44:44:44) cm. (16¾(16¾: 17¼:17¼:17¼) in.), ending with the same patt. row as on back.

Shape Top

Keeping patt. straight, cast off 6(6:6:7:7) sts. at beg. of next 2 rows.

Dec. 1 st. at each end of next and every foll. alt. row until 69(69:73:73:71) sts. rem. Work 1 row, thus ending with a wrong side row.

Now work 39 rows from Chart B, dec. 1 st. at each end of rows as indicated on Chart. [29 sts.]

Next row: in A, p.

Cast off loosely.

NECK BORDER

Sew up right shoulder seam.

With right side facing, 2¾mm. needles and A, pick up and k.24 sts. down left side of neck, k. across sts. from centre front as folls.:

k.2(2:3:4:5), (k.2 tog., k.3) 3 times, k.2 tog., k.2(2:3:4:5), pick up and k. 24 sts. up right side of neck, then k. across sts. from back as folls.:

k.4(4:6:5:6), (k.2 tog., k.5(5:5:6:6)) 5 times, k.2 tog., k.4(4:6:4:5). [104(104:110: 114:118) sts.]

Work in k.1, p.1 rib for 7 cm. (2¾ in.) Cast off loosely in rib, using 3¼mm. needles.

MAKING UP

Sew up left shoulder seam and neck border.

Press according to ball band instructions, omitting ribbing.

Fold neck border in half to wrong side, and slip-hem loosely in position.

Sew up side and sleeve seams

Set in sleeves, matching Fair Isle patt. and easing sleeve top to fit.

Press seams.

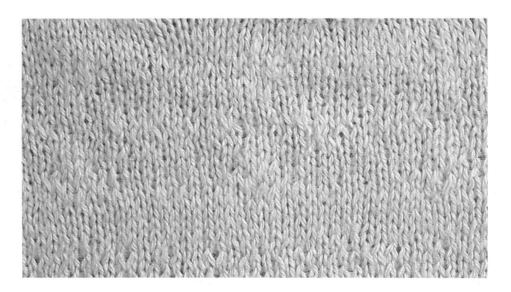

Glittery Evening Sweater

Long-sleeved, eyelet-pattern sweater in metallic yarn, with set-in sleeves and crocheted neck border

★★ Suitable for knitters with some previous experience

MATERIALS

Yarn
Twilley's Double Gold
13(14:15:16) × 50g. balls

Needles
1 pair 3¾mm.
1 3mm. crochet hook

MEASUREMENTS

Bust
82(87:92:97) cm.
32(34:36:38) in.

Length
57(57:59:59) cm.
22¼(22¼:23¼:23¼) in.

Sleeve Seam
45(45:45:45) cm.
17¾(17¾:17¾:17¾) in.

TENSION

26 sts and 36 rows = 10 cm. (4 in.) square over pattern on 3¾mm. needles. If your tension square does not correspond to these measurements, see page 156 for adjustment instructions.

ABBREVIATIONS

k. = knit; p. = purl; st(s). = stitch(es); inc. = increas(ing) (see page 156); dec. = decreas(ing) (see page 157); beg. = begin(ning); rem. = remain(ing); rep. = repeat; alt. = alternate; tog. = together; sl. = slip stitch (transfer one stitch from left needle, knitwise unless otherwise stated, to right hand needle.); cont. = continue; patt. = pattern; foll. = following; folls. = follows; mm. = millimetres; cm. = centimetres; in. = inch(es); st.st. = stocking stitch; d.c. = double crochet.

BACK

Cast on 98(104:110:116) sts.
1st row (right side): * k. next 2 sts. tog. but leave sts. on left-hand needle, then k. first of these sts. again and sl. sts. off left-hand pin *, rep. from * to * to end.
2nd row: p.
3rd row: k.1, rep. from * to * as 1st row to last st., k.1.
4th row: p.

5th row: as 1st row.
Work 7 rows in st.st., beg. with a p. row. These 12 rows form patt.
Cont. in patt., dec. 1 st. each end of next and every foll. 10th row until 90(96:102: 108) sts. rem.
Cont. straight until work measures 18 cm. (7 in.) from beg., ending with a 5th patt. row.
Next row: p.6(12:6:12), (p.2 tog., p.10) to end.
Work 4 rows st.st., beg. with a k. row.
Next row: k.6(12:6:12), (inc. in next st., k.10) to end.
Cont. in patt., inc. 1 st. at each end of next and every foll. 6th row until there are 112(118:124:130) sts., working extra sts. into patt.
Cont. straight until work measures 38 cm. (15 in.) from beg.

Shape Armholes
Cast off 6 sts. at beg. of next 2 rows, then dec. 1 st. at beg. of next 16 rows. [84(90: 96:102) sts.]
Cont. straight in patt. until work measures 57(57:59:59) cm. (22¼(22¼: 23¼:23¼) in.) from beg.

Shape Shoulders
Cast off 7(8:9:10) sts. at beg. of next 6 rows.
Cast off rem. 42 sts. loosely.

FRONT

As back until work measures 54(54:56:56) cm. (21¼(21¼:22:22) in.).

Divide Neck
Patt. 21(24:27:30), cast off centre 42 sts., patt. 21(24:27:30) to end.
Work 3 cm. (1 in.) on last set of sts., ending at armhole edge.

Shape Shoulders
Cast off 7(8:9:10) sts. at beg. of next and foll. 2 alt. rows.
Complete other side of neck to match.

SLEEVES

Cast on 48(48:54:54) sts.
Work in patt. as for back, inc. 1 st. at each end of every 6th row until there are 88(88: 98:98) sts., working extra sts. into patt.
Cont. straight until work measures 45 cm. (17¾ in.) from beg., *ending with same patt. row as back before armhole shaping*, (i.e. 2 complete patts. more than back).

Shape Top
Cast off 6 sts. at beg. of next 2 rows then dec. 1 st. at beg. of next 10 rows. [66(66: 76:76) sts.]
Now dec. 1 st. at each end of every 4th row until 56(56:62:62) sts. rem.
Next row (wrong side): p.2, (p.2 tog., p.1) to end. [38(38:42:42) sts.]
Dec. 1 st. at beg. of next 4 rows. Work 1 row.
Next row (wrong side): p.2, (p.2 tog., p.2) to end. [26(26:29:29) sts.]
Cast off 2 sts. at beg. of next 6 rows.
Cast off.

MAKING UP

Do not press.
Sew up shoulder, side and sleeve seams.
Set in sleeves.
Work 2 rounds of d.c. around neck, sleeve and lower edge.

Mini-check Summer Sweater

Long, roomy sweater with three-colour, slipped-stitch check pattern, set-in sleeves, ribbed cuffs, lower edge, and doubled-over hemmed neck

★★ Suitable for knitters with some previous experience

MATERIALS

Yarn
Phildar Perle 5
6(7:7:7:8:8) × 40g. balls Col. A
3(4:4:4:5:5) × 40g. balls Col. B
3(4:4:4:5:5) × 40g. balls Col. C

Needles
1 pair 2mm.
1 pair 2¾mm.
1 set of 4 double-pointed 2mm.

MEASUREMENTS

Chest
92(97:102:107:112:117) cm.
36(38:40:42:44:46) in.

Length
63(64:65:66:67:68) cm.
24¾(25:25½:26:26¼:26¾) in.

Sleeve Seam
56 cm.
22 in.

TENSION

32 sts. and 60 rows = 10 cm. (4 in.) square over sl. st. patt. on 2¾mm. needles. If your tension square does not correspond to these measurements, see page 156 for adjustment instructions.

ABBREVIATIONS

k. = knit; p. = purl; st(s). = stitch(es); inc. = increas(ing) (see page 156); dec. = decreas-(ing) (see page 157); beg. = begin(ning); rem. = remain(ing); rep. = repeat; alt. = alternate; tog. = together; sl. = slip stitch (transfer one stitch from left needle, knit-wise unless otherwise stated, to right hand needle.); cont. = continue; patt. = pattern; foll. = following; folls. = follows; mm. = millimetres; cm. = centimetres; in. = inch(es); st.st. = stocking stitch.

BACK

Cast on 152(160:168:176:184:192) sts. with 2mm. needles and A, using thumb method. Work 5 cm. (2 in.) in k.1, p.1, rib. Change to 2¾mm. needles and patt. (N.B.: always sl. sts. purlwise. Do not pull yarn tightly when slipping sts.)
1st row (right side): with B, k.3, * sl. 2 purl-wise, k.2, rep. from * to last st., k.1.
2nd row: with B, p.3, * sl. 2, p.2, rep. from * to last st., p.1.
3rd row: with A, k. to end.

4th row: with C, p.1, * sl. 2, p.2, rep. from * to last 3 sts., sl. 2, p.1.
5th row: with C, k.1, * sl. 2, k.2, rep. from * to last 3 sts., sl. 2, k.1.
6th row: with A, p. to end.
These 6 rows form patt. (whole garment, excluding welts, is worked in this patt.)
Cont. in patt. until work measures 40 cm. (15¾ in.).

Shape Armholes
Cast off 6(7:8:9:10:11) sts. at beg. of next 2 rows.
Dec. 1 st. at each end of next and foll. alt. rows until 116(120:126:130:134:138) sts. rem.
Work straight until armhole measures 21(22:23:24:25:26) cm. (8¼(8½:9:9½:9¾: 10¼) in.) on the straight.

Shape Shoulders
Cast off 4 sts. at beg. of next 14(12:8:6:4:2) rows.
Cast off 5 sts. at beg. of next 2(4:8:10:12: 14) rows.
Leave rem. 50(52:54:56:58:60) sts. on a spare needle.

FRONT

Work as for back until armhole measures 15(16:17:18:19:20) cm. (6(6¼:6¾:7:7½:7¾) in.) on the straight, ending with a wrong side row.

Shape Neck
1st row: patt. 49(50:52:53:54:55) sts., turn and leave rem. sts. on a spare needle. Dec. 1 st. at neck edge on next and every foll. alt. row until 33(34:36:37:38:39) sts. rem. Work straight until front matches back to shoulder, ending at armhole edge.

Shape Shoulder
Cast off 4 sts. at beg. of next and every alt. row 7(6:4:3:2:1) times more.
Cast off 5 sts. at beg. of alt. rows 1(2:4:5: 6:7) times.
Slip centre 18(20:22:24:26:28) sts. onto a holder.
Rejoin yarn to rem. 49(50:52:53:54:55) sts. and complete other side of neck to match, reversing shapings.

SLEEVES

Cast on 74(74:78:78:78:82) sts. with 2mm. needles and A.
Work 10 cm. (4 in.) in k.1, p.1 rib, ending with a right side row.
Inc. row (wrong side): p.4(4:6:6:6:8), * p. twice into next st., p.12, rep. from *, end-ing last rep. p.4(4:6:6:6:8). [80(80:84:84:84: 88) sts.]

Change to 2¾mm. needles and cont. in patt. as for back, inc. 1 st. at each end of 13th and every foll. 14th(12th:12th:10th: 10th:10th) row until there are 118(122:126: 130:134:138) sts.
Work straight until sleeve measures 56 cm. (22 in.).

Shape Top
Cast off 6(7:8:9:10:11) sts. at beg. of next 2 rows.
Dec. 1 st. at each end of every alt. row until 88 sts. rem.
Dec. 1 st. at each end of every foll. 3rd row until 60 sts. rem.
Dec. 1 st. at each end of every row until 44 sts. rem.
Cast off 4 sts. at beg. of next 6 rows.
Cast off rem. 20 sts.

NECKBAND

Sew up shoulder seams.
With set of 4 2mm. double-pointed needles and A, and with right side facing, k.50(52:54:56:58:60) sts. from back to neck, k. up 38 sts. down left side of neck, k.18 (20:22:24:26:28) sts. from centre front neck, k. up 38 sts. up right side of neck. [144(148:152:156:160:164) sts.]
Work in rounds in k.1, p.1, rib until neck-band measures 6 cm. (2½ in.).
Cast off loosely in rib.

MAKING UP

Sew up side and sleeve seams.
Sew sleeve top into armhole.
Fold neckband in half and hem cast off edge to wrong side of neck.
Press on wrong side.

Banded Ski Sweater

Thick, unisex sweater in ribbed and two-tone stocking-stitch pattern bands, with set-in sleeves, ribbed polo neck and welts

★★ Suitable for knitters with some previous experience

MATERIALS

Yarn

Sirdar Countrystyle DK
6(7:8:9) × 50g. balls (Main Col. A)
3(4:5:5) × 50g. balls (Contrast Col. B)

Needles

1 pair 3¼mm.
1 pair 4mm.

MEASUREMENTS

Chest

92(97:102:107) cm.
36(38:40:42) in.

Length

64(65:66:67) cm.
25(25½:26:26¼) in.

Sleeve Seam

49 cm.
19¼ in.

TENSION

22 sts. = 10 cm. (4 in.) over 2-colour patt. on 4mm. needles. If your tension does not correspond to these measurements see page 156 for adjustment instructions.

ABBREVIATIONS

k. = knit; p. = purl; st(s). = stitch(es); inc. = increas(ing) (see page 156); dec. = decreas-(ing) (see page 157); beg. = begin(ning); rem. = remain(ing); rep. = repeat; alt. = alternate; tog. = together; sl. = slip stitch (transfer one stitch from left needle, knit-wise unless otherwise stated, to right hand needle.); cont. = continue; patt. = pattern; foll. = following; folls. = follows; mm. = millimetres; cm. = centimetres; in. = inch(es); st.st. = stocking stitch; m.1 = make 1 st.: pick up horizontal loop lying before next st. and work into back of it.

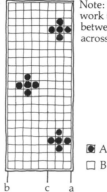

Note: start at 'a' and work to 'b' repeat between 'a' and 'b' across, ending at 'c'

☑ A
☐ B

b   c   a

BACK

Cast on 103(109:115:121) sts. with 3¼mm. needles and A.
1st row: k.1, * p.1, k.1, rep. from * to end.
2nd row: p.1, * k.1, p.1, rep. from * to end.
Rep. 1st and 2nd rows for 8 cm. (3¼ in.) ending with 1st row.
Next row: rib 6(9:12:15), m.1, (rib 13, m.1) 7 times, rib 6(9:12:15).
[111(117:123:129) sts.]
Change to 4mm. needles.
** Joining in and breaking off colours as required, work in st.st., foll. patt. from chart and leaving 2(1:0:3) sts. at each end without patt. [21 rows in 2 colours.]
Next row (wrong side): with A, p.
Next row: with A, k.1, * p.1, k.1, rep. from * to end.
Rep. these 2 rows 10 more times.
Joining in B, work 2-colour patt. starting on the wrong side with a p. row.
Next row: with A, k.
Next row: with A, p.1, * k.1, p.1, rep. from * to end.
Rep. these 2 rows 10 more times.
Rep. from ** for as long as required.
AT THE SAME TIME, when work measures 41 cm. (16 in.), shape armholes.

Shape Armholes

Cast off 5(6:7:8) sts. at beg. of next 2 rows.
Dec. 1 st. at both ends of next and foll. 6(7:7:8) alt. rows. [85(89:93:95) sts.]
Work straight until armhole measures 23(24:25:26) cm. (9(9½:9¾:10½) in.)

Shape Shoulders

Cast off 7 sts. at beg. of next 6 rows.
Cast off 6(8:7:8) sts. at beg. of next 2 rows.
Leave rem. 33(35:37:39) sts. on holder.

FRONT

Work as back to 7 cm. (2¾ in.) below top of centre back.

Shape Neck and Shoulders

Patt. 36(38:37:38) sts.

Leave rem. sts. on spare needle, turn.
Dec. 4 sts. at beg. of next row.
Dec. 2 sts. at neck edge on foll. alt. row.
Dec. 1 st. at neck edge 3 times on foll. alt rows.
Cont. straight to same row as back for shoulder shaping.

Shape Shoulder

Work as for back.
Return to sts. on spare needle.
Sl. 15(17:19:21) sts. onto holder.
Rejoin yarn and work as for left side, reversing all shapings.

SLEEVES

Cast on 53(55:57:59) sts. with 3¼mm. needles and A.
Work in k.1, p.1 rib for 8 cm. (3¼ in.)
Change to 4mm. needles.
1st row: k.1, * p.1, k.1, rep. from * to end.
2nd row: p.
Rep. these 2 rows 10 more times.
Cont. in patt. as on back from ** to **, rep. as required.
AT THE SAME TIME, inc. 1 st. at each end of 3rd row and every foll. 6th row to obtain 79(81:75:77) sts.
Inc. 1 st. at each end of every foll. 5th row to obtain 87(89:93:95) sts.
Cont. straight until work measures approx. 49 cm. (19¼ in.), ending with same row as back at underarm.

Shape Top

Cast off 5(6:7:8) sts. at beg. of next 2 rows.
Dec. 1 st. at each end of next and every foll. alt. row to obtain 39(37:37:33) sts.
Work 1 row.
Cast off 4 sts. at beg. of next 6 rows.
Cast off rem. 15(13:13:9) sts.

POLO COLLAR

Sew up left shoulder seam.
With right side facing, 3¼mm. needles and A, k. up half the sts. on back holder, m.1, k. up rem. sts. on holder, pick up 35 sts. down left front neck, k. up 15(17:19:21) sts. on front holder, pick up 35 sts. up right front neck. [119(123:127:131) sts.]
Work in p.1, k.1 rib for 16 cm. (6¼ in.)
Cast off loosely.

MAKING UP

Press each piece lightly following instructions on ball band.
Sew up right shoulder seam and polo-neck seam.
Sew up side and sleeve seams.
Set in sleeves. Press seams if required.

Acorn and Eyelet Stitch Sweater

1949

Long- or short-sleeved cotton sweater in patterned bands with reversed stocking-stitch neckband, buttoned back opening and ribbed welts

★ Suitable for adventurous beginners

MATERIALS

Yarn
Pingouin Coton Naturel 8 Fils
Short Sleeve Version:
10(10:11:11:12) × 50g. balls
Long Sleeve Version:
11(12:12:13:13) × 50g. balls

Needles
1 pair 3¼mm.
1 pair 4mm.

Buttons
4

MEASUREMENTS

Bust
82(87:92:97:102) cm.
32(34:36:38:40) in.

Length
57(58:59:60:61) cm.
22¼(22¾:23¼:23½:24) in.

Short Sleeve Seam
19 cm.
7½ in.

Long Sleeve Seam
46 cm.
18 in.

TENSION

21 sts. and 28 rows = 10 cm. (4 in.) square over patt. on 4mm. needles. If your tension square does not correspond to these measurements see page 156 for adjustment instructions.

ABBREVIATIONS

k. = knit; p. = purl; st(s). = stitch(es); inc. = increas(ing) (see page 156); dec. = decreas-(ing) (see page 157); beg. = begin(ning); rem. = remain(ing); rep. = repeat; alt. = alternate; tog. = together; sl. = slip stitch (transfer one stitch from left needle, knit-wise unless otherwise stated, to right hand needle.); cont. = continue; patt. = pattern; foll. = following; folls. = follows; mm. = millimetres; cm. = centimetres; in. = inch(es); st.st. = stocking stitch; y.fwd. = yarn forward; m.1 = make 1 st. by pick-ing up horizontal loop lying before next st. and working into back of it; d.c. = double crochet.

BACK

** Cast on 82(86:94:98:106) sts. with 3¼mm. needles.
1st row: k.2, * p.2, k.2, rep. from * to end.
2nd row: p.2, * k.2, p.2, rep. from * to end.
Cont. in rib until work measures 10 cm. (4 in.), inc. 5(7:5:7:5) sts. evenly across last row. [87(93:99:105:111) sts.]
Change to 4mm. needles.
Now work in patt. as folls.:
1st row (right side): p.
2nd row: k.
3rd row: p.4, * (k.1, y.fwd., k.1) in next st., p.5, rep. from * to last 5 sts., (k.1, y.fwd., k.1) in next st., p.4.
4th row: k.4, * p.3, k.5, rep. from * to last 7 sts., p.3, k.4.
5th row: p.4, * k.3, p.5, rep. from * to last 7 sts., k.3, p.4.
6th row: k.4, * p.3 tog., k.5, rep. from * to last 7 sts., p.3 tog., k.4.
7th row: p.
8th row: k.
9th row: p.7, * (k.1, y.fwd., k.1) in next st., p.5, rep. from * to last 2 sts., p.2.
10th row: k.7, * p.3, k.5, rep. from * to last 2 sts., k.2.
11th row: p.7, * k.3, p.5, rep. from * to last 2 sts., p.2.
12th row: k.7, * p.3 tog., k.5, rep. from * to last 2 sts., k.2.
13th row: p.
14th row: k.

15th to 20th rows: as 3rd to 8th.
21st row: k.
22nd row: p.
23rd and 24th rows: as 21st and 22nd.
25th row: k.1, * y.fwd., k.2 tog., rep. from * to end.
26th row: p.
27th row: k.
28th row: p.
29th to 34th rows: rep. 26th to 28th rows twice.
35th row: as 25th.
36th row: p.
37th row: k.
38th row: p.
These 38 rows form patt.
Rep. these 38 patt. rows once more.

Shape Armholes
Keeping patt. correct, cast off 4 sts. at beg. of next 2 rows.
Dec. 1 st. at each end of next 3 rows, then on every foll. alt. row until 69(71:73:77:79) sts. rem. **.
Cont. in patt. until back measures 47(48:49:50:51) cm. (18½(18¾:19¼:19½:20) in.) ending with a wrong side row.
Divide for back opening.
Next row: patt. 34(35:36:38:39), turn and leave rem. sts. on a spare needle.
Cont. in patt. until work measures 57(58:59:60:61) cm. (22¼(22¾:23¼:23½:24) in.) ending with a wrong side row.

Shape Shoulder
Keeping patt. correct, cast off 7 sts. at beg. of next and foll. alt. row.
Work 1 row.
Cast off 6(6:6:7:7) sts.
Leave rem. 14(15:16:17:18) sts. on a spare needle.
With right side facing rejoin yarn to rem. sts.
Cast off 1 st., patt. to end.
Work to match first side, reversing shapings.

FRONT

Work as for back from ** to **.
Cont. in patt. until front measures 51(52:53:54:55) cm. (20(20½:20¾:21¼:21½) in.), ending with a wrong side row.

Shape Neck
Patt. 25(26:27:29:30), work 2 tog., turn and leave rem. sts. on a spare needle.
Dec. 1 st. at neck edge on every row until 20(20:20:21:21) sts. rem.
Work straight until front matches back to shoulder, ending with a wrong side row.

Shape Shoulder

Keeping patt. correct, cast off 7 sts. at beg. of next and foll. alt. row.
Work 1 row.
Cast off rem. 6(6:6:7:7) sts.
With right side facing, slip first 15 sts. onto a spare needle, rejoin yarn to rem. sts., work 2 tog., patt. to end.
Work to match first side, reversing shapings.

SHORT SLEEVES

Cast on 46(46:50:50:54) sts. with 3¼mm. needles and work in rib as on back for 5 cm. (2 in.), inc. 17(17:19:19:21) sts. evenly across last row. [63(63:69:69:75) sts.]
Change to 4mm. needles.
Work 38 patt. rows as on back once only.

Shape Top

Cast off 4 sts. at beg. of next 2 rows.
Dec. 1 st. at each end of next and every foll. 4th row until 47(45:51:49:59) sts. rem.
Work 1 row.
Dec. 1 st. at each end of next and every foll. alt. row until 21 sts. rem.
Work 1 row.
Cast off.

LONG SLEEVES

Cast on 38(38:42:42:46) sts. with 3¼mm. needles and work in rib as on back for 5 cm. (2 in.), inc. 25(25:27:27:29) sts. evenly across last row. [63(63:69:69:75) sts.]
With 4mm. needles work the 38 patt. rows as on back, 3 times.
Shape top as for short-sleeved version.

NECK BORDER

Sew up shoulder seams.
With right side facing and 3¼mm. needles, k.14(15:16:17:18) sts. from left back, k. up 16 sts. down left side of neck, k.15 sts. across centre, k. up 16 sts. up right side of neck, then k.14(15:16:17:18) sts. from right back. [75(77:79:81:83) sts.]
Starting with a k. row, work 8 rows in st.st. Cast off.

MAKING UP

Sew up side and sleeve seams.
Set in sleeves.
Work 2 rows of d.c. round back neck opening, making 4 buttonholes on right side in 2nd row.
DO NOT PRESS. Sew on buttons.

Cashmere, Self-stripe Sweater 1982

Very long, slim, boat-neck, cashmere sweater in textured rib pattern, with drop shoulders, buttoned cuffs and placket on lower edge

★★ Suitable for knitters with some previous experience

MATERIALS

Yarn
Yarn Store Cashmere
360(380)g.
Also available in kit form including buttons by mail order, see page 168.

Needles
1 pair 3mm.
1 pair 3¾mm.
1 circular 3mm.

Buttons
14 shirt-size (included in kit)

MEASUREMENTS

Bust
82–87(92–97) cm.
32–34(36–38) in.

Length
69(72) cm.
27(28¼) in.

Sleeve Seam
38(39) cm.
15(15¼) in.

TENSION

36 sts. and 40 rows = 10 cm. (4 in.) square over patt. on 3¾mm. needles. If your tension square does not correspond to these measurements, see page 156 for adjustment instructions.

ABBREVIATIONS

k. = knit; p. = purl; st(s). = stitch(es); inc. = increas(ing) (see page 156); dec. = decreas(ing) (see page 157); beg. = begin(ning); rem. = remain(ing); rep. = repeat; alt. = alternate; tog. = together; sl. = slip stitch (transfer one stitch from left needle, knitwise unless otherwise stated, to right hand needle.); cont. = continue; patt. = pattern; foll. = following; folls. = follows; mm. = millimetres; cm. = centimetres; in. = inch(es); st.st. = stocking stitch; m.1 = make 1 st.: pick up horizontal loop lying before next st., and k. into back of it; y.r.n. = yarn round needle.

BACK

Cast on 189(201) sts. with 3mm. needles, and work in rib as folls.:
1st row: p.1, sl.1, (k.1, p.1) 5 times, k.1, * sl.1, k.1, p.1, k.1, rep. from * to last 10 sts., (p.1, k.1) 4 times, sl.1, p.1.
2nd row: k.1, k. all k. sts. and p. all p. sts., ending k.1.
Rep. rows 1 and 2 until 50 rows have been worked, ending on wrong side.
51st row: cast off 11 sts., patt. to last 11 sts., cast off. Break yarn, leaving enough for sewing up. [169(179) sts.]

52nd row: k.1, p. to last st., k.1.
Change to 3¾mm. needles and work in patt. as folls.:
1st row: p.1, * sl.1, k.3, rep. from * ending last rep. sl.1, p.1.
2nd row: k.1, p. to last st., k.1.
Rep. patt. until work measures 46(48) cm. (18(18¾) in.) from cast-on edge, ending on wrong side.

Shape Armholes
Keeping continuity of patt., work as folls.:
1st row: p.1, m.1, * sl.1, k.3, rep. from *, ending last rep. sl.1, m.1, p.1.
2nd row: k.1, m.1, p. to last st., m.1, k.1.
3rd row: p.1, k.2, * sl.1, k.3, rep. from *, ending last rep. sl.1, k.2, p.1.
4th row: as 2nd row.
5th row: p.1, m.1, k.2, * sl.1, k.3, rep. from *, ending last rep. k.2, m.1, p.1.
6th row: k.1, p. to last st., k.1.
Rep. 1st to 6th rows until 16 sts. have been inc. on each edge. [199(211) sts.]
Work straight for 60(64) rows, ending on wrong side.

Shape Neck
Keeping continuity of patt. work as folls.:

k.59(63) sts., turn and leave rem. sts. on a spare needle.
Cast off 4 sts., then dec. 1 st. at neck edge on every row until 50(54) sts. rem.
Work 1 row.
Cast off.
Leave centre 81(85) sts. on a holder.
With right side facing, rejoin yarn to rem. 59(63) sts., at centre edge.
Work to match first side.

FRONT

Cast on 167(179) sts. with 3mm. needles, and work in rib as folls.:
Rows 1, 3, 7, 9, 11, 13, 17, 19, 21, 23, 27, 29, 31, 33, 37, 39, 41, 43, 47, 49 and 51: p.1, sl.1, (k.1, p.1) 5 times, k.1, * sl.1, k.1, p.1, k.1, rep. from * to last 10 sts., (p.1, k.1) 4 times, sl.1, p.1.
2nd and alt. rows: k.1, k. all k. sts. and p. all p. sts., ending with k.1.
Rows 5, 15, 25, 35 and 45: p.1, sl.1, k.1, p.1, k.1, y.r.n., k.2 tog., (p.1, k.1) 3 times, * sl.1, k.1, p.1, k.1, rep. from * to last 10 sts., (p.1, k.1) twice, y.r.n., k.2 tog., p.1, k.1, sl.1, p.1.
Change to 3¾mm. needles and work in same way as for back, until work measures 46(48) cm. (18(18¾) in.) from cast-on edge, ending on wrong side.

Shape Armhole
Keeping continuity of patt., work armhole shaping as for back.
Work straight for 42(46) rows, ending on wrong side.

Shape Neck
Keeping continuity of patt., work as folls.:
k.83(88) sts., turn and leave rem. sts. on a spare needle.
Cast off 8 sts., then cast off 4 sts. at beg. of foll. 3 alt. rows.
Now dec. 1 st. at neck edge on every row until 50(54) sts. rem.
Work 4 rows.
Cast off.
Leave centre 33(35) sts. on holder.
With right side facing, rejoin yarn to rem. 83(88) sts. at centre edge.
Work to match 1st side.

SLEEVES

Cast on 79(83) sts. with 3mm. needles and work in rib as folls.:

Left Cuff
1st row: p.1, (sl.1, k.1, p.1, k.1) 4 times, sl.1, (k.1, p.1) 5 times, k.1, * sl.1, k.1, p.1, k.1, rep. from *, ending last rep. with sl.1, p.1.
2nd row: k.1, k. all k. sts. and p. all p. sts., ending with k.1.

Right Cuff
1st row: p.1, (sl.1, k.1, p.1, k.1) 12(13) times, [49(53) sts.], sl.1, (k.1, p.1) 5 times, k.1, (sl.1, k.1, p.1, k.1) 4 times, ending last rep. with sl.1, p.1.
2nd row: k.1, k. all k. sts., and p. all p. sts., ending with k.1.

Both Cuffs
Rep. 1st and 2nd rows until work measures 5 cm. (2 in.), ending on wrong side.

Change to 3¾mm. needles and work in patt. as for back.
Inc. 1 st. at each end of 1st and every foll. 6th row 24(25) times, until there are 127(133) sts.
Patt. straight until work measures 38(39) cm. (15(15¼) in.) from cast-on edge.
Cast off.

NECK RIB

Omitting ribbing, press lightly on wrong side.
Sew up shoulder seams, carefully matching patt.
With 3mm. circular needle and right side facing, k. across centre 81(85) sts. on back neck, then pick up and k.67(68) sts. down left side of neck, 33(35) sts. across centre front neck and 67(68) sts. up right side of neck. [248(256) sts.]
Work neck in rib as on back.
Check that the patt. sequence is in line with patt. on centre back and centre front.
Cont. in circular work until neck rib measures 3 cm. (1 in.).
Cast off.

MAKING UP

Insert sleeves by sewing cast-off edge of sleeve to straight edge of armhole.
Sew sleeve seams and side seams using p. sts. on right side edges for seam.
Sew button extension flaps on back rib to underside of front rib.
Press seams.
Sew 5 buttons onto each back extension and 2 buttons onto each sleeve cuff.

Jacquard Rib Sleeveless Sweater

Fine, lightweight sleeveless sweater in simple, patterned rib, with round neck and ribbed hem, neck and armhole welts

★★ Suitable for knitters with some previous experience

MATERIALS

Yarn
Sunbeam 3 ply
8(8:9:9:10) × 25g. balls

Needles
1 pair 2mm.
1 pair 3mm.

MEASUREMENTS

Chest
87(92:97:102:107) cm.
34(36:38:40:42) in.

Length
61(61:62:64:64) cm.
24(24:24¼:25:25) in.

TENSION

36 sts. and 40 rows = 10 cm. (4 in.) square over patt. on 3mm. needles. If your tension square does not correspond to these measurements see page 156 for adjustment instructions.

ABBREVIATIONS

k. = knit; p. = purl; st(s). = stitch(es); inc. = increas(ing) (see page 156); dec. = decreas-(ing) (see page 157); beg. = begin(ning); rem. = remain(ing); rep. = repeat; alt. = alternate; tog. = together; sl. = slip stitch (transfer one stitch from left needle, knit-wise unless otherwise stated, to right hand needle.); cont. = continue; patt. = pattern; foll. = following; folls. = follows; mm. = millimetres; cm. = centimetres; in. = inch(es); st.st. = stocking stitch.

BACK

Cast on 158(166:174:182:190) sts. with 2mm. needles.
1st row: * p.2, k.2, rep. from * to last 2 sts., p.2.
2nd row: * k.2, p.2, rep. from * to last 2 sts., k.2. Rep. 1st and 2nd rows for 9 cm. (3½ in.), ending with 2nd row.
Change to 3mm. needles and patt.
1st row: k.4(5:6:7:8), * p.2, k.1, p.4, k.4, p.4, k.1, p.2, k.4(5:6:7:8), rep. from * to end.
2nd row: p.4(5:6:7:8), * k.2, p.1, k.4, p.4, k.4, p.1, k.2, p.4(5:6:7:8), rep. from * to end.

21st and 23rd rows: as 9th row.
22nd and 24th rows: as 10th row.
25th row: as 7th row.
26th row: as 8th row.
27th row: as 5th row.
28th row: as 6th row.
29th row: as 3rd row.
30th row: as 4th row.
31st row: as 1st row.
32nd row: as 2nd row.
These 32 rows form patt.
Work until back measures 40(40:40:41:41) cm. (15¾(15¾:15¾:16:16) in.) from beg., ending with a wrong side row.

Shape Armholes

Cast off 10(11:12:13:14) sts. at beg. of next 2 rows.
Now dec. 1 st. at each end of next row, and then every alt. row until 116(122:128: 134:140) sts. rem.
Work until armholes measure 21(21:22: 23:23) cm. (8¼(8¼:8½:9:9) in.) measured straight, ending with a wrong side row.

Shape Shoulders and Neck Border

Cast off 12(13:14:15:16) sts. at beg. of next 6 rows.
Change to 2mm. needles and cont. for neck border:
1st row: p.1, k.2, * p.2, k.2, rep. from * to last st., p.1.
2nd row: k.1, p.2, * k.2, p.2, rep. from * to last st., k.1.
Rep. 1st and 2nd rows 5 times more.
Cast off in rib.

FRONT

Follow instructions for back until armhole shaping has been completed. Work until armholes measure 13(13:14:15:15) cm. (5(5:5½:5¾:5¾) in.) measured on straight, ending with a wrong side row.

Shape Neck

Next row: patt. 48(51:54:57:60) sts., turn, leaving rem. sts. on spare needle.
Cont. on these sts.

Cast off 3 sts. at beg. of next row, and then the 3 foll. alt. rows.
Cont. on rem. 36(39:42:45:48) sts. until armhole measures same as back, ending at armhole edge.

Shape Shoulder

Cast off 12(13:14:15:16) sts. at beg. of next row, and then the foll. alt. row.
Work 1 row.
Cast off 12(13:14:15:16) rem. sts.
Leave centre 20 sts. on a st. holder, rejoin yarn to neck edge of rem. sts. and patt. to end of row.
Work 1 row.
Cast off 3 sts. at beg. of next row, and then the 3 foll. alt. rows. Complete to match first side, working 1 row more, to end at armhole edge, before shaping shoulder.

Neck Border

With 2mm. needles and right side of work facing, k. up 42(42:42:44:44) sts. down left side of front neck edge, 20 sts. from st. holder, and 42(42:42:44:44) sts. up right side of neck.
1st row: k.1, p.2, * k.2, p.2, rep. from * to the last st., k.1.
2nd row: p.1, k.2, * p.2, k.2, rep. from * to the last st., p.1.
Rep. 1st and 2nd rows 5 times more.
Cast off in rib.

MAKING UP AND ARMHOLE BORDERS

Press each piece lightly, following instructions on ball band.
Sew up shoulder and neck border seams.

Armhole Borders

With 2mm. needles and right side of work facing, k. up 176(176:184:192:196) sts. round armhole edge.
Work 12 rows in rib as for front neck border.
Cast off in rib.
Sew up side seams.
Press seams.

3rd row: k.4(5:6:7:8), * p.2, k.1, p.3, k.6, p.3, k.1, p.2, k.4(5:6:7:8), rep. from * to end.
4th row: p.4(5:6:7:8), * k.2, p.1, k.3, p.6, k.3, p.1, k.2, p.4(5:6:7:8), rep. from * to end.
5th row: k.4(5:6:7:8), * p.3, k.1, p.2, k.6, p.2, k.1, p.3, k.4(5:6:7:8), rep. from * to end.
6th row: p.4(5:6:7:8), * k.3, p.1, k.2, p.6, k.2, p.1, k.3, p.4(5:6:7:8), rep. from * to end.
7th row: k.4(5:6:7:8), * p.3, k.1, p.1, k.8, p.1, k.1, p.3, k.4(5:6:7:8), rep. from * to end.
8th row: p.4(5:6:7:8), * k.3, p.1, k.1, p.8, k.1, p.1, k.3, p.4(5:6:7:8), rep. from * to end.
9th row: k.4(5:6:7:8), * p.2, k.1, p.1, k.10, p.1, k.1, p.2, k.4(5:6:7:8), rep. from * to end.
10th row: p.4(5:6:7:8), * k.2, p.1, k.1, p.10, k.1, p.1, k.2, p.4(5:6:7:8), rep. from * to end.
11th row: as 9th row.
12th row: as 10th row.
13th row: k.4(5:6:7:8), * p.1, k.1, p.1, k.4, p.4, k.4, p.1, k.1, p.1, k.4(5:6:7:8), rep. from * to end.
14th row: p.4(5:6:7:8), * k.1, p.1, k.1, p.4, k.4, p.4, k.1, p.1, k.1, p.4(5:6:7:8), rep. from * to end.
15th, 17th and 19th rows: as 13th row.
16th, 18th and 20th rows: as 14th row.

Textured Fair Isle Cardigan

1982

Just below waist-length, three-coloured cardigan with raised geometric pattern and contrast Fair Isle design, set-in sleeves and ribbed edgings

★★★ Suitable for experienced knitters

MATERIALS

Yarn
Patons Clansman DK
10(11) × 50g. balls (Main Col. A)
1(1) × 50g. ball (Contrast Col. B)
1(1) × 50g. ball (Contrast Col. C)

Needles
1 pair 3¼mm.
1 pair 3¾mm.
1 pair 4mm.

Buttons
6

MEASUREMENTS

Bust
82–87 (92–97) cm.
32–34 (36–38) in.

Length
54(55) cm.
21¼(21½) in.

Sleeve Seam
44 cm.
17¼ in.

TENSION

26 sts. and 30 rows = 10 cm. (4 in.) square over patt. on 3¾mm. needles. If your ten-sion square does not correspond to these measurements, see page 156 for adjust-ment instructions.

ABBREVIATIONS

k. = knit; p. = purl; st(s). = stitch(es); inc. = increas(ing) (see page 156); dec. = decreas-(ing) (see page 157); beg. = begin(ning); rem. = remain(ing); rep. = repeat; alt. = alternate; tog. – together; sl. – slip stitch (transfer one stitch from left needle, knit-wise unless otherwise stated, to right hand needle.), cont. – continue; patt. – pattern; foll. = following; folls. = follows; mm. = millimetres; cm. = centimetres; in. = inch(es); st.st. = stocking stitch; sl.1P = sl. 1 st. purlwise; sl.2P = sl. 2 sts. purl-wise; C2R = k. into front of second st. on left-hand needle, then into front of first st. and sl. both sts. off needle tog.; C2L = k. behind first st. on left-hand needle, into front of second st., then k. first st. and sl. both sts. off needle tog.; C2RP = as C2R, but p. the first st. on left-hand needle in-stead of k. it; C2LP – as C2L, but p. the second st. on left-hand needle instead of k. it.

N.B. When working from charts carry yarn not in use across not more than 3 sts. at a time on wrong side of work, to keep fabric elastic.
Read odd rows (k. rows) from right to left, and even rows (p. rows) from left to right.

BACK

Cast on 110(122) sts. with 3¼mm. needles and A, and work in k.2, p.2 rib for 6 cm. (2¼ in.), rows on right side having k.2 at each end, and, ending with a wrong side row, inc. 1 st. at each end of last row on 1st size only. [112(122) sts.]
Change to 3¾mm. needles and work 4 rows in st.st.:
** Work in patt. A as folls.:
1st row: * C2R, k.8, rep. from * to last 2 sts., C2R.
2nd row: p.1, * sl.1P, p.9, rep. from * to last st., p.1.
3rd row: k.1, * C2L, k.6, C2R, rep. from * to last st., k.1.
4th row: p.2, sl.1P, * p.6, sl.1P, p.2, sl.1P, rep. from * to last 9 sts., p.6, sl.1P, p.2.
5th row: * p.2, C2L, k.4, C2R, rep. from * to last 2 sts. p.2.
6th row: k.2, p.1, sl.1P, * p.4, sl.1P, p.1, k.2, p.1, sl.1P, rep. from * to last 8 sts., p.4, sl.1P, p.1, k.2.
7th row: k.2, p.1, * C2LP, k.2, C2RP, p.1, k.2, p.1, rep. from * to last 9 sts., C2LP, k.2, C2RP, p.1, k.2.
8th row: p.2, k.2, * sl.1P, p.2, sl.1P, k.2, p.2. k.2, rep. from * to last 8 sts., sl.1P, p.2, sl.1P, k.2, p.2.
9th row: p.2, k.2, " C2LP, C2RP, k.2, p.2, k.2, rep. from * to last 8 sts., C2LP, C2RP, k.2, p.2.
10th row: k.2, p.2, k.1, * sl.2P, k.1, p.2, k.2, p.2, k.1, rep. from * to last 7 sts., sl.2P, k.1, p.2, k.2.
11th row: k.2, p.2, k.1, * C2R, k.1, p.2, k.2, p.2, k.1, rep. from * to last 7 sts., C2R, k.1, p.2, k.2.
12th row: p.2, k.2, p.1, * sl.2P, p.1, k.2, p.2, k.2, p.1, rep. from * to last 7 sts., sl.2P, p.1, k.2, p.2.
13th row: p.2, k.2, * C2R, C2L, k.2, p.2, k.2, rep. from * to last 8 sts., C2R, C2L, k.2, p.2.

Chart 1

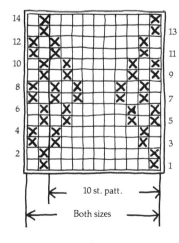

□ A

☒ B

◉ C

Chart 2

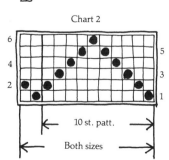

14th row: k.2, p.2, * (sl.1P, p.2) twice, k.2, p.2, rep. from * to last 8 sts., (sl.1P, p.2) twice, k.2.

15th row: k.2, p.1, * C2R, k.2, C2L, p.1, k.2, p.1, rep. from * to last 9 sts., C2R, k.2, C2L, p.1, k.2.

16th row: p.2, k.1, * sl.1P, p.4, sl.1P, k.1, p.2, k.1, rep. from * to last 9 sts., sl.1P, p.4, sl.1P, k.1, p.2.

17th row: * p.2, C2R, k.4, C2L, rep. from * to last 2 sts., p.2.

18th row: k.2, * sl.1P, p.6, sl.1P, k.2, rep. from * to end.

19th row: k.1, * C2R, k.6, C2L, rep. from * to last st., k.1.

20th row: p.1, sl.1P, * p.8, sl.2P, rep. from * to last 10 sts., p.8, sl.1P, p.1.

21st row: as 1st.

22nd row: as 2nd.

These 22 rows form patt. A.

Starting with a k. row, work 4 rows in st.st.

Change to 4mm. needles and, joining in and breaking off B as required, work the 14 rows from chart 1, repeating the 10 patt. sts. 11(12) times across, and working last 2 sts. on k. rows and first 2 sts. on p. rows as indicated.

Change to 3¾mm. needles and, starting with a k. row, work 4 rows st.st.

Now work in patt. B as folls.:

1st row: * C2R, k.8, rep. from * to last 2 sts. C2R.

2nd row: p.1, * sl.1P, p.9, rep. from * to last st., p.1.

3rd row: k.1, * C2L, k.6, C2R, rep. from * to last st., k.1.

4th and every alt. row: p. all p. sts. and sl. the sts. purlwise which have been crossed in front to make the sl. patt.

5th row: * k.2, C2L, k.4, C2R, rep. from * to last 2 sts., k.2.

7th row: k.3, * C2L, k.2, C2R, k.4, rep. from * to last 9 sts., C2L, k.2, C2R, k.3.

9th row: k.4, * C2L, C2R, k.6, rep. from * to last 8 sts., C2L, C2R, k.4.

11th row: k.5, * C2R, k.8, rep. from * to last 7 sts., C2R, k.5.

12th row: p.

These 12 rows form patt. B.

Change to 4mm. needles and, joining in and breaking off C as required, work the 6 rows from chart 2, repeating the 10 patt. sts. 11(12) times across, and working last 2 sts. on k. rows and first 2 sts. on p. rows as indicated.

Change to 3¾mm. needles and, starting with a k. row, work 4 rows st.st. **

From ** to ** forms patt. sequence.

Work the 22 rows of patt. A once more.

Shape Armhole

Keeping continuity of patt. sequence, shape armholes by casting off 7 sts. at beg. of next 2 rows, then 4 sts. at beg. of foll. 2 rows.

Dec. 1 st. at each end of next and foll. 3 alt. rows. [82(92) sts.]

Work straight until ** to ** has been completed twice.

Shape Neck

Cont. in st.st. and shape neck as folls.:

k.27(31), turn and leave rem. sts. on a spare needle.

Dec. 1 st. at neck edge on every row until 22(25) sts. rem.

Work 2(5) rows. Cast off.

With right side facing, rejoin yarn to rem. sts., cast off 28(30) sts., k. to end.

Work to match first side, reversing shapings.

LEFT FRONT

Cast on 66(78) sts. with 3¼mm. needles and A and work in k.2, p.2 rib as on back for 6 cm. (2¼ in.), ending with a right side row.

1st size

Next row: rib 12, leave these 12 sts. on a safety pin, inc. in next st., rib to last st., inc. in last st. [68 sts.]

2nd size

Next row: rib 12, leave these 12 sts. on a safety pin, rib to end.

Change to 3¾mm. needles and cont. on rem. 56(66) sts., and work 4 rows st.st.

Now work the patt. sequence as on back from ** to ** once only, working the extra 4 sts. at front edge on every row into patt. Work the 22 rows of patt. A once more.

Shape Armhole

Keeping continuity of patt. sequence, shape armhole by casting off 7 sts. at beg. of next row, then 4 sts. at beg. of foll. alt. row.

Now dec. 1 st. at armhole edge on foll. 4 alt. rows. [41(51) sts.]

Cont. in patt. as set until the 7th (11th) row of patt. B has been completed.

Shape Neck

Keeping continuity of patt. as on back, shape neck by casting off 9 sts. at beg. of next row, then 6 sts. at beg. of foll. alt. row.

Now dec. 1 st. at neck edge on next 4(6) rows.

Work 16(14) rows. Cast off.

RIGHT FRONT

Work as for left front, reversing shapings, but work a buttonhole on the 8th rib by

casting off the 6th and 7th sts. from front edge and casting them on again on next row.

SLEEVES

Cast on 70(78) sts. with 3¼mm. needles and A, and work in k.2, p.2 rib as on back for 6 cm. (2¼ in.), inc. 1 st. at each end of last row on 1st size. [72(78) sts.].

Change to 3¾mm. needles and work 6 rows in st.st.

Now work in patt. sequence as on back, placing first 2 rows as folls.:

1st row: k.0(3), * C2R, k.8, rep. from * to last 2(5) sts., C2R, k.0(3).

2nd row: p.1(4), * sl.1P, p.9, rep. from * to last 1(4) sts., p.1(4).

These 2 rows set patt. B.

Cont. in patt. sequence of patt. B as on back, (next row = 3rd row), shaping sides by inc. 1 st. at each end of 7th and every foll. 10th row until there are 88(94) sts. taking inc. sts. into patt.

Cont. in patt. sequence until sleeve seam measures approx. 44 cm. (17¼ in.), ending with 22nd row of patt. A.

Shape Armholes

Keeping continuity of patt. sequence, shape armholes by casting off 7 sts. at beg. of next 2 rows, then 4 sts. at beg. of foll. 2 rows.

Now dec. 1 st. at each end of next and foll. 3 alt. rows.

Dec. 1 st. at each end of every foll. 4th row 6 times in all.

Now dec. 1 st. at each end of every row until 34(40) sts. rem. Work 1 row.

Cast off 4 sts. at beg. of next 2 rows. Cast off rem. sts.

FRONT BANDS

Return to band of left front and with 3¼mm. needles cont. to work in k.2, p.2 rib until band reaches to beg. of neck shaping. Do not cast off.

Leave sts. on a safety-pin.

Now work band of right front and make further buttonholes as set, spaced 22 rows apart, until 5 have been worked in all, then cont. in rib to beg. of neck shaping.

Leave sts. on a safety-pin.

MAKING UP AND NECKBAND

Omitting ribbing, press lightly on wrong side following instructions on the ball band.

Sew up shoulder seams. Stitch on front bands.

With right side facing, 3¼mm. needles and A, work over the 12 sts. of right front band in k.2, p.2 rib then pick up and k.36(40) sts. up right side of neck, 40(44) sts. across back of neck, 36(40) sts. down left side of neck, then rib sts. of left front band.

Now work in k.2, p.2 rib for 9 rows, making a further buttonhole as set in centre of neckband. Cast off evenly in rib.

Set in sleeves. Sew sleeve seams and side seams carefully, matching up patts.

Press seams. Sew on buttons.

Epaulet, Wool and Cotton Sweater 1950

Classic, round-neck sweater in stocking stitch, with ribbed welts, garter-stitch stripes on sleeves and shoulders giving an epaulet effect

★ Suitable for beginners

MATERIALS

Yarn
Rowan Cotton DK
7 × 50g. balls

Needles
1 pair 3mm.
1 pair 3¾mm.

MEASUREMENTS

Bust
92 cm.
36 in.

Length
51 cm.
20 in.

Sleeve Seam
43 cm.
16¾ in.

TENSION

11 sts. and 15 rows = 5 cm. (2 in.) square over st.st. on 3¾mm. needles. If your tension square does not correspond to these measurements, see page 156 for adjustment instructions.

ABBREVIATIONS

k. = knit; p. = purl; st(s). = stitch(es); inc. = increas(ing) (see page 156); dec. = decreas-(ing) (see page 157); beg. = begin(ning); rem. = remain(ing); rep. = repeat; alt. = alternate; tog. = together; sl. = slip stitch (transfer one stitch from left needle, knitwise unless otherwise stated, to right hand needle.); cont. = continue; patt. = pattern; foll. = following; folls. = follows; mm. = millimetres; cm. = centimetres; in. = inch(es); st.st. = stocking stitch; g.st. = garter st.: every row k.

BACK

Cast on 120 sts. with 3mm. needles.
Work 6 cm. (2¼ in.) in k.2, p.2 rib.
Change to 3¾mm. needles and st.st.
Cont. until work measures 33 cm. (13 in.).

Shape Armholes
Cast off 6 sts. at beg. of next 2 rows.
Dec. 1 st. at each end of every alt. row until 92 sts. rem. **

Cont. in st.st. until armhole measures 18 cm. (7 in.)

Shape Shoulders
Cast off 8 sts. at beg. of next 4 rows, 7 sts. at beg. of next 2 rows, then 6 sts. at beg. of foll. 2 rows.
Leave rem. sts. on spare needle or st. holder for neckband.

FRONT

Work as for back to **.
Cont. in st.st. until armhole measures 13 cm. (5 in.).

Shape Neck
Next row: k.35, leave next 22 sts. on a spare needle or holder for neckband, and rem. 35 sts. on another holder or spare needle for other side.
Cont. on first set of sts.

Work 1 row, then dec. 1 st. at neck edge on every alt. row 6 times.
Work 1 row.
Cast off 8 sts. at beg. of next and foll. alt. row. Work 1 row. Cast off.
Rejoin yarn to sts. left for other side and work 2 rows.
Dec. 1 st. at neck edge on every alt. row 6 times.
Work 1 row. Cast off 8 sts. at beg. of next and foll. alt. row. Work 1 row. Cast off.

SLEEVES

Cast on 56 sts. with 3mm. needles.
Work in k.2, p.2 rib for 5 cm. (2 in.)
Change to 3¾mm. needles.
Work 8 rows in st.st. Work 4 rows in g.st. These 12 rows form the patt.
Cont. in patt., inc. 1 st. at each end of 5th and every foll. 6th row until there are 98 sts., incorporating extra sts. into patt.
Cont. straight until work measures 43 cm. (16¾ in.).

Shape Top and Epaulet
Cast off 6 sts. at beg. of next 2 rows.
Dec. 1 st. at each end of every alt. row until there are 54 sts.
Dec. 1 st. at each end of every row until there are 20 sts.
Work 12 cm. (4¾ in.) on these sts., for epaulet.
Leave sts. on st. holder or spare needle for neckband.

NECKBAND

Sew sleeve epaulets along back and front shoulders, leaving left back epaulet open. With 3mm. needles pick up and k.20 sts. of left epaulet (on spare needle or holder), pick up 12 sts. down left side of front, k.22 sts. of centre front (on spare needle or holder), pick up and k.12 sts. up right side of front, k.20 sts. of right epaulet (on spare needle or holder), and 34 sts. of back (on spare needle or holder). [120 sts.]
Work in k.2 p.2 rib for 2 cm. (¾ in.)
Cast off in rib.

MAKING UP

Sew up left back epaulet.
Sew up side and sleeve seams.
Set in sleeves.
DO NOT PRESS.

Monogrammed Bathing Suit

Geometric-design bathing suit in stocking stitch, with knitted-in lower hem, and narrowly ribbed neck and armhole borders

1931

★★ Suitable for knitters with some previous experience

MATERIALS

Yarn
Christian de Falbe Studio Yarn in Angora and Lambswool (mail order only, see page 166) N.B. Yarn is *not* pre-shrunk.
12(12:13) × 20g. balls (Main Col. A)
2(3:3) × 20g. balls (Contrast Col. B)

Needles
1 pair 2mm.
1 pair 2¾mm.

Buttons
2 small

MEASUREMENTS

Bust and Hip
82–87(87–92:92–97) cm.
32–34(34–36:36–38) in.

TENSION

32 sts. and 44 rows = 10 cm. (4 in.) square over st.st. on 2¾mm. needles. If your tension square does not correspond to these measurements, see page 156 for adjustment instructions.

ABBREVIATIONS

k. = knit; p. = purl; st(s). = stitch(es); inc. = increas(ing) (see page 156); dec. = decreas-(ing) (see page 157); beg. = begin(ning); rem. = remain(ing); rep. = repeat; alt. = alternate; tog. = together; sl. = slip stitch (transfer one stitch from left needle, knit-wise unless otherwise stated, to right hand needle.); cont. = continue; patt. = pattern; foll. = following; folls. = follows; mm. = millimetres; cm. = centimetres; in. = inch(es); st.st. = stocking stitch.

FRONT

Begin at the bottom of one leg.
Cast on 70(74:78) sts. with 2¾mm. needles and A. N.B. Cast on using 2 needle method: as cable method, but putting needle *into* each st., not between each st., to make next st.
Work 7 cm. (2¾ in.) in st.st.
Make hem by folding work in half and k. tog. 1 st. from needle and 1 loop from cast on edge, all across row. **
Cont. in st.st. until work measures 11 cm (4¼ in.).
Leave sts. on holder and work 2nd leg to match.
*** Join legs: k. across sts. from 1st leg,

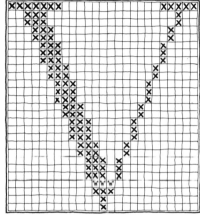

⊠ B, darned

cast on 1 st., k. across sts. from 2nd leg. [141(149:157) sts.]
Cont. until work measures 23 cm. (9 in.).

Shape Hips
Dec. 1 st. at each end of next and every foll. 4th row until 129(137:145) sts. rem.
Dec. 1 st. at each end of every foll. alt. row until 123(131:139) sts. rem.
Cont. until work measures 43 cm. (16¾ in.).

Shape Upper Body
Inc. 1 st. at each end of next and every foll. 6th row until there are 131(139:147) sts.
Cont. in st.st., starting coloured inset by working centre st. in B, and enlarging inset by 1 st. at each side of B sts. of previous row, until all sts. are worked in B. *At the same time* inc. 1 st. at each end of 9th and foll. 10th row. [135(143:151) sts.]
Work 2 rows in B.

Shape Armholes and Neck
Cast off 6(7:8) sts. at beg. of next 4 rows.
Next row: k.44(45:46), cast off 23(25:27), k. to end.
Working on 1st set of sts., dec. 1 st. at each end of next and every foll. alt. row until 14(13:14) sts. rem.
Cont. on these sts. until shoulder strap (from beg. of decs.), measures 20 cm. (7¾ in.).
Cast off.
Rejoin yarn to 2nd set of sts. and work to match 1st set. ***

BACK

Work as for front to **.
Cont. in st.st. until work measures 14 cm. (5½ in.).
Leave sts. on holder and work 2nd leg to match.
Work from *** to *** as for front.

GUSSET

Cast on 3 sts. with 2¾mm. needles. and A.
K.1 row.
Working in st.st., inc. 1 st. at beg. of every row until there are 47 sts.
Work 1 row.
Now dec. 1 st. at each end of every row until 3 sts. rem.
Cast off.

FINISHING

Sew up right shoulder strap seam.
With 2mm. needles and B, pick up and k.160(164:168) sts. round armhole.
Work 1 row in k.1, p.1 rib.
Cast off in rib.
Sew up side seams.
With 2mm. needles and B, pick up and k.326(336:346) sts. round neck.
Work 1 row in k.1, p.1 rib.
Cast off in rib.
Work 2nd armhole trim to match first, but pick up and k. sts. from shoulder to shoulder.

Make Buttonhole Border
With 2mm. needles and A, pick up and k.15 sts. across left front shoulder strap.
1st row: k.1, p.1, cast off 2 sts., rib 7, cast off 2 sts., p.1, k.1.
2nd row: as 1st row, casting on 2 sts. over those cast off in 1st row.
3rd row: work in k.1, p.1 rib.
Cast off in rib.

MAKING UP

Sew 2 small buttons to left back shoulder strap, to match buttonholes in left front.
Sew in gusset between legs: the smaller edges of diamond to the front legs above hem line, the longer edges to the back legs.
Sew front and back legs tog. (hems only).
Press garment using damp cloth and warm iron.
Swiss darn the motif in A onto centre of B front section, as shown in pictures.

Knitted Shirt-style Sweater

Stretchy-rib, long sweater with set-in sleeves, buttoned front placket, patterned collar and ribbed welts

★★ Suitable for knitters with some previous experience

MATERIALS

Yarn
Sirdar Countrystyle 4 ply
10(11:11:12) × 50g. balls

Needles
1 pair 2¾mm.
1 pair 3¼mm.

Buttons
3

MEASUREMENTS

Chest
92(97:102:107) cm.
36(38:40:42) in.

Length
65(66:67:68) cm.
25½(26:26¼:26¾) in.

Sleeve Seam
48 cm.
18¾ in.

TENSION

30 sts. and 36 rows = 10 cm. (4 in.) square over patt. on 3¼mm. needles. If your tension square does not correspond to these measurements see page 156 for adjustment instructions.

ABBREVIATIONS

k. = knit; p. = purl; st(s). = stitch(es); inc. = increas(ing) (see page 156); dec. = decreas(ing) (see page 157); beg. = begin(ning); rem. = remain(ing); rep. = repeat; alt. = alternate; tog. = together; sl. = slip stitch (transfer one stitch from left needle, knitwise unless otherwise stated, to right hand needle.); cont. = continue; patt. = pattern; foll. = following; folls. = follows; mm. = millimetres; cm. = centimetres; in. = inch(es); st.st. = stocking stitch; y.r.n. = yarn round needle.

BACK

Cast on 146(154:162:170) sts. with 2¾mm. needles.
1st row: k.2, * p.2, k.2, rep. from * to end.
2nd row: p.2, * k.2, p.2, rep. from * to end.
Rep. 1st and 2nd row for 5 cm. (2 in.) ending with 2nd row. Change to 3¼mm. needles and work in patt.:
1st row: k.2., * y.r.n., k.2, pass the y.r.n. over the 2 sts. just worked, k.2, rep. from * to end.
2nd row: p.2, * k.2, p.2, rep. from * to end.

These 2 rows form the patt.
Cont. in patt. until work measures 44 cm. (17¼ in.), ending with a 2nd row.

Shape Armholes
Keeping patt. correct, cast off 6 sts. at beg. of next 2 rows.
Cast off 2 sts. at beg. of next 4 rows.
Dec. 1 st. at each end of next and foll. 3(5:7:9) alt. rows. [118(122:126:130) sts.]
Cont. straight until armholes measure 21(22:23:24) cm. (8¼(8½:9:9½) in.), ending with a 2nd row.

Shape Shoulders
Cast off 8(8:8:8) sts. at beg. of next 4 rows.
Cast off 8(8:8:9) sts. at beg. of next 2 rows.
Cast off 8(8:9:9) sts. at beg. of next 2 rows.
Cast off 8(9:9:9) sts. at beg. of next 2 rows.
Cast off rem. 38(40:42:44) sts.

FRONT

Work as back to 1 row less than needed for armholes.

Divide for Front Opening
Next row (wrong side): patt. 70(74:78:82) sts., cast off 6, patt. to end.
Cont. on last 70(74:78:82) sts., leaving rem. sts. on spare needle.

Shape Armhole
Cast off 6 sts. at beg. of next row.
Cast off 2 sts. at beg. of foll. 2 alt. rows.
Dec. 1 st. at beg. of foll. 4(6:8:10) alt. rows. [56(58:60:62) sts.]
Cont. straight until armhole measures 14(14:15:15) cm. (5½(5½:5¾:5¾) in.,) ending with 1st row.

Shape Neck and Shoulder
Cast off 6(7:8:9) sts. at beg. of next row.
Cast off 4 sts. at beg. of foll. alt. row.
Cast off 2 sts. at beg. of foll. 2 alt. rows.
Dec. 1 st. at beg. of foll. 2 alt. rows. [40(41:42:43) sts.]
Cont. straight until armhole measures the same as on back, ending with 2nd row.
Cast off shoulder as on back.
Return to sts. on spare needle.
Rejoin yarn and work as for left front, reversing all shapings.

SLEEVES

Cast on 66(70:70:74) sts. with 2¾mm. needles.
Work in k.2, p.2 rib as on back for 8 cm. (3¼ in.) ending with 2nd row.
Change to 3¼mm. needles.
Cont. in patt. as on back.
AT THE SAME TIME, inc. 1 st. at each end of 1st and every foll. 4th row until there are 110(114:118:122) sts.

Cont. straight until sleeve measures 48 cm. (18¾ in.) or required length, ending with 2nd row.

Shape Top
Cast off 6 sts. at beg. of next 2 rows.
Dec. 1 st. at each end of next and foll. 15 alt. rows, ending with a 2nd row.
Cast off 2 sts. at beg. of next 16(18:20:22) rows.
Cast off 3 sts. at beg. of next 4 rows.
Cast off 4 sts. at beg. of next 2 rows.
Cast off rem. 14 sts.

FRONT BANDS

With 2¾mm. needles and right side facing, pick up 44(44:48:48) sts. evenly along right front edge of opening.
1st row (wrong side): k.1, * p.2, k.2, rep. from * to last 3 sts., p.2, k.1.
2nd row: k.3, * p.2, k.2, rep. from * to last st., k.1.
Work 1st and 2nd row 3 more times.
Cast off in rib.
Pick up sts. from left edge and work as for right band for 3 rows.
4th row: rib 3, (cast off 2, rib 14) twice, cast off 2, rib 7(7:11:11).
5th row: rib to end, casting on 2 sts. over each 2 cast off.
Rib 3 more rows. Cast off in rib.

COLLAR

Cast on 38(38:42:42) sts. with 3¼mm. needles.
Work in patt. as on back.
AT THE SAME TIME, cast on 4 sts. at beg. of 2nd and foll. 11 rows.
Cast on 8(8:10:10) sts. at beg. of next 2 rows, ending with 1st row. [102(102:108:108) sts.]
Next row: k.2, patt. to last 2 sts., k.2.
Cont. in patt., keeping 2 sts. at each end in garter st., for 4 rows.
Next row: k.2, inc. 1 by picking up loop between sts. and k. into the back of it, patt. to last 2 sts., inc. 1, k.2.
Cont. inc. on every 4th row until side edge measures 7(7:8:8) cm. (2¾(2¾:3¼:3¼) in.), ending with 2nd row.
Cast off loosely in patt.

MAKING UP

Press work, if required, following instructions on ball band.
Sew up shoulder seams. Set in sleeves.
Sew up side and sleeve seams.
Sew up lower edges of front bands.
Sew on collar, starting and ending in centre of front bands.
Press seams if required. Sew on buttons.

Sweater with Garter-stitch Insert

Simple, unisex, thick sweater with V-shaped garter-stitch front 'insert', set-in sleeves and ribbed welts

★ Suitable for beginners

MATERIALS

Yarn
Lister-Lee Motoravia DK
9(9:10:11:11:12) × 50g. balls

Needles
1 pair 3¼mm.
1 pair 4mm.

MEASUREMENTS

Bust/Chest
82(87:92:97:102:107) cm.
32(34:36:38:40:42) in.

Length
54(57:60:62:65:67) cm.
21¼(22¼:23½:24¼:25½:26¼) in.

Sleeve Seam
49(49:49:52:52:52) cm.
19¼(19¼:19¼:20½:20½:20½) in.

TENSION

22 sts. and 28 rows = 10 cm. (4 in.) square over st.st. on 4mm. needles. If your tension square does not correspond to these measurements see page 156 for adjustment instructions.

ABBREVIATIONS

k. = knit; p. = purl; st(s). = stitch(es); inc. = increas(ing) (see page 156); dec. = decreas(ing) (see page 157); beg. = begin(ning); rem. = remain(ing); rep. = repeat; alt. = alternate; tog. = together; sl. = slip stitch (transfer one stitch from left needle, knitwise unless otherwise stated, to right hand needle.); cont. = continue; patt. = pattern; foll. = following; folls. = follows; mm. = millimetres; cm. = centimetres; in. = inch(es); st.st. = stocking stitch; g.st.

= garter stitch: all rows k.; m.1 = make 1 st.: pick up horizontal loop lying before next st. and work into back of it.

BACK

Cast on 87(91:97:103:109:113) sts. with 3¼mm. needles.
1st row: k.1, * p.1, k.1, rep. from * to end.
2nd row: p.1, * k.1, p.1, rep. from * to end.
Rep. 1st and 2nd rows for 10 cm. (4 in.) ending with 1st row.
Next row: k.1, m.1, rib 5(2:5:5:4:6), m.1, * rib 15(12:12:13:14:11), m.1, rep. from * to last 6(4:7:6:6:7) sts., rib to end. [94(100:106:112:118:124) sts.]
Change to 4mm. needles.
Cont. in st.st. until work measures 36(38:41:42:44:46) cm. (14(15:16:16½:17¼:18) in.), ending with a p. row.

Shape Armholes
Cast off 5 sts. at beg. of next 2 rows.
Dec. 1 st. at each end of next and foll. alt. rows 5(6:7:7:8:10) times. [74(78:82:88:92:94) sts.]
Cont. straight until work measures 54(57:60:62:65:67) cm. (21¼(22¼:23½:24½:25½:26¼) in.], ending with a p. row.

Shape Shoulders
Cast off 7(8:8:9:9:9) sts. at beg. of next 4 rows.
Cast off 7(7:8:9:10:10) sts. at beg. of next 2 rows.
Leave rem. 32(32:34:34:36:38) sts. on holder.

FRONT

Work as back until front measures 18 cm. (7 in.), ending with a k. row.

Work Insert
1st row: p.46(49:52:55:58:61), k.2, p. to end.
2nd and every alt. row: k.
3rd row: rep. 1st row.
5th row: p.45(48:51:54:57:60), k.4, p. to end.
7th row: rep. 5th row.
9th row: p.44(47:50:53:56:59), k.6, p. to end.
Cont. to work 1 more st. each side of g.st. panel every 4th row to end of work.
AT THE SAME TIME, shape armholes as for the back, until work measures 48(51:54:55:58:60) cm. (18¾(20:21¼:21½:22¾:23½) in.) from beg. ending with a p. row.

Shape Neck
Next row: patt. 30(32:33:36:37:37) sts., turn work and leave rem. sts. on spare needle.

Dec. 1 st. at neck edge on every row 5 times.
Dec. 1 st. at neck edge on alt. rows 4 times. [21(23:24:27:28:28) sts.]
Cont. straight, shaping shoulder as on back.
Return to sts. on spare needle.
Sl. 14(14:16:16:18:20) sts. onto a holder.
Rejoin yarn and work to match first side, reversing all shapings.

SLEEVES

Cast on 41(43:45:49:51:53) sts. with 3¼mm. needles.
Work in k.1, p.1 rib for 9 cm. (3½ in.), ending with a 1st row.
Next row: rib 2(3:4:6:3:4), m.1, * rib 4(4:4:4:5:5), m.1, rep. from * to last 3(4:5:7:3:4) sts., rib to end. [51(53:55:59:61:63) sts.]
Change to 4mm. needles.
Cont. in st.st.
AT THE SAME TIME, inc. 1 st. at each end of 3rd and every foll. 8th row. [73(75:77:81:83:85) sts.]
Cont. straight until work measures 49(49:49:52:52:52) cm. (19¼(19¼:19¼:20½:20½:20½) in.), ending with a p. row.

Shape Top
Cast off 5 sts. at beg. of next 2 rows.
Dec. 1 st. at each end of next and every foll. alt. row 13(14:15:16:17:18) times. [37(37:37:39:39:39) sts.]
Cast off 6 sts. at beg. of next 4 rows.
Cast off rem. 13(13:13:15:15:15) sts.

NECKBAND

Sew up right shoulder seam.
With 3¼mm. needles and right side facing, pick up and k.17(18:19:21:21:21) sts. down left front neck, k.14(14:16:16:18:20) from front holder, pick up and k.17(18:19:21:21:21) sts. up right front neck, k.15(15:16:16:17:18) sts. from back holder, k.2 sts. tog., k. rem. 15(15:16:16:17:18) sts. from holder. [79(81:87:91:95:99) sts.]
Work in p.1, k.1 rib for 4 cm. (1½ in.).
Cast off loosely in rib.

MAKING UP

Press each piece following instructions on ball band and stretching g.st. insert if required.
Sew up left shoulder seam, including neckband.
Sew up side seams. Sew up sleeve seams.
Set in sleeves.
Press seams if required.

Norwegian Sweater

1962

Two-tone, hip-length, stocking stitch sweater with raglan sleeves, firm-rib welts, and patterned yoke knitted in the round

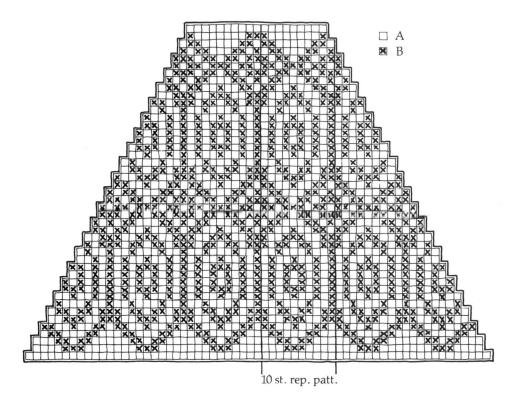

☐ A
☒ B

10 st. rep. patt.

★ Suitable for adventurous beginners

MATERIALS

Yarn
Phildar Sagittaire
8(8:9:9:10:10:11) × 50g. balls (Col. A)
1(1:1:1:1:2:2) × 50g. balls (Col. B)

Needles
1 pair 3mm.
1 pair 3¾mm.
1 circular 3¾mm.
1 set of 4 double-pointed 3mm.

MEASUREMENTS

Bust
82(87:92:97:102:107:112) cm.
32(34:36:38:40:42:44) in.

Length
64(65:66:67:68:69:70) cm.
25(25½:26:26¼:26¾:27¼:27½) in.

Sleeve Seam
45(45:46:46:47:47:47) cm.
17¾(17¾:18:18:18½:18½:18½) in.

TENSION

22 sts. and 32 rows = 10 cm. (4 in.) square over st.st. on 3¾mm. needles. If your tension square does not correspond to these measurements see page 156 for adjustment instructions.

ABBREVIATIONS

k. = knit; p. = purl; st(s). = stitch(es); inc. = increas(ing) (see page 156); dec. = decreas(ing) (see page 157); beg. = begin(ning); rem. = remain(ing); rep. = repeat; alt. = alternate; tog. = together; sl. = slip stitch (transfer one stitch from left needle, knit-wise unless otherwise stated, to right hand needle.); cont. = continue; patt. = pattern; foll. = following; folls. = follows; mm. = millimetres; cm. = centimetres; in. = inch(es); st.st. = stocking stitch.

BACK

Cast on 102(106:112:118:124:128:134) sts. with 3mm. needles and A.
Work 6 cm. (2¼ in.) in k.1, p.1, rib and inc. 1 st. at end of last row. [103(107:113:119:125:129:135) sts.]
Change to 3¾mm. needles and cont. in st.st. until work measures 42(43:44:44:44:45:45) cm. (16½(16¾:17¼:17¼:17¼:17¾:17¾) in.), ending with a wrong side row.

Shape Raglan
Cast off 3(4:4:5:6:5:6) sts. at beg. of next 2 rows.

Dec. 1 st. at each end of next and every alt. row until 73(73:83:83:93:93) sts. rem.
P.1 row. Leave sts. on a spare needle.

FRONT

Work as for back until front matches back to armholes, ending with a wrong side row.

Shape Raglan And Yoke Curve
Cast off 3(4:4:5:6:5:6) sts. at beg. of next 2 rows.
Dec. 1 st. at each end of next and every alt. row until 89(89:99:99:99:109:109) sts. rem.
P.1 row.
1st row: k.2 tog., k.34(34:39:39:39:44:44), turn, leave rem. sts.
2nd and alt. rows: p. to end.
3rd row: k.2 tog., k.29(29:33:33:33:37:37), turn.
5th row: k.2 tog., k.24(24:27:27:27:30:30), turn.
7th row: k.2 tog., k.19(19:21:21:21:23:23), turn.
9th row: k.2 tog., k.14(14:15:15:15:16:16), turn.
11th row: k.2 tog., k.9, turn.
13th row: k.2 tog., k.4, turn.
15th row: k.2 tog., cont. across all sts., k. to last 2 sts., k.2 tog.
Next row: p.35(35:40:40:40:45:45), turn.
Cont. to dec. 1 st. at raglan edge and to

work curve to match other side, reversing shaping, until 13th row has been worked. *Next row:* p. across all sts. [73(73:83:83:83: 93:93) sts.]

Leave sts. on a spare needle.

SLEEVES

Cast on 52(54:56:60:62:62:64) sts. with 3mm. needles and A.

Work 8 cm. (3¼ in.) in k.1, p.1, rib and inc. 1 st. at end of last row. [53(55:57: 61:63:63: 65) sts.]

Change to 3¾mm. needles, cont. in st.st. Inc. 1 st. at each end of 7th and every foll. 8th row until there are 75(69:67:71:75:75: 77) sts. and then every foll. 6th row until there are 83(87:91:95:97:97:99) sts.

Work straight until sleeve measures 45(45: 46:46:47:47:47) cm. (17¾(17¾:18:18:18½: 18½:18½) in.)

Shape Raglan

Cast off 3(4:4:5:6:5:6) sts. at beg. of next 2 rows. Work 2 rows.

Dec. 1 st. at each end of next and every foll. 4th row 4(4:0:1:3:0:2) times more. [67(69:81:81:77:85:81) sts.]

Dec. 1 st. at each end of every alt. row until 63 sts. rem.

P.1 row. Leave sts. on a spare needle.

YOKE

With 3¾mm. circular needle and right side of work facing, work across 73(73:83: 83:83:93:93) sts. from back following chart thus: ** k.2 tog. A, k.3 A, * k.3 B, k.7 A, rep. from * to last 8 sts., k.3 B, k.3 A, k.2 tog. A, ** place coloured thread to mark dec. point, rep. from ** to ** across 63 sts. for sleeve, rep. from ** to ** across 73(73: 83:83:83:93:93) sts. for front, and rep. again

across 63 sts. for other sleeve, placing markers between each dec. point.

Cont. in rounds, following patt. from chart and dec. 1 st. each side of markers every alt. round as shown on chart.

Complete chart. [96(96:116:116:136: 136) sts.]

Cont. in A and cont. to dec. as before on alt. rounds 0(0:2:1:0:2:2) times more. [96(96:100:108:116:120:120) sts.]

Change to set of 4 double-pointed 3mm. needles, arrange sts. on 3 needles and cont. in k.1, p.1 rib.

Work 12 rounds.

Cast off loosely in rib.

MAKING UP

Sew up raglan seams.

Sew up side and sleeve seams.

Press lightly on wrong side.

Cabled Mittens

1953

Simple, shetland wool mittens in stocking stitch with cable- and moss-stitch backs, and ribbed welts

★★ Suitable for knitters with some previous experience

MATERIALS

Yarn
Wendy Shetland DK
1 × 50g. ball

Needles
1 set of 4 double-pointed 3¼mm.
1 cable needle

MEASUREMENTS

average woman's size

TENSION

26 sts and 36 rows = 10 cm. (4 in.) square over st.st. on 3¼mm. needles. If your tension square does not correspond to these measurements see page 156 for adjustment instructions.

ABBREVIATIONS

k. = knit; p. = purl; st(s). = stitch(es); inc. = increas(ing) (see page 156); dec. = decreas- (ing) (see page 157); beg. = begin(ning); rem. = remain(ing); rep. = repeat; alt. = alternate; tog. = together; sl. = slip stitch (transfer one stitch from left needle, knit- wise unless otherwise stated, to right hand needle.); cont. = continue; patt. = pattern; foll. = following; folls. = follows; mm. = millimetres; cm. = centimetres; in. = inch(es); st.st. = stocking stitch; m.st. = moss st.; p.s.s.o. = pass slipped stitch over; rem. = remain; t.b.l. = through back

of loops; cable 10 = sl. next 5 sts. onto cable needle, leave at the back of the work, k.5, then k.5 from cable needle.

RIGHT MITT

Cast on 40 sts. with set of 4 3¼mm. needles and join into a round.

Work 30 rounds in k.2, p.2 rib then cont. in patt. as folls.:

1st round: p.1, (k.1, p.1) twice, k.10, p.1, (k.1, p.1) twice, k.20.

2nd round: k.1, (p.1, k.1) twice, k.10, k.1, (p.1, k.1) twice, k.1, inc. 1 by picking up loop between sts., and k. into the back of it, k.3, inc. 1, k.16.

3rd round: m.st. 5 as on 1st round, cable 10, m.st. 5, k. to end.

4th round: m.st. 5 as on 2nd round, k.10, m.st. 5, k.1, inc. 1, k.5, inc. 1, k.16.

Cont. to inc. 2 sts. on every alt. round, until there are 54 sts., then work 6 rounds, at the same time working cable 10 on 19th round.

21st round: patt. 20, sl. next 17 sts. onto a thread, cast on 3 sts., k. to end. [40 sts.]

Cont. in patt., working cable 10 on every 16th round until 54 rounds have been worked in patt.

Shape Top

1st round: patt. 4, sl. 1, k.1, p.s.s.o., k.8, k.2 tog., patt. 4, k.4, sl. 1, k.1, p.s.s.o., k.8, k.2 tog., k.4.

2nd round: patt. 4, sl. 1, k.1, p.s.s.o., k.6, k.2 tog., patt. 4, k.4, sl. 1, k.1, p.s.s.o., k.6, k.2 tog., k.4.

3rd round: patt. 4, sl. 1, k.1, p.s.s.o., k.4,

k.2 tog., patt. 4, k.4, sl. 1, k.1, p.s.s.o., k.4, k.2 tog., k.4.

4th round: patt. 4, sl. 1, k.1, p.s.s.o., k.2, k.2 tog., patt. 4, k.4, sl. 1, k.1, p.s.s.o., k.2, k.2 tog., k.4.

5th round: patt. 4, sl. 1, k.1, p.s.s.o., k.2 tog., patt. 4, k.4, sl. 1, k.1, p.s.s.o., k.2 tog., k.4.

6th round: patt. 3, sl. 1, k.1, p.s.s.o., k.2 tog., patt. 3, k.3, sl. 1, k.1, p.s.s.o., k.2 tog., k.3.

7th round: patt. 2, sl. 1, k.1, p.s.s.o., k.2 tog., patt. 2, k.2, sl.1, k.1, p.s.s.o., k.2 tog., k.2. [12 sts.]

Break off yarn, thread through sts., draw up and fasten off.

Sl. the 17 thumb sts. back onto needles, pick up and k.3 sts. from cast on sts. at base of thumb, k. to end and join into a round. [20 sts.]

Cont. in rounds of st.st. for 4 cm. (1½ in.).

Shape Thumb Top

1st round: (k.3, k.2 tog.) to end.

2nd, 4th and 6th rounds: k.

3rd round: (k.2, k.2 tog.) to end.

5th round: (k.1, k.2 tog.) to end.

7th round: k.2 tog. to end.

Break off yarn, thread through sts., draw up and fasten off.

LEFT MITT

Work as right mitt until rib is completed.

Next round: k.20, p.1, (k.1, p.1) twice, k.10, p.1, (k.1, p.1) twice.

Cont. to match right mitt, reversing patt. and all shapings.

124

Raised Leaf-pattern Top

1961

Allover leaf-design top, with three-quarter length set-in sleeves, ribbed welts and round neckline

★★ Suitable for knitters with some previous experience

MATERIALS

Yarn
Sirdar Countrystyle DK
10(10) × 50g. balls

Needles
1 pair 3¼mm.
1 pair 4(4½)mm.
2 stitch holders

MEASUREMENTS

Bust
92(97) cm.
36(38) in.

Length
58(59) cm.
22¾(23¼) in.

Sleeve Seam
28 cm.
11 in.

TENSION

13 sts. and 15 rows (12 sts. and 14 rows) = 5 cm. (2 in.) square over patt. on 4(4½)mm. needles. If your tension square does not correspond to these measurements, see page 156 for adjustment instructions.

ABBREVIATIONS

k. = knit; p. = purl; st(s). = stitch(es); inc. = increas(ing) (see page 156); dec. = decreas-(ing) (see page 157); beg. = begin(ning); rem. = remain(ing); rep. = repeat; alt. = alternate; tog. = together; sl. = slip stitch (transfer one stitch from left needle, knit-wise unless otherwise stated, to right hand needle.); cont. = continue; patt. = pattern; foll. = following; folls. = follows; mm. = millimetres; cm. = centimetres; in. = inch(es); st.st. = stocking stitch; y.o. = yarn over, to make 1 st.; p.s.s.o. = pass the slipped st. over; p.u. = pick up the loop before next st. and k. or p. into the back of it.
N.B. The 2nd size is worked over the same number of sts. as the 1st size, but using larger needles.

BACK

Cast on 121 sts. with 3¼mm. needles.
Work in k.1, p.1 rib for 5 cm. (2 in.), inc. in last row as folls.:
(Rib 11, p.u.) 10 times, rib 11. [131 sts.]
Change to 4(4½)mm. needles and work as folls.:
1st row: k.3, * y.o., p.3, sl.1, k.1, p.s.s.o., k.3, k.2 tog., p.3, y.o., k.1, rep. from * to last 2 sts., k.2.
2nd row: p.4, * k.3, p.5, k.3, p.3, rep. from * to last st., p.1.
3rd row: k.3, * y.o., k.1, p.3, sl.1, k.1, p.s.s.o., k.1, k.2 tog., p.3, k.1, y.o., k.1, rep. from * to last 2 sts., k.2.
4th row: p.5, * k.3, p.3, k.3, p.5, rep. from * to end.
5th row: k.3, * y.o., k.2, p.3, sl.1, k.2 tog., p.s.s.o., p.3, k.2, y.o., k.1, rep. from * to last 2 sts., k.2.
6th row: p.6, * k.3, p.1, k.3, p.7, rep. from * to end, ending last rep. p.6.
7th row: k.6, * p.7, k.7, rep. from * to end, ending last rep. k.6.
8th row: p.6, * k.7, p.7, rep. from * to end, ending last rep. p.6.
9th row: k.3, * k.1, k.2 tog., p.3, y.o., k.1, y.o., p.3, sl.1, k.1, p.s.s.o., k.2, rep. from * to last 2 sts., k.2.
10th row: as 4th row.
11th row: k.3, * k.2 tog., p.3, k.1, y.o., k.1, y.o., k.1, p.3, sl.1, k.1, p.s.s.o., k.1, rep. from * to last 2 sts., k.2.
12th row: as 2nd row.
13th row: k.2, k.2 tog., * p.3, k.2, y.o., k.1., y.o., k.2, p.3, sl.1, k.2 tog., p.s.s.o., rep. from * to end, ending last rep. sl.1, k.1, p.s.s.o., k.2.
14th row: p.3, * k.3, p.7, k.3, p.1, rep. from * to last 2 sts., p.2.
15th row: as 8th row.
16th row: as 7th row.
Rep. these 16 patt. rows throughout.
Work straight until back measures 38 cm. (15 in.) from beg.
Place a marker at both ends of work.
Work straight until back measures 56(57) cm. (22(22¼) in.) from beg.

Shape Neck

* Patt. 48 sts., turn. Leave rem. sts. on a holder.
Dec. 1 st. at neck edge on next row.

Work 1 row.
Cast off 2 sts. at beg. of next row.
Dec. 1 st. at neck edge on next and foll. alt. rows until 43 sts. rem.*
Work straight until 8 rows have been completed from beg. of neck shaping.
Cast off.
Return to rem. sts.
With right side facing, sl. the next 35 sts. onto a holder.
Rejoin yarn and patt. to end of row.
Dec. 1 st. at neck edge on next row.
Cast off 2 sts. at neck edge on next row.
Dec. 1 st. at neck edge on foll. 2 alt. rows.
Work 1 row. Cast off.

FRONT

Work as for back until 16 rows less than back have been worked.

Shape Neck

Work as for back from * to *.
Work straight until same length as back.
Cast off.
Return to rem. sts.
Sl. the next 35 sts. onto a holder, then complete to match first side, reversing all shapings.

SLEEVES

Cast on 59 sts. with 3¼mm. needles.
Work in k.1, p.1 rib for 10 rows, inc. on last row as folls.:

Rib 1, p.u., (rib 2, p.u.,) 28 times, rib 1, p.u., rib 1. [89 sts.]
Change to 4(4½)mm. needles and work in patt. as given for back.
Work straight until 64(60) rows of patt. have been worked.

Shape Top

Inc. 1 st. at both ends of the next and every foll. alt. row until there are 105 sts., working the extra sts. at both ends in st.st.
Cast off.

NECKBAND

Sew up left shoulder seam.
With right side facing and 3¼mm. needles, pick up and k.11 sts. from right side back neck, k. across 35 sts. at centre back neck, pick up and k.11 sts. from left side back neck and 17 sts. from left side front neck, k. across 35 sts. from centre front neck, and pick up and k.17 sts. from right side front neck.
Work in k.1, p.1 rib for 5 cm. (2 in.).
Cast off fairly loosely in rib.

MAKING UP

Press work on wrong side under a damp cloth.
Sew up right shoulder and neckband seam.
Fold neckband in half onto wrong side, and sew down.
Sew sleeves into armholes between markers.
Sew up side and sleeve seams.

Mock Cable Sweater

1958

Guernsey wool, V-neck sweater in a mock cable pattern, with set-in sleeves and single-ribbed welts

★★ Suitable for knitters with some previous experience

MATERIALS

Yarn
Poppleton Guernsey 5 ply
6(7:7:8:8) × 100g. balls

Needles
1 pair 2¾mm.
1 pair 3¼mm.
1 set of 4 double-pointed 2¾mm.

MEASUREMENTS

Chest
92(97:102:107:112) cm.
36(38:40:42:44) in.

Length
64(65:67:68:69) cm.
25(25½:26¼:26¾:27) in.

Sleeve Seam
46(47:48:48:49) cm.
18(18½:18¾:18¾:19¼) in.

TENSION

30 sts. and 35 rows = 10 cm. (4 in.) square over patt. on 3¼mm. needles. If your tension square does not correspond to these measurements see page 156 for adjustment instructions.

ABBREVIATIONS

k. = knit; p. = purl; st(s). = stitch(es); inc. = increas(ing) (see page 156); dec. = decreas(ing) (see page 157); beg. = begin(ning); rem. = remain(ing); rep. = repeat; alt. = alternate; tog. = together; sl. = slip stitch (transfer one stitch from left needle, knitwise unless otherwise stated, to right hand needle.); cont. = continue; patt. = pattern; foll. = following; folls. = follows; mm. = millimetres; cm. = centimetres; in. = inch(es); st.st. = stocking stitch; p.s.s.o. = pass slipped stitch over.

BACK

** Cast on 131(137:143:149:155) sts. with 2¾mm. needles.
1st row: k.2, * p.1, k.1, rep. from * to last st., k.1.
2nd row: * k.1, p.1, rep. from * to last st., k.1.
Rep. 1st and 2nd rows for 10 cm. (4 in.), ending with 2nd row.
Next row: k.10(8:8:10:5), * k. twice into next st., k.10(9:8:7:7), rep. from * to last 11(9:9:11:6) sts., k. twice into next st., k. to end. [142(150:158:166:174) sts.]
Change to 3¼mm. needles and patt.
1st row (wrong side): * k.2, p.2, rep. from * to last 2 sts., k.2.
2nd row: * p.2, k.2, rep. from * to last 2 sts., p.2.

3rd row: as 1st row.

4th row: * p.2, take the needle in front of first st. on left hand needle and k. the 2nd st., keeping needle at front, now k. the first st., sl. both sts. off the needle tog., rep. from * to last 2 sts., p.2.

These 4 rows form patt.

Work until back measures 42(42:43:44:46) cm. (16½(16½:16¾:17¼:18) in.) from beg., ending with a wrong side row. **

Shape Armholes

Cast off 5(6:7:8:9) sts. at beg. of next 2 rows.

Now dec. 1 st. at each end of next 3 rows, and then the 5(6:7:7:7) following alt. rows. [116(120:124:130:136) sts.]

Work until armholes measure 22(23:23: 24:24) cm. (8½(9:9:9½:9½) in.) measured straight, ending with a wrong side row.

Shape Shoulders

Cast off at beg. of next and foll. rows, 8 sts. 8 times, and 5(6:7:8:9) sts. twice.

Slip rem. 42(44:46:50:54) sts. onto a st. holder.

FRONT

Follow instructions for back from ** to **.

Shape Armholes and Neck

Next row: cast off 5(6:7:8:9) sts., patt. 66(69:72:75:78) sts. including st. on needle, turn, leaving rem. sts. on spare needle.

Cont. on these sts.

Next row: k.2 tog., work to end.

Cont. to dec. for neck on every 3rd row, and at the same time dec. 1 st. at armhole edge on the next 3 rows, and then the 5(6: 7:7:7) foll. alt. rows.

Now keeping armhole edge straight, cont. to dec. for neck on every 3rd row until 37(38:39:40:41) sts. rem.

Work until armhole measures same as back, ending at armhole edge.

Shape Shoulder

Cast off at beg. of next and foll. alt. rows, 8 sts. 4 times.

Work 1 row.

Cast off 5(6:7:8:9) rem. sts.

Rejoin yarn to rem. sts. at neck edge, patt. to end.

Next row: cast off 5(6:7:8:9) sts., patt. to last 2 sts., k.2 tog. Complete to match first side, working 1 row more to end at armhole edge before shaping shoulder.

SLEEVES

Cast on 63(63:67:67:71) sts. with 2¾mm. needles and work 8 cm. (3 in.) in rib as for back.

Next row: k.1(1:3:3:5), * k. twice into next st., k.5, rep. from * to last 2(2:4:4:6) sts., k. twice into next st., k.1(1:3:3:5). [74(74:78: 78:82) sts.]

Change to 3¼mm. needles and patt. Work 4 rows.

Inc. 1 st. at each end of next row, and then every 6th(6th:6th:5th:5th) row until there are 106(112:118:124:130) sts.

Work until sleeve measures 46(47:48: 48:49) cm. (18(18½:18¾:18¾:19¼) in.) from beg., ending with a wrong side row.

Shape Top

Cast off 5(6:7:8:9) sts. at beg. of next 2 rows.

Now dec. 1 st. at each end of every row until 86(86:90:90:94) sts. rem., and then every alt. row until 58 sts. rem.

Cast off at beg. of next and foll. rows, 2 sts. twice, 3 sts. twice, 4 sts. twice, and 5 sts. 4 times.

Cast off rem. 20 sts.

MAKING UP AND NECK BORDER

Press each piece lightly, foll. instructions on ball band.

Sew up shoulder seams.

Neck Border

With right side of work facing, and double-pointed needles, k. up sts. round neck as folls.:

1st needle – 42(44:46:50:54) sts. from holder at back, 2nd needle – 70(74:78: 82:86) sts. down left side of neck to centre front, 3rd needle – 69(73:77:81:85) sts. up right side of neck. [181(187:201:213:225) sts.]

1st round: 1st needle – (k.1, p.1) to end; 2nd needle – (k.1, p.1) to last 2 sts., sl.1, k.1, p.s.s.o.; 3rd needle – k.2 tog., (p.1, k.1) to last st., p.1.

2nd round: 1st needle – (k.1, p.1) to end; 2nd needle – (k.1, p.1) to last st., k.1; 3rd needle – k.1, (p.1, k.1) to last st., p.1.

3rd round: 1st needle – (k.1, p.1) to end; 2nd needle – (k.1, p.1) to last 3 sts., k.1, sl.1, k.1, p.s.s.o.; 3rd needle – k.2 tog., (k.1, p.1) to end.

4th round: 1st needle – (k.1, p.1) to end; 2nd needle – (k.1, p.1) to end; 3rd needle – (p.1, k.1) to last st., p.1.

Rep. last 4 rounds twice more.

Cast off firmly in rib.

Sew up side and sleeve seams.

Sew sleeves into armholes.

Press seams.

Aran Sweater with Rounded Yoke   1957

Thick, stocking-stitch, unisex sweater with heart, chevron and cable designs on circular-knitted yoke, and ribbed welts

★★★ For experienced knitters only

MATERIALS

Yarn

Hayfield Brig Aran
13(14:15:16:17:17) × 50g. balls

Needles

1 pair 3¾mm.
1 pair 4½mm.
1 set of 4 double-pointed 3¾mm.
1 circular 4½mm. (60 cm. long).
1 circular 4½mm. (100 cm. long).

MEASUREMENTS

Bust/Chest

87(92:97:102:107:112) cm.
34(36:38:40:42:44) in.

Length

60(61:62:63:64:65) cm.
23½(24:24½:24¾:25:25½) in.

Sleeve Seam

46(47:48:49:50:50) cm.
18(18½:18¾:19¼:19½:19½) in.

TENSION

18 sts. and 26 rows = 10 cm. (4 in.) square over st.st. on 4½mm. needles. If your tension square does not correspond to these measurements see page 156 for adjustment instructions.

ABBREVIATIONS

k. = knit; p. = purl; st(s). = stitch(es); inc. = increas(ing) (see page 156); dec. = decreas(ing) (see page 157); beg. = begin(ning);

rem. = remain(ing); rep. = repeat; alt. = alternate; tog. = together; sl. = slip stitch (transfer one stitch from left needle, knit-wise unless otherwise stated, to right hand needle.); cont. = continue; patt. = pattern; foll. = following; folls. = follows; mm. = millimetres; cm. = centimetres; in. = inch(es); st.st. = stocking stitch; t.b.l. = through back of loop(s); C2B = cable 2 back: sl. 1 st. purlwise onto cable needle and leave at back of work, k. next st., then p. the st. from cable needle; C2F = cable 2 front: sl. 1 st. purlwise onto cable needle and leave at front of work, p. next st., then k. the st. from cable needle through back of loop; C3B = cable 3 back: sl. 1 st. purl-wise onto cable needle and leave at back of work, k. next 2 sts. through back of loops, then p. st. from cable needle; C3F = cable 3 front: sl. 2 sts. purlwise onto cable needle and leave at front of work, p. next st., then k. the 2 sts. from cable needle through back of loops; C4B = cable 4 back: sl. 2 sts. purlwise onto cable needle and leave at back of work, k. next 2 sts., then k. the 2 sts. from cable needle; C4F = cable 4 front: sl. 2 sts. purlwise onto cable needle and leave at front of work, k. next 2 sts., then k. the 2 sts. from cable needle.

BACK

Cast on 78(82:86:90:94:98) sts. with 3¾mm. needles.
1st row: k.2, * p.2, k.2, rep. from * to end.
2nd row: p.2, * k.2, p.2, rep. from * to end.
Rep. 1st and 2nd rows for 8 cm. (3¼ in.), ending with 1st row.
Next row: still in rib, inc. 6(7:8:9:10:11) sts. evenly across row. [84(89:94:99:104:109) sts.]
Change to 4½mm. needles.
Cont. in st.st., starting with a k. row.
Work until back measures 39(40:41:42:43:44) cm. (15¼(15¾:16:16½:16¾:17¼) in.) from beg., ending with a p. row.

Shape Armholes
Cast off 8 sts. at beg. of next 2 rows.
Leave rem. 68(73:78:83:88:93) sts. on spare needle.

FRONT

Work exactly as back.

SLEEVES

Cast on 38(42:42:46:46:50) sts. with 3¾mm. needles.
Work in rib as on back for 8 cm. (3¼ in.), ending with 1st row.
Next row: still in rib, inc. 2(0:2:0:2:0) sts. evenly across row. [40(42:44:46:48:50) sts.]
Change to 4½mm. needles.
Cont. in st.st. starting with a k. row.
AT THE SAME TIME, inc. 1 st. at each end of 9th and every foll. 8th row to obtain 62(64:66:68:70:72) sts.
Cont. straight until sleeve measures 46(47:48:49:50:50) cm. (18(18½:18¾:19¼:19½:19½) in.), ending with a p. row.

Shape Top
Cast off 8 sts. at beg. of next 2 rows.

Leave rem. 46(48:50:52:54:56) sts. on spare needle.

YOKE

Start with back.
With 100 cm. long 4½mm. circular needle and right side facing, sl. 1st back st. purl-wise, k. to last back st., k. tog. last back st. and 1st left sleeve st., k. to last left sleeve st., k. tog. last left sleeve st. and 1st front st., k. to last front st., k. tog. last front st. and 1st right sleeve st., k. to last right sleeve st., k. tog. last right sleeve st. and sl. st. from back. [224(238:252:266:280:294) sts.]
Next round: k.33(36:38:41:43:46) to centre back.
All foll. rounds start here.
Make a loop with contrasting yarn and place it round needle as marker.
Sl. loop from left to right on every round.
Work in patt. as folls.:
1st and 2nd rounds: k.
3rd round: * k.1, p.1, rep. from * to end.
4th and 5th rounds: k.
6th and 7th rounds: p.

Work Heart Patt.
8th round: p.6, * sl. 1 st. purlwise onto cable needle and leave at back of work, k.1 t.b.l., then k. st. from cable needle, sl. 1 st. purlwise onto cable needle and leave at front of work, k.1, then k. st. from cable needle t.b.l., p.10, rep. from * ending last rep. p.4.
9th round: p.6, * k.4, p.10, rep. from * ending last rep. p.4.
10th round: p.5, * C3B, C3F, p.8, rep. from * ending last rep. p.3.
11th round: p.5, * k.2, p.2, k.2, p.8, rep. from * ending last rep. p.3.
12th round: p.4, * C3B, p.2, C3F, p.6, rep. from * ending last rep. p.2.
13th round: p.4, * k.2, p.4, k.2, p.6, rep. from * ending last rep. p.2.
14th round: p.3, * C3B, p.4, C3F, p.4, rep. from * ending last rep. p.1.
15th round: p.3, * k.2, p.6, k.2, p.4, rep. from * ending last rep. p.1.
16th round: * p.2, C3B, p.1, k.4, p.1, C3F, rep. from * to end.
17th round: * p.2, k.2, p.2, k.4, p.2, k.2, rep. from * to end.
18th and 19th rounds: as 17th round.
20th round: * p.2, (C3F, C3B) twice, rep. from * to end.
21st round: p.
Change to 60 cm. long 4½mm. circular needle.
22nd round: k., dec. 69(73:87:91:95:99) sts. evenly across round. [155(165:165:175:185:195) sts.]
23rd and 24th rounds: p.

Work Chevron Patt.
25th round: * C2F, p.3, rep. from * to end.
26th round: p.1, * k.1, p.4, rep. from * ending last rep. p.3.
27th round: p.1, * C2F, p.3, rep. from * ending last rep. p.2.
28th round: p.2, * k.1, p.4, rep. from * ending last rep. p.2.
29th round: p.2, * C2F, p.3, rep. from * ending last rep. p.1.

30th round: p.3, * k.1, p.4, rep. from * ending last rep. p.1.
31st round: p.2, C2B, p.3, rep. from * ending last rep. p.1.
32nd round: as 28th round.
33rd round: p.1, * C2B, p.3, rep. from * ending last rep. p.2.
34th round: as 26th round.
35th round: * C2B, p.3, rep. from * to end.
36th round: p.
37th round: k., dec. 56(57:57:58:59:60) sts. evenly across round. [99(108:108:117:126:135) sts.]
38th and 39th rounds: p.

Work Cable Patt.
40th round: * k.8, p.1, rep. from * to end.
41st round: * C4B, C4F, p.1, rep. from * to end.
42nd to 47th rounds: as 40th round.
48th round: * C4F, C4B, p.1, rep. from * to end.
49th round: p.
Change to set of double-pointed 3¾mm. needles.
50th round: k., dec. 7(12:12:17:22:27) sts. evenly across round. [92(96:96:100:104:108) sts.]
51st and 52nd rounds: p.

NECKBAND

Work in k.2, p.2 rib for 16 rounds.
Cast off loosely in rib.

MAKING UP

Press according to instructions on ball band, being careful not to flatten the patt.
Sew up side and sleeve seams.
Fold neckband in half to inside and slip-stitch.
Press seams if required.

Harlequin Sweater

Long, diamond-patterned, circular-knitted, V-neck sweater with sleeves worked downwards from picked-up armhole stitches

★★★ Suitable for experienced knitters

MATERIALS

Yarn
Templeton's H & O Shetland Fleece
7(7:8:8) × 25g. balls (Main Col. A)
7(7:8:8) × 25g. balls (Contrast Col. B)

Needles
1 set of 4 double-pointed 3mm. (ribbing)
1 circular 3mm. (ribbing)
1 set of 4 double-pointed 3¼(3¾:3¼:3¾)mm. (sleeves)
1 circular 3¼(3¾:3¼:3¾)mm. (body)
1 pair 3¼(3¾:3¼:3¾)mm. (upper body)

MEASUREMENTS

Bust
87(92:97:102) cm.
34(36:38:40) in.

Length
61(61:65:65) cm.
24(24:25½:25½) in.

Sleeve Length
45(45:47:47) cm.
17¾(17¾:18½:18½) in.

TENSION
Approx. 27 sts. = 10 cm. (4 in.) over patt. on 3¾mm. needles. Approx. 28 sts. = 10 cm. (4 in.) over patt. on 3¼mm. needles. If your tension does not correspond to these measurements see page 156 for adjustment instructions.

ABBREVIATIONS
k. = knit; p. = purl; st(s). = stitch(es); inc. = increas(ing) (see page 156); dec. = decreas-(ing) (see page 157); beg. = begin(ning); rem. = remain(ing); rep. = repeat; alt. = alternate; tog. = together; sl. = slip stitch (transfer one stitch from left needle, knit-wise unless otherwise stated, to right hand needle.); cont. = continue; patt. = pattern; foll. = following; folls. = follows; mm. = millimetres; cm. = centimetres; in. = inch(es); st.st. = stocking stitch; t.b.l. = through back of loop.

FRONT AND BACK (worked together)

Cast on 252(258:282:288) sts. with 3mm. circular needle and B.
Join into a circle, placing a contrast yarn marker at join, and work in rounds to armholes as folls.:

1st round: with B, * k.4, p.2, rep. from * to end.
2nd round: with A, * k.4, p.2, rep. from * to end.
Rep. these 2 rounds until rib measures 5 cm. (2 in.), ending with a 1st round.
Change to 3¼(3¾:3¼:3¾)mm. circular needle and cont. in st.st.
N.B.: *All* st.sts. and patt. sts. are k. sts. when worked in the round.
1st round: with A, k.
2nd round: with B, k., inc. 14(8:12:6) sts.

evenly on round. [266(266:294:294) sts.]
Cont. in 2 col. patt.
1st round: * 1A, 1B, rep. from * to end.
2nd round: * 1B, 1A, rep. from * to end.
3rd round: * 1A, 1B, 3A (1B, 1A) twice, 3B, 1A, 1B, rep. from * to end.
4th round: * 1B, 5A, 1B, 1A, 5B, 1A, rep. from * to end.
5th round: * 7A, 7B, rep. from * to end.
6th round: as 4th round.
7th round: as 3rd round.
8th round: as 2nd round.
These 8 rounds form the patt. and are repeated throughout.
Cont. in patt. until work measures 41(42:43:44) cm. (16(16½:16¾:17¼) in.) or required length to armhole.
Slip next 10(10:8:8) sts. to right needle tip, rejoin yarn to next st. and cast off 8(8:12:12) sts. for left armhole, patt. a further 131(131:141:141) sts. for front, cast off next 8(8:12:12) sts. for right armhole and patt. a further 117(117:127:127) sts. for back. [132(132:142:142) sts. in front; 118(118:128:128) sts. in back].

Work Back
With 3¼(3¾:3¼:3¾)mm. needles, cont. on back sts., working in rows.
N.B.: When working on 2 needles, all wrong side patt. rows are p., all right side patt. rows are k.
Keeping patt. correct, work 56(56:64:64) rows.
Cast off.

Work Front
With wrong side of rem. sts. facing, rejoin yarn and cont. in patt.
Work 1 row.
Keeping patt. correct, dec. 1 st. at each end of next and every alt. row until there are 118(118:128:128) sts.
Work 1(1:5:5) rows more.

Divide for Neck
1st row: patt. 59(59:64:64), turn and complete left side of neck, leaving rem. sts. on holder.
Keeping patt. correct, dec. 1 st. at centre front edge on next 8 rows, then on every right side row until there are 39(39:42:42) sts.
Work 9 rows.
Cast off.
With right side facing rejoin yarn to rem. sts. for right side of neck and work to correspond with left side, reversing shapings.
Sew up shoulder seams.

SLEEVES

With right side of armhole facing and set of 3¾(3¾:3¼:3¾)mm. needles, beg. at underarm and using A and B alternately, k. up 112(112:126:126) sts. evenly round armhole and arrange on 3 needles, marking end of round as for body. Work in rounds of two col. patt. as for body, beg. with a 2nd row.

Work 1 complete patt.

Cont. keeping patt. correct, dec. 1 st. at each end of next and every 8th round until 102(102:116:116) sts. rem., then dec. 1 st. at each end of every 4th round until there are 70(70:84:84) sts.

Cont. until sleeve measures 40(40:42:42) cm. (15¾(15¾:16½:16½) in.) or 5 cm. (2 in.) less than required finished sleeve length.

Next round: with B, k.

Next round: with A, k., dec. 22(16:24:24) sts. evenly. [48(54:60:60) sts.]

Change to set of 3mm. needles.

Now work 5 cm. (2 in.) cuff in rib patt. as given at start of body. Cast off loosely.

NECKBAND

With set of 3mm. needles and B, and with right side of neck facing, k. up 50(50:54:54) sts. down left side of neck, with 2nd needle k. up 50(50:54:54) sts. up right side of neck, and with 3rd needle k. up 42(42:46:46) sts. from back. [142(142:154:154) sts.]

1st round: 1st needle – * k.2, p.2, rep. from * to last 2 sts., k.2 tog., 2nd needle – k.2 tog. t.b.l., * p.2, k.2, rep. from * to end, 3rd needle – p.2, * k.2, p.2, rep. from * to end. Keeping rib as set, work 3 more rows, dec. at end of 1st needle and beg. of 2nd needle on each round as for 1st round.

Cast off loosely in rib, working centre front dec. on this row also.

MAKING UP

Roll finished work in damp towel and leave for 1 hour. Pin out to size. Leave until dry before unpinning.

Basketwork-check Waistcoat

1963

Warm waistcoat in three-colour, stocking-stitch check pattern, with doubled-over, ribbed front and armhole bands, single-rib hem welt

★★ Suitable for knitters with some previous experience

MATERIALS

Yarn
Pingouin Confort
4(4:5:5:6) × 50g. balls (Main Col. A)
2(2:3:3:3) × 50g. balls (Contrast Col. B)
2(2:3:3:3) × 50g. balls (Contrast Col. C)

Needles
1 pair 3mm.
1 pair 4mm.

Buttons
5

MEASUREMENTS

Chest
92(97:102:107:112) cm.
36(38:40:42:44) in.

Length
57(58:60:61:62) cm.
22¼(22¾:23½:24:24¼) in.

TENSION

26 sts. and 22 rows = 10 cm. (4 in.) square over patt. on 4mm. needles. If your tension square does not correspond to these measurements, see page 156 for adjustment instructions.

ABBREVIATIONS

k. = knit; p. = purl; st(s). = stitch(es); inc. = increas(ing) (see page 156); dec. = decreas-

(ing) (see page 157); beg. = begin(ning); rem. = remain(ing); rep. = repeat; alt. = alternate; tog. = together; sl. = slip stitch (transfer one stitch from left needle, knitwise unless otherwise stated, to right hand needle.); cont. = continue; patt. = pattern; foll. = following; folls. = follows; mm. = millimetres; cm. = centimetres; in.

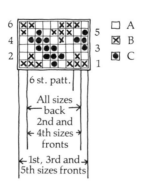

= inch(es); st.st. = stocking stitch; m.1 = make 1 st.: pick up horizontal loop lying before next st., and work into back of it.

N.B.: When working from chart, carry yarns not in use loosely across wrong side of work to keep fabric elastic. Read odd rows (k. rows) from right to left, and even rows (p. rows) from left to right.

BACK

Cast on 105(111:117:123:129) sts. with 3mm. needles and A, and work in k.1, p.1 rib, rows on right side having k.1 at each end, for 6 cm. (2¼ in.), ending with a right side row.

Next row: rib 2(3:2:2:1), m.1, (rib 4(0:6:6:0), m.1) 5(9:7:13:0) times, (rib 5(5:5:5:6), m.1) 16(21:14:8:21) times, rib to end. [127(133:139:145:151) sts.]

Change to 4mm. needles.

Work in patt. from chart, rep. the 6 patt. sts. 21(22:23:24:25) times across, working first st. on k. rows and last st. on p. rows as indicated, until back measures 35 cm. (13¾ in.), ending with a wrong side row.

Shape Armholes

Cast off 5(5:6:6:7) sts. at beg. of next 2 rows.
Dec. 1 st. at each end of next 5(7:7:9:9) rows.
Work 1 row.
Dec. 1 st. at each end of next and foll. 3(2: 2:1:1) alt. rows. [99(103:107:111:115) sts.]
Work straight until armhole measures 22(23:25:26:27) cm. (8½:9:9¾:10¼:10½) in.), ending with a wrong side row.

Shape Shoulders

Cast off 7(7:7:8:8) sts. at beg. of next 6 rows, and 7(8:9:7:8) sts. at beg. of foll. 2 rows.
Cast off rem. 43(45:47:49:51) sts.

LEFT FRONT

Cast on 53(57:59:63:65) sts. with 3mm. needles and A, and work in rib as for back, ending with a right side row.
Next row: rib 4(1:2:4:5), m.1, (rib 5(6:6:6:6), m.1) 9 times, rib to end. [63(67:69:73:75) sts.]
Change to 4mm. needles and work in patt. from chart, rep. the 6 patt. sts. 10(11: 11:12:12) times across, working first 2(1:2: 1:2) sts. and last 1(0:1:0:1) st. on k. rows, and first 1(0:1:0:1) st. and last 2(1:2:1:2) sts. on p. rows as indicated until front matches back to armhole, ending with a wrong side row.

Shape Armhole and Front Slope

Keeping patt. correct, work as folls.:
1st row: cast off 5(5:6:6:7) sts., patt. to last 2 sts., k.2 tog.
2nd row: patt.
Dec. 1 st. at armhole edge on next 5(7:7:9:9) rows then on every alt. row 3(2:2:1:1) times, at the same time dec. 1 st. at front slope on next and every foll. alt. row until 43(46:47:50:51) sts. rem.
Cont. dec. 1 st. at front slope *only* on every alt. row until 28(29:30:31:32) sts. rem.
Work straight until armhole matches back to shoulder, ending with a wrong side row.

Shape Shoulder

Cast off 7(7:7:8:8) sts. at beg. of next and foll. 3 alt. rows.
Work 1 row.
Cast off rem. 7(8:9:7:8) sts.

RIGHT FRONT

Work as for left front, reversing shapings.

FRONT BORDERS

Cast on 15 sts. with 3mm. needles and A.
1st row: k.7, sl.1, k.7.
2nd row: p.
Rep. these 2 rows throughout.
Work straight until border fits up right front from lower edge, around back neck to front slope shaping on left front.
Mark position for 5 buttons on right front, first to come level with front slope, last to

come 2 cm. (¾ in.) from lower edge and the others spaced evenly between.
Work 1st buttonhole as folls.:
Next row: k.3, cast off 2 sts., k.2 including st. used in casting off, sl.1, k.2, cast off 2 sts., k. to end.
Next row: p., casting on 2 sts. over each set cast off.
Work 4 more sets of buttonholes to correspond with button markers.
Complete border.
Cast off.

ARMHOLE BORDERS

Cast on 11 sts. with 3mm. needles and A.

1st row: k.5, sl.1, k.5.
2nd row: p.
Rep. these 2 rows until border fits around armhole when slightly stretched.
Cast off.

MAKING UP

Sew up shoulder and side seams.
Fold front border in half to wrong side and sew in position.
Buttonhole-stitch around double buttonholes.
Join armhole borders into a circle, fold in half to wrong side and sew to armholes.
Press. Sew on buttons.

Thick Cotton Sweater

Loose T-shape, stocking-stitch sweater in two broad bands of colour, with grafted shoulder seam and ribbed hem welt

★ Suitable for beginners

MATERIALS

Yarn
Pingouin Coton Naturel 8 Fils
9(10) × 50g. balls in A (lower col.)
7(8) × 50g. balls in B (top col.)

Needles
1 pair 3¼mm.
1 pair 4mm.
1 crochet hook 4mm.

MEASUREMENTS

Bust
82–87(92–97) cm.
32–34(36–38) in.

Length
66(69) cm.
26(27) in.

Sleeve Seam
26(28) cm.
10¼(11) in.

TENSION

22 sts. and 28 rows = 10 cm. (4 in.) square over st.st. on 4mm. needles. If your tension square does not correspond to these measurements, see page 156 for adjustment instructions.

ABBREVIATIONS

k. = knit; p. = purl; st(s). = stitch(es); inc. = increas(ing) (see page 156); dec. = decreas(ing) (see page 157); beg. = begin(ning); rem. = remain(ing); rep. = repeat; alt. = alternate; tog. = together; sl. = slip stitch (transfer one stitch from left needle, knitwise unless otherwise stated, to right hand needle.); cont. = continue; patt. = pattern; foll. = following; folls. = follows; mm. = millimetres; cm. = centimetres; in. = inch(es); st.st. = stocking stitch; m.1 = make 1 st.: pick up the horizontal loop lying before next st. and k. into the back of it.

BACK

Cast on 121(125) sts. with 3¼mm. needles and A.
Work 8 cm. (3¼ in.) in k.1, p.1 rib, ending with wrong side facing.

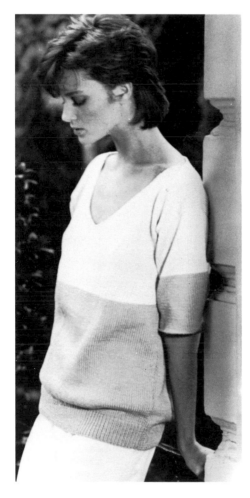

Change to 4mm. needles and dec. as folls.:
1st row: * k.7, k.2 tog., rep. from * to last 4(8) sts., k.4(8). [108(112) sts.]
2nd row: p. to end.
Cont. to work in st.st. until work measures 33(35) cm. (13(13¾) in.) from cast-on edge. Change to B and work in st.st. for a further 13 cm. (5 in.).

Shape Neck
With right side facing, work as folls.:
K.53(55), cast off centre 2 sts., k. to end.
Leave rem. sts. on a st. holder.
Dec. 1 st. at neck edge on the next 11(13) rows, then dec. 1 st. at neck edge on the foll. 22 alt. rows.
Work 1 row.
Leave 20 shoulder sts. on a st. holder.
Work other side to match first side.

FRONT

Work as for back, changing to B 33(35) cm. (13(13¾) in.) from cast on edge, and cont. to work straight until work measures 66(69) cm. (26(27) in.) from cast-on edge.

Shape Neck
With right side facing, work as folls.:
K.20, cast off centre 68(72) sts., work to end.
Leave each group of rem. 20 sts. on holder.

SLEEVES

Cast on 84(88) sts. with 4mm. needles and A. Work in st.st., and change to B when work measures 10 cm. (4 in.) from cast-on edge. Now inc. 1 at each end of first and every foll. 8th row until there are 100(106) sts. Cast off.

FINISHING

Omitting ribbing, press pieces on wrong side.

Right Shoulder Seam
Holding front and back of shoulder with right sides tog., and needles parallel, work as folls.: beg. at opposite side to rem. tail of yarn, take first st. from needle of front onto crochet hook, then take first st. from back needle and draw this st. through first st. on hook. Now take 2nd st. from front needle and draw this through st. on crochet hook, as before.
Rep. to end of sts., pulling tail of yarn through last st. to cast off.

Neck Border
With 4mm. needles and B, right side facing, pick up and k. 68(72) sts. across front neck, 57(59) sts. down right side, then 57(59) sts. up left side of back neck. [182(190) sts.]
Turn work and cast off on next row.

Left Shoulder Seam
Work as for right shoulder seam.

MAKING UP

Sew cast off edge of sleeve to body by positioning centre top of sleeve to shoulder seamline.
Sew up sleeve and side seams.
Press seam.

Softly Ribbed Ski Sweater

Long, loose, ski sweater with huge, divided collar and set-in sleeves, knitted throughout in fisherman's rib

★★★ Suitable for experienced knitters

MATERIALS

Yarn
Patons Clansman DK
11(12:13:14) × 50g. balls

Needles
1 pair 3¼mm.
1 pair 4mm.

MEASUREMENTS

Bust
82(87:92:97) cm.
32(34:36:38) in.

Length
59(60:61:62) cm.
23¼(23½:24:24¼) in.

Sleeve Seam
36 cm.
14 in.

TENSION

18 sts. and 48 rows = 10 cm. (4 in.) square over patt. on 4mm. needles. If your tension square does not correspond to these measurements, see page 156 for adjustment instructions.

ABBREVIATIONS

k. = knit; p. = purl; st(s). = stitch(es); inc. = increas(ing) (see page 156); dec. = decreas(ing) (see page 157); beg. = begin(ning); rem. = remain(ing); rep. = repeat; alt. = alternate; tog. = together; sl. = slip stitch (transfer one stitch from left needle, knitwise unless otherwise stated, to right hand needle.); cont. = continue; patt. = pattern; foll. = following; folls. = follows; mm. = millimetres; cm. = centimetres; in. = inch(es); st.st. = stocking stitch; p.s.s.o. = pass the slipped st. over; k.1 blw. = k. 1 below: k. into next st. one row below, at the same time slipping off st. above.

BACK

** Cast on 70(74:76:80) sts. with 3¼mm. needles and work in fisherman's rib as folls.:
1st row (wrong side): k.
2nd row: * p.1, k.1 blw., rep. from * to last 2 sts., k.2.
Rep. 2nd row throughout.
Work straight for 7 cm. (2¾ in.).
Change to 4mm. needles and, keeping rib correct, shape sides by inc. 1 st. at each end of next and every foll. 6th row until there are 78(82:88:92) sts., taking inc. sts. into rib.
Work straight until back measures 45 cm. (17¾ in.).

Shape Armholes
Cast off 2 sts. at beg. of next 4 rows.
Dec. 1 st. at each end of next and every foll. alt. row until 58(64:68:74) sts. rem., ending with a wrong side row.
Dec. 1 st. at each end of next and every foll. 4th row until 42(44:48:50) sts. rem. Work 3 rows. **
Dec. 1 st. at each end of next and every alt. row until 22(24:26:28) sts. rem., ending with a wrong side row.
Cast off rem. sts.

FRONT

Work as for back from ** to **.
Dec. 1 st. at each end of next and every foll. alt. row until 34(36:38:40) sts. rem., ending with a right side row.

Shape Neck
Next row: rib 14, cast off 6(8:10:12) sts., patt. to end.
Work left side first.
Dec. 1 st. at armhole and neck edge on next and every foll. alt. row until 2 sts. rem., ending with a wrong side row.
Cast off rem. 2 sts.

With right side facing, rejoin yarn to rem. sts. and complete to match first side, reversing shapings.

SLEEVES

Cast on 40(44:44:48) sts. with 3¼mm. needles and work in rib as given for back for 8 rows.
Change to 4mm. needles and shape sides by inc. 1 st. at each end of next and every foll. 10th(10th:8th:8th) row until there are 64(68:72:76) sts., taking inc. sts. into patt.
Work straight until sleeve seam measures 36 cm. (14 in.).

Shape Top
Cast off 2 sts. at beg. of next 4 rows.
Dec. 1 st. at each end of next and every foll. 4th row until 52(48:42:40) sts. rem.
Work 3 rows.
1st, 2nd and 3rd sizes:
Dec. 1 st. at each end of next and every foll. 6th row until 40 sts. rem.
Work 5 rows.

Shape Shoulder Dart
All sizes:
1st row: rib 19, sl.1, k.2 tog., p.s.s.o., patt. 18.
Work 4(4:6:6) rows.
Next row: rib 17, sl.1, k.2 tog., p.s.s.o., patt. 18.
Work 4(4:6:6) rows.
Next row: rib 17, sl.1, k.2 tog., p.s.s.o., patt. 16.
Work 4(4:6:6) rows.
Next row: rib 15, sl.1, k.2 tog., p.s.s.o., patt. 16.
Work 4 rows.
Cont. to dec. 2 sts. in centre on every 5th row until 18 sts. rem.
Cast off.

COLLAR

Cast on 114(118:122:126) sts. with 4mm. needles. Work in rib for 16 cm. (6¼ in.).
Cast off 6 sts. at beg. of next 8 rows.
Cast off rem. sts.

MAKING UP

Sew up shoulder seams and set in sleeves.
Sew up side and sleeve seams.
Turn in two sts. along straight edges of collar, and sew down rib on wrong side, pulling stitching tight to give a straight line.
Overlap ends of collar for 5 cm. (2 in.) and pin cast-off edge of collar to neck, placing overlap to centre front and easing collar to fit.
Sew collar to sweater.

V-neck Casual Sweater

Unisex, V-neck sweater with cable-twist and stocking-stitch panels, set-in sleeves and ribbed welts

★★ Suitable for knitters with some previous experience

MATERIALS

Yarn
Emu Super Match DK
12(12:13:13:14) × 50g. balls

Needles
1 pair 3¼mm.
1 pair 4mm.

MEASUREMENTS

Chest
92(97:102:107:112) cm.
36(38:40:42:44) in.

Length
61(62:63:65:66) cm.
24(24¼:24¾:25½:26) in.

Sleeve Seam
50(51:52:52:53) cm.
19½(20:20½:20½:20¾) in.

TENSION

24 sts. and 30 rows = 10 cm. (4 in.) square over patt. on 4mm. needles. If your tension square does not correspond to these measurements see page 156 for adjustment instructions.

ABBREVIATIONS

k. = knit; p. = purl; st(s). = stitch(es); inc. = increas(ing) (see page 156); dec. = decreas-(ing) (see page 157); beg. = begin(ning); rem. = remain(ing); rep. = repeat; alt. = alternate; tog. = together; sl.. = slip stitch (transfer one stitch from left needle, knit-wise unless otherwise stated, to right hand needle.); cont. = continue; patt. = pattern; foll. = following; folls. = follows; mm. = millimetres; cm. = centimetres; in. = inch(es); st.st. = stocking stitch; C3B = cable 3 back: sl. 2 sts. onto cable needle and leave at back of work, k. next st. then p.1, k.1 from cable needle; C3F = cable 3 front: sl. 1 st. onto cable needle and leave at front of work, k. next st., p. the foll. st., then k. the st. on cable needle; p.s.s.o. = pass the sl. st. over.

BACK

Cast on 117(123:129:135:141) sts. with 3¼mm. needles.

1st row: k.1, * p.1, k.1, rep. from * to end.
2nd row: p.1, * k.1, p.1, rep. from * to end.
Rep. 1st and 2nd rows until work measures 9(9:10:10:11) cm. (3½(3½:4:4: 4¼) in.), ending with 2nd row.
Change to 4mm. needles and work in patt. as folls.:
1st row: k.16(16:19:19:22), * p.1, C3B, p.1, k.1, p.1, k.6(7:7:8:8), rep. from * to last 10(9:12:11:14) sts., k. to end.
2nd row: p.16(16:19:19:22), * (k.1, p.1) 3 times, k.1, p.6(7:7:8:8), rep. from * to last 10(9:12:11:14) sts., p. to end.
3rd row: k. the k. sts. and p. the p. sts.
4th row: as 2nd row.
5th row: k.16(16:19:19:22), * p.1, k.1, p.1, C3F, p.1, k.6(7:7:8:8), rep. from * to last 10(9:12:11:14) sts. k. to end.
6th row: p.16(16:19:19:22), * (k.1, p.1) 3 times, k.1, p.6(7:7:8:8), rep. from * to last 10(9:12:11:14) sts., p. to end.
7th row: k. the k. sts. and p. the p. sts.
8th row: as 6th row.
Rep. 1st to 8th row throughout.

AT THE SAME TIME, when work measures 39(39:39:40:40) cm. (15¼(15¼: 15¼:15¾:15¾) in.) ending with a wrong side row, shape armholes.

Shape Armholes

Cast off 6(6:7:8:9) sts. at beg. of next 2 rows.
Dec. 1 st. at each end of next row and foll. 5(6:7:7:8) alt. rows. [93(97:99:103:105) sts.]
Cont. straight until work measures 20(21: 22:23:24) cm. (7¾(8¼:8½:9:9½) in.) from beg. of armhole shaping, ending with a wrong side row.

Shape Shoulders

Cast off 7(8:8:9:9) sts. at beg. of next 4 rows.
Cast off 8 sts. at beg. of foll. 4 rows.
Cast off rem. 33(33:35:35:37) sts.

FRONT

Work as on back up to 6th row of armhole shapings, ending with a wrong side row. [101(107:111:115:119) sts.]
Cont. as back but AT THE SAME TIME shape neckline.

Shape Neckline

Next row: patt. to centre st. (4th st. on 4th cable), place centre st. unworked on safety pin, turn work and leave rem. sts. on spare needle.
Next row: p.1, sl. 1 purlwise, p.1, p.s.s.o., patt. to end.
Cont. in patt., dec. 1 st. at neck edge (as in previous row) on every alt. row 15(15:16: 16:17) times. [30(32:32:34:34) sts.]
Cont. straight until front reaches same row as back for shoulder shaping.

Shape Shoulder

Work as for back.
Return to sts. on spare needle, and rejoin yarn.
Next row: k.1, sl. 1 knitwise, k.1, p.s.s.o., patt. to end.
Finish to match first side, dec. as just indicated, and reversing all shapings.

SLEEVES

Cast on 57(59:61:63:65) sts. with 3¼mm. needles.
Work in k.1, p.1 rib as on back for 9(9:10:10:11) cm. (3½(3½:4:4:4½) in.), ending with 2nd row.
Change to 4mm. needles.

Next row: k.12(12:13:13:14), * p.1, C3B, p.1, k.1, p.1, k.6(7:7:8:8), rep. from * to last 6(5:6:5:6) sts., k. to end.
Cont. in patt. as set on this row.
AT THE SAME TIME, inc. 1 st. at each end of 3rd row, then inc. 1 st. at each end of every foll. 6th row 18 times, working all incs. in st.st. [95(97:99:101:103) sts.]
Cont. straight until work measures 50(51: 52:52:53) cm. (19½(20:20½:20½:20¾) in.), ending with a wrong side row.

Shape Top
Cast off 6(6:7:8:9) sts. at beg. of next 2 rows.
Dec. 1 st. at each end of every foll. alt. row 26(27:27:27:27) times. [31 sts.]
Dec. 6 sts. at beg. of next 2 rows.
Cast off rem. 19 sts.

NECKBAND
Sew up right shoulder seam.
With 3¼mm. needles and right side facing, pick up 50(50:52:52:54) sts. down left front neck, 1 st. from safety pin (mark with loop of contrasting yarn), 50(50:52: 52:54) sts. up right front neck and 33(33: 35:35:37) sts. from back neck. [134(134: 140:140:146) sts.]
1st row: p.1, * k.1, p.1, rep. from * to 2 sts. before marked st., k.2 sts. tog., p. marked st., k.2 sts. tog., * p.1, k.1, rep. from * to end.
2nd row: p.1, * k.1, p.1, rep. from * to 2 sts. before marked st., sl. 1, p.1, p.s.s.o., k. marked st., k.2 sts. tog., * p.1, k.1, rep. from * to end.
Rep. 1st and 2nd row for 3 cm. (1¼ in.).
Cast off in rib, dec. as usual.

MAKING UP
Press each piece following instructions on ball band.
Sew up left shoulder seam and neckband.
Sew up side and sleeve seams.
Set in sleeves. Press seams if required.

Classic, Aran-style Sweater 1957

Hip-length sweater in moss, ladder and cable patterns, with set-in sleeves and ribbed welts

★★ Suitable for knitters with some previous experience

MATERIALS
Yarn
Lister-Lee Motoravia DK
13(14:15) × 50g. balls

Needles
1 pair 3¼mm.
1 pair 4mm.
1 cable needle

MEASUREMENTS
Chest
97(102:107) cm.
38(40:42) in.

Length
69 cm.
27 in.

Sleeve Seam
47(47:48) cm.
18½(18½:18¾) in.

TENSION
22 sts. and 32 rows = 10 cm. (4 in.) square over moss st. (every row * k.1, p.1, rep. from * to last st., k.1, on an uneven number of sts.) on 4mm. needles. If your tension square does not correspond to these measurements see page 156 for adjustment instructions.

ABBREVIATIONS
k. = knit; p. = purl; st(s). = stitch(es); inc. = increas(ing) (see page 156); dec. = decreas-(ing) (see page 157); beg. = begin(ning); rem. = remain(ing); rep. = repeat; alt. = alternate; tog. = together; sl. = slip stitch (transfer one stitch from left needle, knit-wise unless otherwise stated, to right hand needle.); cont. = continue; patt. = pattern; foll. = following; folls. = follows; mm. = millimetres; cm. = centimetres; in. = inch(es); st.st. = stocking stitch; C6B = cable 6 back: sl. 3 sts. onto cable needle and leave at back of work, k. next 3 sts., then k.3 sts. from cable needle; k.1 t.f.b. = k.1 st. first through the front and then through the back of its loop.

BACK
Cast on 130(134:138) sts. with 3¼mm. needles.
1st row: k.2, * p.2, k.2, rep. from * to end.
2nd row: p.2, * k.2, p.2, rep. from * to end.
Rep. 1st and 2nd row for 9 cm. (3½ in.), ending with 2nd(1st:2nd) row.
Adjust sts. for patt.

Chest 97 cm. (38 in.) only:
Next row: (k.2, p.2) twice, k.2 tog., (p.2, k.2) 3 times, p.2, k.2 tog., (p.2, k.2) 7 times, p.2, k.2 tog., p.2, k.2, p.2, k.2 tog. (centre st.), p.2, k.2, p.2, k.2 tog., (p.2, k.2) 9 times, p.2, k.2 tog., (p.2, k.2) to last 4 sts., p.2, k.2 tog. [123 sts.]
Chest 102 cm. (40 in.) only:
Next row: p.2 tog., rib 64, k.2 tog. (centre st.), rib to last 2 sts., p.2 tog. [131 sts.]
Chest 107 cm. (42 in.) only:
Next row: (p.2, k.2) 4 times, p.2, k.1 t.f.b., k.1, (p.2, k.2) 7 times, p.2, k.1 t.f.b., k.1, (p.2, k.2) 3 times, p.2, k.2 tog. (centre st.), (p.2, k.2) 3 times, p.2, k.1 t.f.b., k.1, (p.2, k.2) 7 times, p.2, k.1 t.f.b., k.1, (p.2, k.2) to last 4 sts., p.2, k.2 tog. [139 sts.]
All sizes:
Change to 4mm. needles and cont. in patt. as folls.:
1st row: (k.1, p.1) 4(5:6) times, * p.1, k.6, p.1, k.7(8:9), p.1, k.6, * p.1, (p.1, k.1) 4 times, rep. from * to * twice, p.1, (k.1, p.1) 4 times, rep. from * to *, p.1, (k.1, p.1) 4(5:6) times.
2nd row: (p.1, k.1) 4(5:6) times, k.1, * p.6, k.1, p.7(8:9), k.1, p.6, k.1, * (p.1, k.1) 4 times, k.1, rep. from * to * twice, k.1, (p.1, k.1) 4 times, rep. from * to *, (p.1, k.1) 4(5:6) times.
3rd row: as 1st row.
4th row: as 2nd row.
5th row: as 1st row.
6th row: as 2nd row.
7th row: (k.1, p.1) 4(5:6) times, * p.1, C6B, p.9(10:11), C6B, * p.1, (p.1, k.1) 4 times, rep. from * to * twice, p.1, (k.1, p.1) 4 times, rep. from * to *, p.1, (k.1, p.1) 4(5:6) times.
8th row: as 2nd row.
Rep. 1st to 8th rows throughout.

Work until back measures 47(46:45) cm. (18½(18:17¾) in.).

Shape Armholes
Cast off 4(6:8) sts. at beg. of next 2 rows.
Dec. 1 st. at each end of next and foll. 3 alt. rows. [107(111:115) sts.]
Cont. straight until work measures 69 cm. (27 in.), ending with a wrong side row.

Shape Shoulders
Cast off 7 sts. at beg. of next 6 rows.
Cast off 7(8:9) sts. at beg. of foll. 2 rows.

Work Neckband
Change to 3¼mm. needles.
Next row: k.25(26:27), k.1 t.f.b., k. to end. [52(54:56) sts.]
Work 9 rows in k.2, p.2 rib, starting with 2nd row.
Cast off loosely in rib.

FRONT

Work as back until front measures 5 cm. (2 in.) less than back to shoulder shaping, ending with a wrong side row.

Shape Neckline
Next row: patt. 41(42:43) sts., turn work and place rem. sts. on spare needle.
Cast off 3 sts. at neck edge at beg. of next row and foll. alt. row.
Cast off 2 sts. at neck edge on next alt. row.
Dec. 1 st. at neck edge on every alt. row 5 times. [28(29:30) sts.]
Cont. straight.
AT THE SAME TIME, starting on the same row as back, shape shoulder as on back.
Return to sts. on spare needle.
Sl. centre 25(27:29) sts. onto holder, rejoin

yarn and work to match first side, reversing all shapings.

Work Neckband
With 3¼mm. needles and right side facing, pick up 20 sts. down left side of neck, k.12(13:14) sts. from holder, k.1 t.f.b., k. rem. 12(13:14) sts. on holder, pick up 20 sts. up right side of neck. [66(68:70) sts.]
Work 9 rows in k.2, p.2 rib, starting with 2nd row.
Cast off in rib.

SLEEVES

Chest 97 cm. (38 in.) only:
Cast on 68 sts. with 3¼mm. needles.
1st row: k.1, * p.2, k.2, rep. from * to last 3 sts., p.2, k.1.
Cont. in rib as set in 1st row for 10 cm. (4 in.), ending with 1st row.
Next row: p.1, (k.2, p.2) 6 times, k.2 tog., (p.2, k.2, p.2, k.2 tog.) twice, (p.2, k.2) to last st., p.1. [65 sts.]
Chest 102 cm. (40 in.) only:
Cast on 72 sts. with 3¼mm. needles.
1st row: p.1, k.2, * p.2, k.2, rep. from * to last st., p.1.
Cont. in rib as set in 1st row for 10 cm. (4 in.), ending with 1st row.
Next row: k.1, (p.2, k.2) 8 times, p.2, k.2 tog., rib to end. [71 sts.]
Chest 107 cm. (42 in.) only:
Cast on 74 sts. with 3¼mm. needles.
1st row: p.2, * k.2, p.2, rep. from * to end.
Cont. in rib as set in 1st row for 10 cm. (4 in.), ending with 1st row.
Next row: k.2 tog., (p.2, k.2) 4 times, p.2, k.1 t.f.b., k.1, (p.2, k.2) 3 times, p.2, k.2 tog., (p.2, k.2) 3 times, p.2, k.1 t.f.b., k.1, (p.2, k.2) to last 4 sts., p.2, k.2 tog. [73 sts.]
All sizes:
Change to 4mm. needles and cont. in patt.:
1st row: (k.1, p.1) 5(6:6) times, * p.1, k.6, p.1, k.7(8:9), p.1, k.6, rep. from * once, p.1, (k.1, p.1) to end.
2nd row: (p.1, k.1) 5(6:6) times, * k.1, p.6, k.1, p.7(8:9), k.1, p.6, rep. from * once, k.1, (p.1, k.1) to end.
Cont. in patt. as now set.
AT THE SAME TIME, inc. 1 st. at each end of next and 16(15:16) foll. 6th rows, working incs. in moss st. [99(103:107) sts.]
Cont. straight until work measures 47(47:48) cm. (18½(18½:18¾) in.).

Shape Top
Cast off 3(4:5) sts. at beg. of next 2 rows.
Dec. 1 st. at each end of next 13 rows.
Dec. 1 st. at each end of every alt. row 4(5:6) times. [59 sts.]
Dec. 1 st. at each end of next 6 rows. [47 sts.]
Cast off 6 sts. at beg. of next 4 rows.
Cast off rem. 23 sts.

MAKING UP

Press following instructions on ball band, taking care not to flatten the patt.
Sew up shoulder and neckband seams.
Sew up side and sleeve seams.
Set in sleeves.
Press seams if required.

Cable-panelled Slipover 1942

Round-necked sleeveless slipover with three cable panels on front and back, stocking-stitch neck and armhole borders, ribbed hem welt

★★ Suitable for knitters with some previous experience

MATERIALS

Yarn
Maxwell Cartlidge Pure Silk
5(5:6) × 50g. balls

Needles
1 pair 2¾mm.
1 pair 3¼mm.
1 cable needle

MEASUREMENTS

Bust
82(87:92) cm.
32(34:36) in.

Length
58 cm.
22¾ in.

TENSION

16 sts. and 19 rows = 5 cm. (2 in.) square

over patt. on 3¼mm. needles. If your tension square does not correspond to these measurements, see page 156 for adjustment instructions.

ABBREVIATIONS

k. = knit; p. = purl; st(s). = stitch(es); inc. = increas(ing) (see page 156); dec. = decreas(ing) (see page 157); beg. = begin(ning); rem. = remain(ing); rep. = repeat; alt. = alternate; tog. = together; sl. = slip stitch (transfer one stitch from left needle, knitwise unless otherwise stated, to right hand needle.); cont. = continue; patt. = pattern; foll. = following; folls. = follows; mm. = millimetres; cm. = centimetres; in. = inch(es); st.st. = stocking stitch.

FRONT

Cast on 128(136:144) sts. with 2¾mm. needles.
Work in k.2, p.2 rib for 29 rows.
Change to 3¼mm. needles and patt.
1st row (wrong side): p.18(22:26), k.2, * p.16, k.2, rep. from * to last 18(22:26) sts., p.18(22:26).
2nd row: k.18(22:26), p.2, * k.16, p.2, rep. from * to last 18(22:26) sts., k.18(22:26).
3rd row: as 1st row.
4th row: as 2nd row.
5th row: as 1st row.
6th row: k.18(22:26), * p.2, sl. next 4 sts. onto a cable needle and leave at back of work, k. next 4 sts., then k.4 sts. from cable needle, sl. next 4 sts. onto cable needle, leave at front of work, k. next 4 sts., then k.4 sts. from cable needle, p.2, k.16, rep. from *, ending last rep. k.22 in place of k.16.
7th row: as 1st row.
8th row: as 2nd row.
These 8 rows form patt.
Cont. in patt. until work measures 38 cm. (15 in.).

Shape Armholes
Cast off 6 sts. at beg. of next 2 rows, 2(4:4) sts. at beg. of foll. 2 rows, and 2 sts. at beg. of next 5(6:6) rows. [104 sts.] **
Cont. without shaping until work measures 51 cm. (20 in.).

Shape Neck
Next row: patt. 44 sts., cast off 16 sts., patt. to end.
Cont. on first group of sts.
Work 1 row, thus ending at neck edge.
Next row: cast off 2 sts., work to end.

Rep. last 2 rows twice more.
Work 1 row.
Dec. 1 st. at neck edge on next and every alt. row 6 times. [32 sts.]
Work 10 rows without shaping. Cast off 11 sts. at shoulder edge on next 2 alt. rows.
Work 1 row.
Cast off rem. 10 sts.
Rejoin yarn to neck edge of rem. group of sts., and work to match first side, reversing shapings

BACK

Work as for front to **.
Cont. without shaping until back measures same as to beg. of shoulder shaping on front.

Shape Shoulders
Next row: cast off 11, patt. 23 (including st. on needle after casting off), cast off 36, work to end.
Cont. on first group of sts.
1st row: cast off 11 sts., work to end.
2nd row: k.2 tog., work to end.
3rd row: as 1st row.
4th row: as 2nd row.
Cast off rem. sts.
Rejoin yarn to neck edge of second group of shoulder sts., and work as folls.:
1st row: k.2 tog., work to end.
2nd row: cast off 11 sts., work to end.
3rd row: as 1st row.
Cast off rem. sts.

BORDERS

Neck Border
Sew up left shoulder seam. With 2¾mm. needles, pick up and k.5 sts. at right side of back, 36 sts. at centre, 5 sts. at left side of back, 37 sts. down left side of front, 16 sts. at centre front, 37 sts. at left side of front. [136 sts.]
Work in k.2, p.2 rib for 2 cm. (¾ in.).
Cast off in rib.

Armhole Borders
Sew up right shoulder seam.
With 2¾mm. needles pick up 156 sts. evenly around armhole.
Work in k.2, p.2 rib for 2 cm. (¾ in.).
Cast off in rib.

MAKING UP

Sew up side seams.
Press lightly using damp cloth and warm iron.

Cotton Socks

Simple, stocking-stitch socks with ribbed top and heel and grafted toe

★★ Suitable for knitters with some previous experience

MATERIALS

Yarn
Pingouin Fil d'Ecosse no. 5
3(3) × 50g. balls

Needles
1 set of 4 double-pointed 2¾mm.

MEASUREMENTS

Foot Length (adjustable)
23(26) cm.
9(10¼) in.

Length to Base from Top (turned over)
29(30) cm.
11¼(11¾) in.

TENSION

16 sts. = 5 cm. (2 in.) over st.st. on 2¾mm. needles. If your tension does not correspond to this measurement, see page 156 for adjustment instructions.

ABBREVIATIONS

k. = knit; p. = purl; st(s). = stitch(es); inc. = increas(ing) (see page 156); dec. = decreas-(ing) (see page 157); beg. = begin(ning); rem. = remain(ing); rep. = repeat; alt. = alternate; tog. – together; sl. = slip stitch (transfer one stitch from left needle, knit-wise unless otherwise stated, to right hand needle.); cont. = continue; patt. = pattern; foll. = following; folls. = follows; mm. = millimetres; cm. = centimetres; in. = inch(es); st.st. = stocking stitch; p.s.s.o. = pass the slipped st. over.

Cast on 80(84) sts.: 26(28) sts. on each of 2 needles, and 28(28) sts. on 3rd needle. Join, being careful not to twist sts. Work 9 cm. (3½ in.) in k.2, p.2 rib. Turn work inside out to reverse turnover top.
Inc. round: * k.39(41), inc. in next st., rep. from * once more. [82(86) sts.]

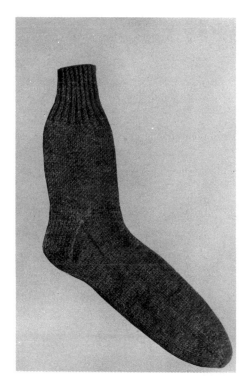

Now cont. in st.st. until work measures 19 cm. (7½ in.) from cast-on edge. (Adjust length here if required.)

Shape Leg
1st round: k.1, sl.1, k.1, p.s.s.o., k. to last 2 sts., k.2 tog.
2nd–5th rounds: k.
Rep. last 6 rounds 12 more times. [58(62) sts.]
Cont. straight until work measures 34(35) cm. (13¼(13¾) in.) from cast-on edge, (or length required).

Divide for Heel and Instep
Sl. the last 14(15) sts. and the first 15(16) sts. onto one needle for heel, leave the rem. 29(31) sts. on 2 needles for instep. Rejoin yarn to right side of heel sts. and work 22 rows in st.st.

Turn Heel
Next row: k.17(19), k.2 tog., turn.
Next row: p.6(8), p.2 tog., turn.
Next row: k.7(9), k.2 tog., turn.
Next row: p.8(10), p.2 tog., turn.
Cont. in this way, working 1 more st. before the dec. on every row until all sts. have been worked, ending with a p. row. [17(19) sts.]
Next round:
1st needle – k.17(19), then with same needle pick up and k.12 sts. along side of heel;
2nd needle – k. across 29(31) instep sts.;
3rd needle – pick up and k.12 sts. along other side of heel, [70(74) sts.], then k.8(9) heel sts. from 1st needle (thus ending at centre of heel).
K.1 round.

Shape Instep
Next round:
1st needle – k. to last 3 sts., k.2 tog., k.1.;
2nd needle – k.;
3rd needle – k.1, sl.1, k.1, p.s.s.o., k. to end.
K. 1 round.
Rep. last 2 rounds 4 times more. [60(64) sts.]
Cont. in st.st. without further shaping until foot measures 17(20) cm. (6½(7¾) in.) from back of heel (adjust length here if required), ending with 3rd needle.
Now transfer 1 st. from end of 1st needle on to 2nd needle. [15(16), 31(32), 15(16) sts.]

Shape Toe
Next round: 1st needle – k. to last 3 sts., k.2 tog., k.1; 2nd needle – k.1, sl.1, k.1, p.s.s.o., k. to last 3 sts., k.2 tog., k.1; 3rd needle – k.1, sl.1, k.1, p.s.s.o., k. to end.
K.1 round.
Rep. last 2 rounds until 24 sts. rem.
Place the 2 sets of 6 sts. onto one needle. Cast off both sets of sts. tog.: hold 2 needles parallel and cast off 1 st. from each needle alternately, to end.
Press work on wrong side with a damp cloth, omitting ribbing.

147

Alpaca Socks with Clocks

Furry, ankle-length socks in stocking stitch with Swiss-embroidered contrast side clocks, ribbed heel and top welt

★★ Suitable for knitters with some previous experience

MATERIALS

Yarn
Jaeger Alpaca
2(2:3) × 50g. balls (Main Col. A)
1(1:1) × 50g. ball (Contrast Col. B)

Needles
1 set of 4 double-pointed 2¾mm.

MEASUREMENTS

Length of Foot
24(27:28) cm.
9½(10½:11) in.

Length from Top to Base of Heel
41 cm.
16 in.

TENSION

32 sts. and 40 rows = 10 cm. (4 in.) square over st.st. on 2¾mm. needles. If your tension square does not correspond to these measurements, see page 156 for adjustment instructions.

ABBREVIATIONS

k. = knit; p. = purl; st(s). = stitch(es); inc. = increas(ing) (see page 156); dec. = decreas-(ing) (see page 157); beg. = begin(ning); rem. = remain(ing); rep. = repeat; alt. = alternate; tog. = together; sl. = slip stitch (transfer one stitch from left needle, knit-wise unless otherwise stated, to right hand needle.); cont. = continue; patt. = pattern; foll. = following; folls. = follows; mm. = millimetres; cm. = centimetres; in. = inch(es); st.st. = stocking stitch; p.s.s.o. = pass the slipped st. over; tbl. = through back of loop; m.1 = make 1 st.: pick up horizontal loop lying before next st. and work into back of it; sl.1K = sl. 1 st. knit-wise; sl.1P = sl. 1 st. purlwise.

Cast on 68 sts.: 24 sts. on each of 1st and 3rd needles, and 20 sts. on 2nd needle. Work in rounds of k.2, p.2 rib for 8 cm. (3¼ in.).
Next round: (k.17, m.1) 4 times. [72 sts.]
Place a coloured marker at end of last round to mark centre back.
Work in patt. as folls.:

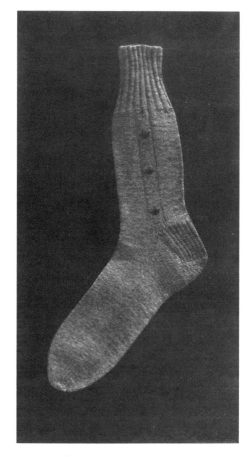

 ☑ B, darned

Next round: k.16, p.1, k.6, p.1, k.24, p.1, k.6, p.1, k.16.
Rep. this round until work measures 20 cm. (7¾ in.).

Shape Leg
1st round: k.1, k.2 tog., patt. to last 3 sts., sl. 1K, k.1, p.s.s.o., k.1.
Work 2nd to 6th rounds in patt.
Rep. last 6 rounds 5 times more. [60 sts.]
Work straight until work measures 33 cm. (13 in.).

Divide for Heel
Next round: k.14, sl. last 15 sts. of round onto end of same needle, (these 29 sts. are for heel).

Divide rem. sts. onto two needles and leave for instep.

Shape Heel
1st row: sl.1P, p. to end.
2nd row: sl. 1K, * k.1, keeping yarn at back of needle, sl.1P, rep. from * to last 2 sts., k.2.
Rep. last 2 rows 16 times more, then 1st row again.

Turn Heel
1st row: k.17, sl.1K, k.1, p.s.s.o., turn.
2nd row: p.6, p.2 tog., turn.
3rd row: k.7, sl.1K, k.1, p.s.s.o., turn.
4th row: p.8, p.2 tog., turn.
Cont. to dec. until all sts. are worked onto one needle.
Next row: k.9, thus completing heel (8 sts. rem. unworked on left hand needle).
Sl. all instep sts. onto one needle.
Using spare needle, k.8 heel sts. k. up 18 sts. along side of heel, using 2nd needle k. across instep sts., using 3rd needle k. up 18 sts. along other side of heel, k.9 heel sts. [84 sts.]

Shape Instep
1st round: k.
2nd round: 1st needle – k. to last 3 sts., k.2 tog., k.1.
2nd needle – k.
3rd needle – k.1, k.2 tog. tbl., k. to end.
Rep. these 2 rounds until 58 sts. rem.
Cont. on these sts. until foot measures 16(18:19) cm. (6¼(7:7½) in.) from where sts. were knitted up at heel.
Sl. 1st st. of 2nd needle onto end of 1st needle, and last st. of 2nd needle onto 3rd needle.

Shape Toe
1st round: 1st needle – k. to last 3 sts., k.2 tog. k.1.
2nd needle – k.1, k.2 tog. tbl., k. to last 3 sts., k.2 tog., k.1.
3rd needle – k.1, k.2 tog. tbl., k. to end.
2nd round: k.
Rep. these rounds until 26 sts. rem.
K. sts. from 1st needle onto end of 3rd needle.
Cast off sts. from two needles tog.: hold 2 needles parallel and cast off 1 st. from each needle alternately to end. With B, Swiss darn 3 stars as shown in chart between the p. sts. on side of socks.

Textured Shawl

*Huge, warm shawl with fringed ends, in simple
moss-stitch pattern throughout*

★ Suitable for beginners

MATERIALS

Yarn
Sunbeam Aran Bainin
18 × 50g. balls

Needles
1 pair 6½mm.

MEASUREMENTS

Length
230 cm.
90 in.

Width
51 cm.
20 in.

TENSION

16 sts. = 10 cm. (4 in.) over patt. on
6½mm. needles. If your tension does not
correspond to these measurements see
page 156 for adjustment instructions.

ABBREVIATIONS

k. = knit; p. = purl; st(s). = stitch(es); inc. =
increas(ing) (see page 156); dec. = decreas-
(ing) (see page 157); beg. = begin(ning);
rem. = remain(ing); rep. = repeat; alt. =
alternate; tog. = together; sl. = slip stitch
(transfer one stitch from left needle, knit-
wise unless otherwise stated, to right
hand needle.); cont. = continue; patt. =
pattern; foll. = following; folls. = follows;
mm. = millimetres; cm. = centimetres; in.
= inch(es); st.st. = stocking stitch.

STOLE

Cast on 81 sts. with 6½mm. needles.
1st row: k.1, * p.1, k.1, rep. from * to end.
This one row forms the patt.
Work until stole is 230 cm. (90 in.) long.
Cast off in patt., i.e. work each st. in patt.
before casting it off.

FRINGE AND MAKING UP

Using 6 strands of yarn 51 cm. (20 in.) long
for each tassel (or length required), work
a fringe along cast on and cast off edges,
working a tassel into every 4th st., using
crochet hook to pull yarn through stole.
Knot each tassel. Press stole.

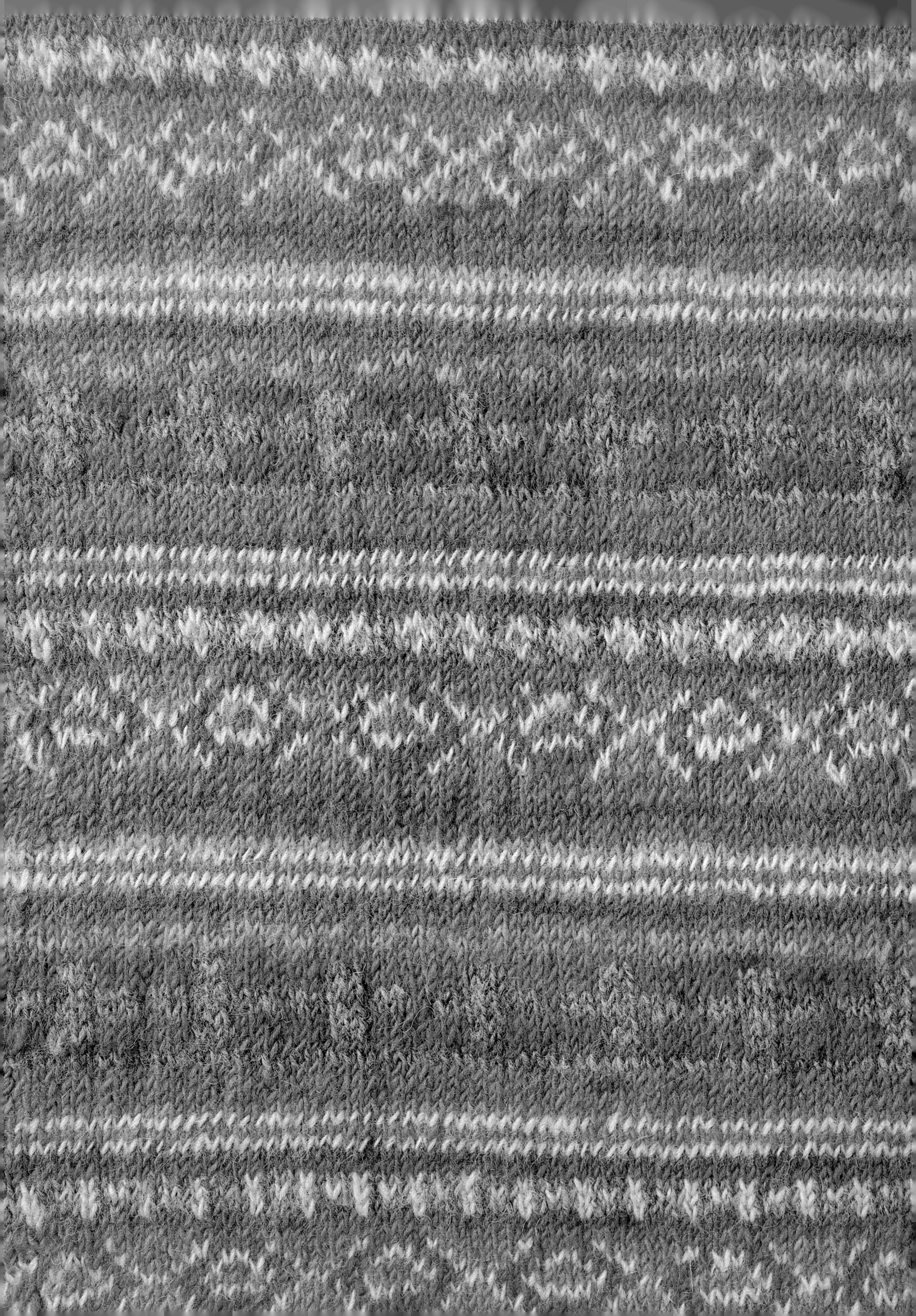

KNITTING KNOW-HOW

Starting to Knit from a Pattern

Here are all the knitting basics which you will need to know in order to make full use of 'Knitting in Vogue'. Whether you're a beginner, or need a refresher course, it's a good idea to familiarize yourself with the techniques drawn and described on the following pages before you begin to knit. There are sections covering all the knitting basics: casting on, knitting and purling, notes on simple stitch patterns, tension, increasing and decreasing, the finishing touches, casting off and making up. And if a disaster occurs, there is a problem section with diagrams to show you how, for example, to pick up dropped stitches, how to unpick your work. Finally, there is a section covering care of knitted garments, with notes on cleaning, and explanations of the international code symbols used on yarn ball bands.

Yarn Use the yarn specified in the pattern (or the equivalents detailed on page 164) to achieve perfect results. The weight and type of yarn used for each pattern has been chosen for two reasons: firstly, because it can be knitted at a tension which produces standard sizings, and secondly, because it corresponds as closely as possible in character to the yarn originally used. Buy all your yarn at once, checking that dye lots are identical. Colour differences between lots are often marked and you will not achieve satisfactory results from a mixture.

Tension Always check by knitting a sample square (see page 156 for more tension details) and, if necessary, change your needle size. The needle size given in the pattern will, in many cases, produce the correct tension but, since every knitter's tension varies slightly, there can be no one yarn/needle combination to suit everyone.

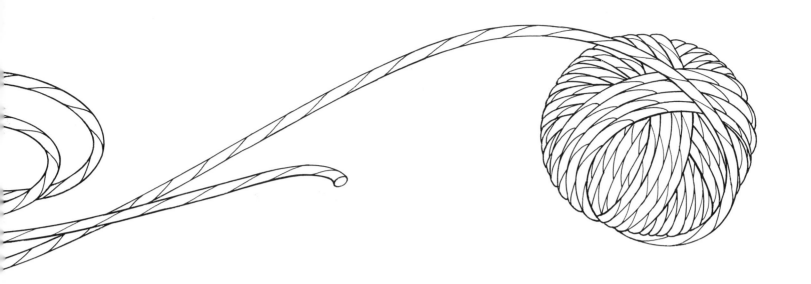

Sizes The smallest size is always printed first, larger sizes following in brackets. This system applies throughout the pattern wherever instructions differ according to size, and wherever one instruction is given, it applies to all sizes. It is a good idea to mark the size you are knitting, in pencil (which can, of course be rubbed out later), throughout the pattern to prevent mistakes.

Abbreviations These are used to save space in knitting instructions and are explained at the head of each pattern. It is advisable to familiarize yourself with these before starting to knit. Asterisks (*) are used where a section of the pattern is to be repeated, in order to save space. The asterisk will appear beside a pattern section. Where the pattern is to be repeated the wording reads 'repeat from *'. Where more than one section is to be repeated, two or three asterisks may be used for differentiation.

Charts These are used for multi-coloured patterns. Each square of the graph paper denotes one stitch and one row. Colours are indicated by symbols. When working in stocking stitch row 1 (at the bottom of the chart) and all odd-numbered rows are knit rows, worked from right to left. Even numbered rows are purl, and worked from left to right. For further details on multicoloured knitting see page 158.

Keeping your place Mark your pattern at each stage. The easiest way to make a mistake is to lose your place. Use a ruler to underline the row which you have reached, or a card marker. Where you have to count rows, for example when increasing, use a stitch counter (available from knitting departments and shops) on your needle, or make a note of each row you knit.

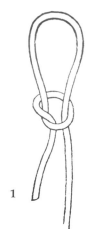

1

Casting On

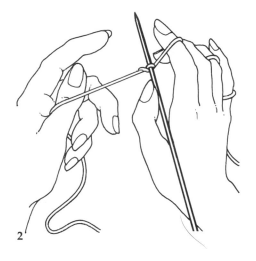

2

There are several methods of casting on stitches, each of which creates a slightly different first row of loops on the needle. The simplest method to learn is the thumb method, which is therefore a good starting point for beginners. All the methods begin with a slip loop (fig 1), which is made as follows:

1. Make an X twist of wool around your thumb.

2. Pull lower right half of this X through upper right half using needle point, and pull yarn end to tighten.

Thumb method

1. Make a slip loop as above, leaving an end of yarn about a metre (yard) long. Put loop on needle.

2. Draw up both ends of yarn to tighten the loop. Take the needle in your right hand (fig 2), holding the yarn end in your left hand, main yarn in your right hand, as shown.

3. Wind the yarn around your left hand in an X shape and put the needle through the loop (fig 3). Wind the main yarn around the needle and draw this loop through (fig 4).

4. Leave this stitch on the needle and repeat the process from step **3.** until the required number of stitches have been made. For an extra strong edge, you can double the loose end of yarn.

This method of casting on produces an elastic, hard-wearing edge.

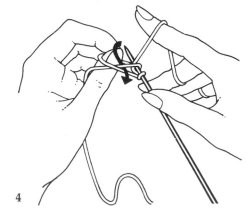

3

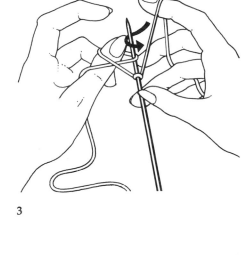

4

Cable method with 2 needles

1. Make a slip loop on the left-hand needle.

2. Put the right-hand needle into the loop and wind the yarn round it (fig 5).

3. Draw the yarn through the loop on the left-hand needle with right needle and transfer loop to the left-hand needle (fig 6).

4. Put the right-hand needle between the last two stitches on the left-hand needle (fig 7), and wind the yarn around the right-hand needle as before. Draw the loop through and transfer the stitch onto the left-hand needle (fig 8).

5. Repeat step **4.** until the required number of stitches have been made.

This method of casting on produces a firm edge, and can be used where casting on is necessary within the garment as well as to begin the work. For a slightly less firm finish, put the needle into the stitch *knitwise* in step **4.** instead of between stitches.

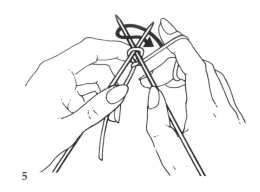

5

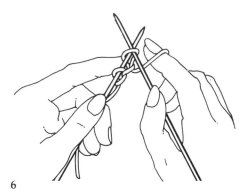

6

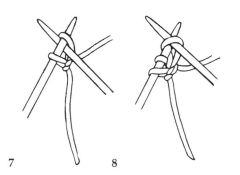

7   8

Cable method with 4 needles

Use four needles with points at both ends for this method.

1. With two needles, cast on the number of stitches for one needle on first needle.

2. With the third and second needles cast on the required number of stitches for the second needle, likewise with the following needle.

3. Ensure that the stitches are not twisted, draw the last stitch on the third needle up close to the first stitch on the first needle, for the next row, forming a triangle (fig 9). The right side of the work will always be on the outside of the triangle.

This method of casting on produces a firm edge.

Knitting and Purling

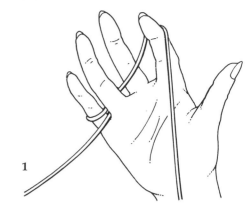

1

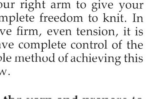

2

Casting on with a circular needle

1. Cast on the required number of stitches using the cable method for two needles.
2. Draw the last stitch on the needle up close to the first to prevent a loose stitch. The right side of the work is always on the outside of the circle.

Looped method with 1 needle

1. Make a slip loop on the needle, which should be held in the right hand.
2. Loop the yarn around the left thumb, and put the loop on the needle (fig 10).
3. Repeat step **2.** until the required number of stitches have been made.
This method of casting on produces a very loose cast on edge, which is suitable for lacy patterns and for hems which are to be knitted up.

Once you have created your first row of loops, or stitches, (see preceding pages) you can begin to knit. Use long, firm needles, for they are the easiest to manipulate, and the right needle can be held under your right arm to give your right hand complete freedom to knit. In order to achieve firm, even tension, it is essential to have complete control of the yarn, one simple method of achieving this is shown below.

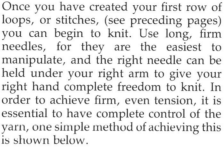

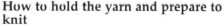

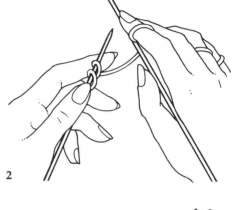

3

How to hold the yarn and prepare to knit

1. Wind the yarn around the little finger of your right hand, over your third finger, under the second and over the index finger (fig 1).
2. Rest the right-hand needle between thumb and the palm of the hand. Allow the needle to slide between thumb and hand, using only the index finger to manipulate the yarn (fig 2).

Knit stitch

1. With the needle containing the cast on stitches in your left hand and the wool at the back of the work, put the right-hand needle through the front of the first stitch from right to left (fig 3).
2. Wind the yarn around the right-hand needle around the two needle points with the index finger (fig 4), and turn the right needle slightly to pull the new loop of wool through the old loop and onto the right-hand needle. Slip the old stitch off the left-hand needle.
Repeat this process until all the stitches are knitted. *Abbreviation: 'k.'.* The side of the work facing you while knitting is known as the 'knit' side.

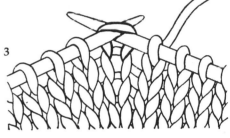

4

Purl stitch

1. With the needle containing the cast on stitches in your left hand and the wool at the front of the work, put the right-hand needle through the front of the first stitch, from right to left (fig 5).
2. Wind the yarn around the right-hand needle from above with the index finger (fig 6), and turn the right-hand needle slightly to pull the new loop of yarn through the old loop and onto the right-hand needle. Slip the old stitch off the left-hand needle.
Repeat this process until all the stitches are purled. *Abbreviation: 'p.'.* The side of

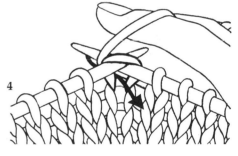

5

6

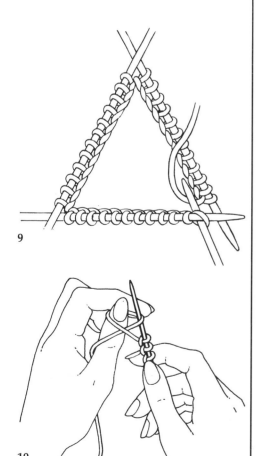

9

10

the work facing you while purling is called the 'purl' side.

Stitch notes

Some knitters find that slipping the first stitch in every row and knitting the last gives an extra firm and even selvedge to the work.

Garter stitch

This is one of the simplest for beginners, achieved by knitting every row. Purling every row would achieve a similar effect. *Abbreviation: 'g.st.'.*

Stocking stitch

One row purl, one row knit. *Abbreviation: 'st.st.'.* The knit side of the fabric is usually treated as the 'right' side, but some patterns are worked in 'reversed stocking stitch' (*abbreviated as rev.st.st.*), when the purl side is treated as the right side.

Ribbing

Ribbing can be worked in various widths, the most usual being one stitch knit, one stitch purl. This is worked as follows: k.1, *bring the yarn forward, p.1, bring the yarn back, k.1, rep. from * to end. On the following row all the knit sts. (which appear as purl sts. on the opposite side) will be purled, and all the purl sts. (which appear as knit sts. on the opposite side) will be knitted. For a chunkier rib, the stitch combination might be k.2, p.3, or k.2, p.2, instead of k.1, p.1, but the pattern will be worked in exactly the same way, reversing the type of stitch on the following row. Ribbing is usually referred to in patterns as 'rib'.

Moss stitch

This stitch is derived from ribbing. On the first row the stitches are alternated as for ribbing, and as for ribbing the number of stitches worked in each block vary. On the second row all the knit stitches are knitted, and all the purl stitches are purled. A 'single' moss stitch pattern, i.e. one stitch purl, one stitch plain, will work thus on an even number of stitches: k.1, p.1 to end; the second row will work thus: p.1, k.1 to end. *Abbreviation: 'm.st.'.*

Tension

'Tension' means the number of rows and stitches in a given measurement over the knitted fabric. Since every knitting pattern is based on a particular ratio of these, it is essential to check your tension before beginning to knit a new pattern. Personal tension is very variable and adjustments in needle sizes are often necessary. In particular, when the yarn suggested in the pattern is unavailable and an equivalent has to be used, great care in checking tension is necessary. There are tremendous variations in thickness between yarns of the same 'ply': the importance of checking tension cannot be overstressed.

How to check your tension

1. Work a small square, measuring at least 10 cm. (4 in.), in the pattern stitch or that mentioned in tension section.
2. Put the work on a flat surface, and, using a rigid ruler, measure 5 cm. (2 in.), (or the measurement suggested in the pattern) across stitches and rows. Carefully mark this square with pins.
3. If there are more rows or stitches in the pinned area than there should be, your tension is too tight and you should work a new sample using larger needles.
4. If there are too few stitches or rows in the pinned area, your tension is too loose and you should work a new sample using smaller needles.
Continue in this way until you have achieved the correct tension for the pattern. A variation from that suggested in the pattern by even as much as ½ stitch or row could mean that the garments will be a size smaller or larger, and the effect of the stitch too loose or tight for the design. Where a substitute yarn has been used it is sometimes impossible to obtain the correct width and depth tension. In this case the width tension should be obtained and the depth adjusted by working more or less rows as required.

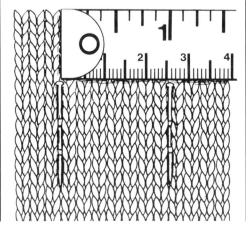

Shaping: Increasing

Knitting is shaped by the addition and subtraction of stitches. There are many different ways of doing this, some purely functional, some decorative too. Single stitches can be increased or decreased at any point in the row, groups of stitches are increased or decreased by casting on and casting off at the end of rows.

Casting on

This method is used where blocks of stitches are to be added. Cast on the required number of stitches at the beginning of a row using the cable method (see page 154), or at the end of a row by the looped method (see page 155).

Simple increasing

1. On a knit row: increase one stitch by knitting first into the front and then into the back of the same stitch. Slip stitch off left-hand needle, (fig 1).
On a purl row: increase one stitch by purling first into the front and then into the back of the same stitch. *Abbreviation: 'inc. 1 st.'.*

2. On a knit or a purl row: increase one stitch by knitting (or purling) the stitch below the next stitch on the left-hand needle, and then knitting (or purling) the next stitch on the left-hand needle, (fig 2). *Abbreviation: 'k.1 up'.*

3. On a knit or a purl row: increase one stitch by picking up the loop lying between the needles, knitwise or purlwise, using the right-hand needle. Put the loop onto the left-hand needle and knit or purl into the back of it, (fig 3). *Abbreviation: 'm. 1'.*

Decorative increasing

These methods produce a series of holes in the fabric which can be used to create lacy patterns.
1. On a knit row: increase one stitch by bringing the yarn forward between needles (as for a purl stitch), then carrying the yarn over the needle to knit the stitch in the usual way, (fig 4). *Abbreviation: 'y.fwd.'.*

2. On a purl row: increase one stitch by bringing the yarn over and round the right-hand needle, then purling the stitch in the usual way, (fig 5). *Abbreviation: 'y.r.n.'.*

3. Between a purl and a knit stitch: increase one stitch by taking the yarn from the front of the work over the needle, then knitting the next stitch in the usual way, (fig 6). *Abbreviation: 'y.o.n.'.*

Shaping: Decreasing

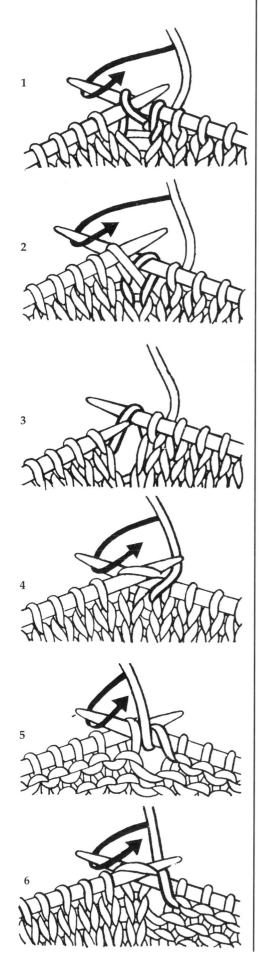

Casting off

This method is used where blocks of stitches are to be removed, for example at shoulder or neck. Casting off should be worked loosely, particularly at the neck (to allow for stretch in wear), and it is often helpful to use a size larger needle.

Simple decreasing

1a. On a knit row: decrease one stitch by putting the right-hand needle knit-wise into second and then first stitch, then knitting them together in the usual manner (fig 1). *Abbreviation: 'k.2 tog.'.*

b. On a purl row: decrease one stitch by putting the right-hand needle purl-wise through the first and then second stitches and purling them together in the usual manner (fig 2). *Abbreviation: 'p.2 tog.'*

c. On a purl row: decrease one stitch by putting the right-hand needle through the back of the first and then second stitches on the left-hand needle and purling them together in the usual manner (fig 3). *Abbreviation: 'p.2 tog. t.b.l'.*

2. On a knit row: decrease one stitch by slipping the next stitch purlwise on to the right-hand needle. Knit the next stitch, put the point of the left-hand needle purl-wise into the slipped stitch and slip it over the knitted stitch and off the needle (fig 4). *Abbreviation: 'sl. 1, k. 1, p.s.s.o.'.*

3. On a knit row: decrease two stitches by putting the right-hand needle through the next three stitches and knitting them together in the usual manner (fig 5). *Abbreviation: 'k.3 tog.'.*

4. On a knit row: decrease two stitches by slipping the next stitch purlwise. Knit the next two stitches together, then put the point of the left-hand needle purlwise into the slipped stitch and slip it over the stitches knitted together and off the needle (fig 6). *Abbreviation: 'sl. 1, k. 2 tog., p.s.s.o.'.*

Decorative decreasing

Decreased stitches lean either to left or right. Different methods of decreasing, *see above*, can thus be used to create patterns. For example, 'sl. 1, k. 1, p.s.s.o.' is used on the decreased edge of raglan sleeves. Of the methods above:
1a., **1b.** and **4.** lean to the right;
1c., **2.** and **3.** lean to the left.

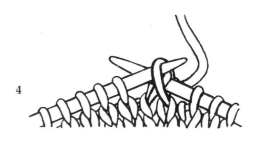

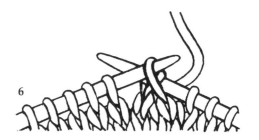

Problems

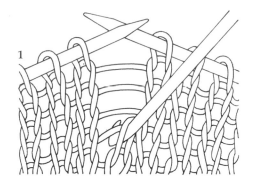

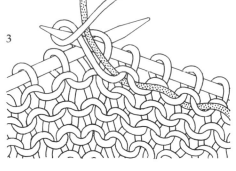

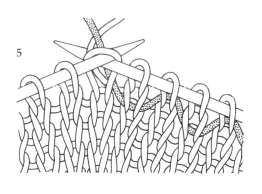

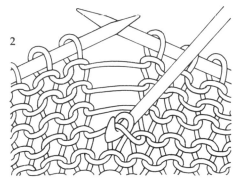

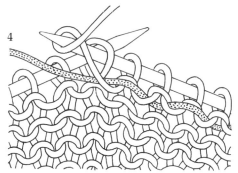

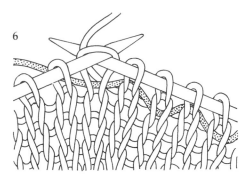

Keeping work clean and evenly knitted

Never leave your knitting in the middle of a row, or an uneven stitch will result. Don't stick your needles into the ball of wool, because this splits the yarn. When knitting very furry or pale yarns, it may be helpful to pin a polythene bag or linen cloth over the finished work to keep it clean.

Dropped stitches

Even if the stitch has dropped several rows, it is usually very simple to pick it up again using a crochet hook.

1. On a knit row (fig 1), with right side facing:

a. Insert crochet hook from the front into the dropped stitch.

b. Put hook under the thread above the stitch and pull it through the stitch.

c. Continue in this way until the dropped stitch is level with the rest of the work.

2. On a purl row (fig 2), with wrong side facing:

a. Insert the crochet hook between the bottom and second threads lying above the dropped stitch, then into the stitch from back to front.

b. Draw the thread through the stitch.

c. Put the new stitch onto a spare needle. Insert hook between the next two threads as in step **a.** pick up stitch from needle and draw thread through.

If you are knitting in pattern, it may be impossible to pick up dropped stitches in this manner. Unpicking will then be necessary.

Unpicking mistakes

If you make a mistake don't tear your work off the needles. Unpicking may be time-consuming, but it is simple and, when worked as below, will prevent your dropping any stitches in the process.

1. On a knit row:

a. With the knit side facing you, put the right-hand needle into the stitch below the first stitch on your left-hand needle.

b. Gently pull the first stitch off the left-hand needle and pull the yarn out of the stitch on your left-hand needle, leaving it at the back of the work.

c. Continue in this way until you have unpicked the required number of stitches.

2. On a purl row:

With the purl side of the work facing you, proceed as above, remembering that the yarn will unravel at the front of the work instead of the back.

Running out of yarn

Yarn should always be joined in at the end of a row, for best results, with a loose knot which can later be untied, and the yarn ends darned in. Splicing, an invisible method of joining yarn, is sometimes used by experienced knitters in mid-row, but it creates a weak join. If you inadvertently run out of yarn in mid-row, unpick to the beginning of the row and join there.

Snagging

If you catch your work and pull a thread, you can rectify this by easing the stitches on the same row gently with a crochet

hook or a knitting needle until the loop disappears. If the snag is really bad, you can either unpick, or pull the loop through to the back of the work and ease the stitches around it.

Working with several colours:

There are two methods of dealing with the spare colours running behind the work. Over small pattern repeats, up to four or five stitches, the stranding method is used, over large pattern repeats the weaving method is used. Some patterns combine the two.

Weaving method

Carry the yarn not in use over the yarn in use for one stitch (fig 3, purl row; fig 5, knit row), and under it for the next stitch (fig 4, purl row; fig 6, knit row), on the wrong side of the work. As with the stranding method, the yarns should be carried loosely to prevent pulling of the work.

Stranding method

Carry the yarn not in use loosely along the back of the work, being careful not to pull it too tightly when picking it up to use again (fig. 7).

See page 153 for notes on working from pattern charts.

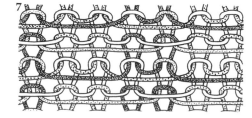

Casting Off

Casting off is used both at the end of a piece of work, to fasten off all the stitches, and also to decrease blocks of stitches within the work, such as at shoulder and underarm. Casting off should be worked loosely, often a larger size needle makes this easier. Where a block of stitches is cast off at the end of a row, the yarn must be broken off and rejoined at the beginning of the following row.

Simple casting off

On a knit row
1. Knit the first two stitches.
2. Lift the first stitch over the second with the point of the left-hand needle (fig 1).
3. Drop the first stitch off the needle leaving the second on the right-hand needle.
4. Knit one stitch.
5. Repeat steps 2. to 4. inclusive until the required number of stitches have been cast off. If block decreasing, cast off number of stitches required and knit to end of row (fig 2). If finishing off work, continue until one stitch remains. Break off yarn leaving an end of 15 cm. (5¾ in.). Draw end through remaining stitch and pull tight.

On a purl row
1. Purl the first two stitches. Keep yarn forward.
2. As above (fig 3).
3. As above.
4. Purl one stitch.
5. Repeat steps 2. to 4. inclusive until the required number of stitches have been cast off. If block decreasing, cast off the number of stitches required and purl to end of row (fig 4). If finishing off work, continue until one stitch remains. Break off yarn leaving an end of 15 cm. (5¾ in.). Draw end through remaining stitch and pull tight.

Casting off in pattern

Cast off each stitch by knitting or purling it according to the pattern being knitted. Where casting off a block, cast off in pattern and continue to work in pattern to end of row.

Casting off on 4 needles

This is done exactly as on two needles, except for the adjoining stitches at each end of needles, worked as follows each time:
1. Cast off to last stitch on needle.
2. Knit (or purl) first stitch on next needle.
3. Cast off last stitch on needle by lifting it over the first on the next needle.

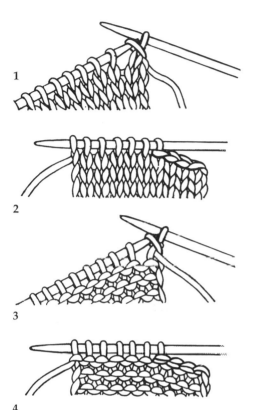

Finishing Touches

Knitting with sequins
Thread sequins onto yarn as follows:
1. Fold a 25 cm. (9¾ in.) length of sewing cotton in half, thread a needle with the cut ends.
2. Pass 20 cm. (7¾ in.) of the knitting yarn through the cotton loop, and thread the sequins onto the needle, over the cotton and onto the yarn.

When a sequin is required
1. Knit to position of sequin, slide sequin down yarn and position close to work.
2. Knit the next stitch through the back of the loop in the usual manner, pushing the sequin through the stitch to the front of the work (fig 1).

Swiss darning

Swiss darning is a type of embroidery used on knitted fabric to create a pattern which appears knitted-in. It is worked on stocking stitch, using a yarn of similar weight to that of the piece of work.

1. Thread a blunt darning needle with the yarn. Insert needle from back to front of the work at the centre of the first stitch to be embroidered over.
2. Following fig 2, insert the needle behind both strands of the stitch above.
3. Then thread the needle through the two next strands below, as marked by the arrow in fig 2. Be careful to ensure that the tension of the embroidery matches that of

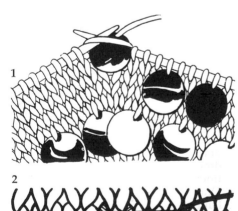

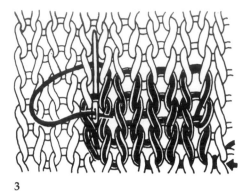

3

the original work, to prevent the fabric pulling.

4. Where the embroidery is to cover several rows, complete one row as above and insert the needle under the upper loop of the last stitch (fig 3). Turn the work upside down and continue with steps 1. to 3. and reverse again for following row.

Buttonholes

The patterns detail how and when buttonholes are to be made. You can alter their size by adding or taking away stitches to be cast off (on the armhole edge) on a horizontal buttonhole, or by increasing or decreasing the number of rows worked for a vertical buttonhole.

Horizontal buttonholes

1. Loosely cast off required number of stitches. The stitch remaining after casting off is counted as part of the row, NOT of the buttonhole.
2. In the next row, cast on the same number of stitches as were cast off in the previous row (figs 4 and 5).

Vertical buttonholes

1. Divide stitches to form the sides of the buttonhole.

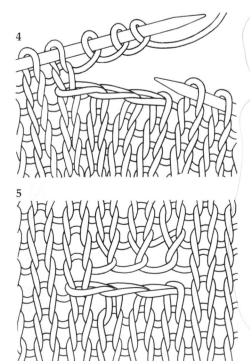

4

5

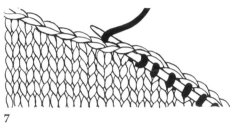

6

7

2. Work individually to required height, rejoin the two sides.
3. Later, work buttonhole stitch with the end of yarn left when the two sides were joined together, to strengthen the buttonhole.

Working separate front bands

When separate front bands have to be worked, as for a cardigan, it is a good idea to knit both bands simultaneously to ensure that they are exactly the same length. As you knit the buttonholes mark the button position on the other band.

When measuring the band length ensure that the band is *very* slightly stretched against the main work, otherwise the band will sag in wear.

Knitting up stitches

Always ensure that stitches are picked up evenly, thus count rows or stitches and compare with the number of stitches to be picked up before starting.

Knitting up vertically, used for knitted-on front bands

1. Compare number of stitches to be picked up with number of rows.
2. To pick up each stitch: having yarn at back of work, put needle from front to back of work, pick up a loop of yarn and bring it through to front (fig 6).

Knitting up along straight or curved edges

1. Compare number of stitches to be picked up with the number of stitches along the edge to be worked on.
2. To pick up each stitch: having yarn at back of work, put needle from front to back of work, pick up a loop of yarn and bring it through to front (fig 7).

Making Up

Careful making up is essential to the success of your work. There are pressing and making up instructions on each pattern, which you should follow. Below there are further details on how to block, press, and how to sew up seams to achieve a professional finish.

Blocking and pressing

Only press where this is specifically mentioned in the pattern.

Where the pattern instructs you to press the finished pieces of your garment, proceed as follows (fig 6):
1. Pin each piece, right side downwards, onto a well-padded surface. Do NOT stretch any part of the fabric, be careful to keep rows and stitches in straight lines.
2. Press the fabric, excluding any ribbing, under a damp cloth if specified.
3. Allow fabric to cool and remove pins.
4. Push ribbing together so that only the knit stitches show, pin out carefully and press lightly, again under a damp cloth if specified.

Sewing up seams

Use your knitting yarn to sew up seams wherever possible. If the yarn is very heavy, or very textured, substitute a similar-coloured 4 ply yarn. Your pattern will tell you the order in which to sew up the pieces you have knitted. There are several methods of sewing up seams, of which the backstitch and flat seam methods, below, are the most popular. Backstitch can be used for most seams except ribbing, where flat seaming is used. Flat seaming is also used on fabrics knitted in very fine yarns.

Flat Seam (fig 2)

1. Put the right sides of the two pieces together, matching rows if working on a straight edge.
2. Put your left forefinger between the two pieces of work. Join in yarn with several

1

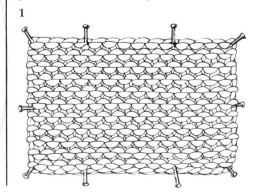

running stitches one over the other at the beginning of the seam.

3. Bring the needle from front to back close to the edge of the fabric, pull yarn through, create a small running stitch by putting needle through the fabric again from back to front, one stitch further on along the fabric.

4. Continue to end, ensuring that the stitches are not drawn too tightly, thus pulling the work. Press (if pressing is recommended for the yarn) under a damp cloth.

Backstitch Seam (fig 3)

1. Put the right sides of the two pieces together, matching rows if working on a straight edge.

2. Join in yarn with several running stitches one over the other at the beginning of the seam.

3. Put needle into right-hand end of the running stitches and bring out at front of work one stitch from the edge of the fabric, and one stitch beyond the left-hand end of the running stitches.

4. Put needle back into work at left-hand end of the running stitches, and bring out to front of work one stitch beyond the stitch created in step **3**. Continue in this way taking care not to split stitches. Use running stitches as in step **2.** to finish the end of the seam. Press (if pressing is recommended for the yarn) under a damp cloth.

Special seam notes

Shoulder seams: match shapings on both pieces. When stitching, work in a straight line across these shaping steps, in firm backstitch. Press seams on the wrong side. Reinforce with tape, in the case of very heavy garments.

Sleeve and side seams: join with backstitch, using flat seaming for ribbing (and throughout for jumpers in very fine yarns).

Set-in sleeves: mark the centre top of the sleeve and pin to shoulder seam, match cast off stitches in sleeve and armhole and pin together. Pin remaining sloping sides of sleeve evenly into the armhole. Backstitch as near the edge as possible, using fine stitches.

Raglan sleeves: match raglan seams row for row, and stitch using a flat seam, with very small stitches.

Sewn on collars: with right side of collar facing wrong side of the work, pin centre of collar to centre of neckline, and each end of the collar to neckline edges, or position marked in the pattern. Stitch, taking care not to stretch the neckline, as close to the edge as possible.

Hems: where the hem has been marked by a line of knit stitches, or where a length of fabric is to be turned up as hem, this should be pressed, and slipstitched in place.

Lapped seams: place parts to be joined right sides together, with the underneath fabric extending 12mm. (½ in.) beyond the upper part. Backstitch close to the edge, turn to the right side and backstitch again through both layers of fabric 12mm. (½ in.) from the original seam, using small, neat stitches.

Front Bands: sew on using a flat seam.
Zips (fig 4): nylon zips are normally the best type for knitwear. Reinforce the edges of the knitting with a row of double crochet, if necessary, and pin zip in place, taking care not to stretch the knitting. With right side facing, using small backstitches, sew in with fine thread (to match yarn) and needle, as close to the edge of the knitting as possible. Stitch from top to bottom on both sides of the zip. Later, slipstitch the zip edges on the inside.

Yarn ends

Thread each end in turn into a blunt-ended darning needle. Darn neatly into the back of the work, including a couple of back stitches to hold it firmly. Trim end close to work.

Where more than one colour has been used, darn the ends of each into its own colour area.

Ribbon facing

Choose ribbon in a colour to match your yarn. You should allow at least a 6 mm. (¼ in.) hem on either side of the button bands, and a 12mm. (½ in.) hem at top and bottom of both bands.

1. Press the work lightly. Cut the button and buttonhole band facings together so that their length is identical.

2. Fold in all the turnings and press lightly.

3. Pin to the bands on the wrong side, checking that buttonholes are evenly spaced: ease work to adjust this. Slipstitch around the ribbon with matching fine cotton, using tiny stitches.

4. Mitre corners: slipstitch outer seam, fold ribbon at corner and stitch.

5. Cut buttonholes along grain, oversew ribbon and knitting together with sewing cotton, then work buttonhole stitch on top using the original yarn.

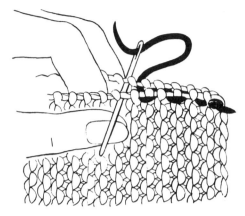

2

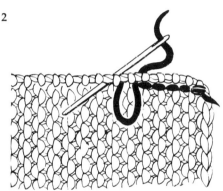

3

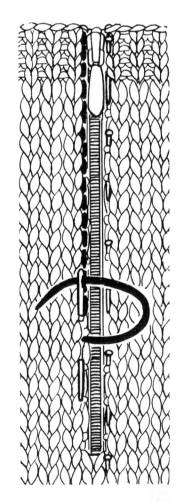

4

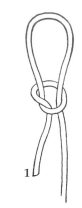

Crochet Finishes

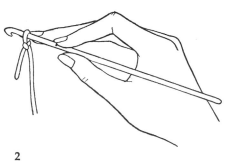

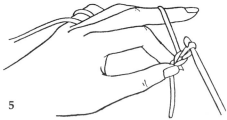

Crochet is sometimes used to finish hand-knitting, either as a border or to create patterns on the knitted fabric.

Like knitting, crochet is begun with a slip loop (fig 1), which is made as follows:

1. Make an X twist of yarn around your thumb.
2. Pull lower right half of this X through upper right half, using hook point, and pull yarn end to tighten.

Hold the hook like a pencil with the shank resting between your thumb and first finger, using your first and second fingers to guide the work (fig 2).

The yarn should be held in the left hand (fig 3), wound over the first and second fingers, under the third finger and then looped over the fourth finger, so that the new yarn runs first over and then round the fourth finger.

Chain stitch

Chains are used as the basis of most crochet work. The first row of any crochet garment is worked in chain stitch. Chains are worked at the end of crochet rows before turning work for the next row, their number depending on the stitch being used.

Chains are worked as follows:

1. Make a slip loop as above.
2. Hold the end of the slip loop with thumb and first finger of the left hand.
3. Put hook under yarn from left to right, then back over the yarn from right to left (fig 4).
4. Pull yarn through the loop (fig 5).

Repeat steps 2 to 4 to lengthen the chain. Chain stitch can be used on knitted fabric to create patterns, and is particularly useful where knitted-in contrast is unsatisfactory, such as in the case of narrow vertical lines.

When working over a fabric, work as for simple chain, but keep the new end of yarn behind the fabric, working with right side facing, as follows:

1. Make a slip loop, take it off the hook, put hook through fabric from front to back in position where first chain stitch is to be and put loop back on hook. Pull loop through to front of fabric, leaving the knot at back of fabric.
2. Put hook through fabric from front to back at required point, one chain's length from previous hole, put hook under and over yarn as in step 3 above.
3. Pull yarn through fabric and through loop on right side surface of fabric.

Repeat steps 2 and 3 to required length of line or design.

Double crochet

Double crochet edging on knitted fabric is worked as follows:

1. Attach yarn to edge of garment which is to be finished.
2. Put hook through edge of fabric along cast-off edge, from front to back, loop yarn around hook as in step 3 of chain stitch above, and pull resulting loop to front.
3. Now put hook through fabric from front to back again, a stitch further along cast-off edge, loop yarn around hook as before and pull through the fabric to front. There are now two stitches on the hook.
4. Loop yarn around hook once more and pull through both stitches.

Repeat steps 3 and 4 to end of edge requiring finishing.

If only one row of double crochet is indicated by the pattern, break off the yarn and end it in neatly, likewise neaten in the slip loop end.

If further rows are required, work 1 chain before turning work to begin the next row.

Care of Knitwear

Pilling

Many yarns are prone to pilling: this means that loose balls of fibre appear on the surface of the garment. These can be removed very simply with a strip of sticky tape, or with gentle brushing.

Snagging

This, too, can usually be remedied, see description of the process on page 158.

Cleaning knitted garments

The great variety of yarns now on the market has meant that washing instructions need to be individually described for each type: thus ball bands carry cleaning and pressing instructions in the International Textile Care Labelling Code. The symbols are explained briefly opposite.

General guidelines

1. Where the garment should be hand-washed, ensure that soap flakes are thoroughly dissolved before immersing the knitwear, or use Woolite cold water wash. Never use very hot water to wash wool, follow the temperature suggested on the ball band.
2. Rinse thoroughly in tepid water.
3. NEVER wring knitwear roughly by hand, spin briefly in a machine, or squeeze gently, to remove moisture.
4. Unless otherwise stated in the pattern, knitwear should be gently pulled into shape and dried on a clean flat surface.

60°C = Hot, hotter than the hand can bear, the temperature of water from a domestic hot tap.
50°C = Hand-hot, as hot as the hand can bear.
40°C = Warm, pleasantly warm to the hand.
30°C = Cool to the touch.

Can safely be washed by hand or machine. Number above line denotes washing process for machines, figure below it denotes water temperature in °C, see above for temperature details.

Wash *only* by hand.

Must *not* be washed.

Dry cleanable in all solvents.

Dry cleanable in perchloroethylene, white spirit, Solvent 113 and Solvent 11.

Goods sensitive to dry cleaning which may be cleaned with solvents shown for **P**, but with strict limitation on the addition of water during cleaning and/or restrictions concerning mechanical action or drying temperature or both.

Dry cleanable in white spirit and Solvent 113.

Goods sensitive to dry cleaning which may be cleaned with solvents shown for **F** but with a strict limitation on the addition of water during cleaning and/or certain restrictions concerning mechanical action or drying temperature or both.

Do *not* dry clean.

Tumble drying beneficial.

Do *not* tumble dry.

Where a triangle contains the letters **CL** the article can be treated with chlorine bleach. Where the triangle is crossed out chlorine bleach may *not* be used.

Hot iron up to 210°C.

Warm iron up to 160°C.

Cool iron up to 120°C.

Do not iron.

Yarn Conversion Chart

U.K.	U.S.A.	Australia
A.N.I. Shetland Homespun	A.N.I. Shetland Homespun	Mail order
A.N.I. Shetland 2 ply	A.N.I. Shetland 2 ply	Mail order
Chat Botté Petrouchka	Chat Botté Petrouchka	Mail order
Emu Filigree	Emu Filigree	Emu Filigree
Emu Scotch Superwash Wool 4 ply	Emu Scotch Superwash Wool 4 ply	Emu Scotch Superwash Wool 4 ply
Emu Shetland DK	Emu Shetland DK	Emu Shetland DK
Christian de Falbe studio yarn	Mail order	Mail order
Hayfield Brig Aran	Hayfield Brig Aran	Hayfield Brig Aran
Hayfield Gaucho	Hayfield Gaucho	Hayfield Gaucho
Hayfield Grampian 4 ply	Hayfield Grampian 4 ply	Hayfield Grampian 4 ply
Jaeger Alpaca	Jaeger Alpaca	Jaeger Alpaca
Jaeger Botany Wool 3 ply	York Fingering 3 ply (Patons)	Jaeger Botany Wool 3 ply
Jaeger Luxury Spun DK	Jaeger MatchMaker DK	Jaeger Spiral Spun DK
Jaeger Naturgarn	Jaeger Naturgarn	Jaeger Naturgarn
Jaeger Wool-Silk	any 4 ply (without silky effect) or mail order	Jaeger Wool-Silk
Lister-Lee Motoravia 4 ply	Lister-Lee Motoravia 4 ply	Lister-Lee Motoravia 4 ply
Lister-Lee Motoravia DK	Lister-Lee Motoravia DK	Lister-Lee Motoravia DK
Karen Naismith-Robertson Cable Cotton	Mail order	Mail order
Karen Naismith-Robertson Mercerised Cotton	Mail order	Mail order
Natural Dye Company Cotton	Mail order	Mail order
Natural Dye Company Wool	Mail order	Mail order
Patons Clansman 4 ply	Lady Galt Kroy 4 ply (Patons)	Patons/Jaeger MatchMaker 4 ply
Patons Clansman DK	Patons Beehive DK or Patons MatchMaker DK	Patons Husky DK or Patons Hurdwick DK
Phildar Perle 5	Phildar Perle 5	Mail order
Phildar Sagittaire	Phildar Sagittaire	Mail order
Phildar Shoot	Phildar Shoot	Mail order
Picaud Laine et Coton	Picaud Laine et Coton	Picaud Laine et Coton
Picaud Orient Express	Picaud Orient Express	Picaud Orient Express
Pingouin Confort DK	Pingouin Confort DK	Pingouin Confort DK or mail order
Pingouin Confortable Sport	Pingouin Confortable Sport	Pingouin Confortable Sport
Pingouin Coton Naturel 8 fils	Pingouin Coton Naturel 8 fils	Pingouin Coton Naturel 8 fils or mail order
Pingouin Fil d'Ecosse no 5	Pingouin Fil d'Ecosse no 5	Pingouin Fil d'Ecosse no 5 or mail order
Pingouin Pingolaine 4 ply	Pingouin Pingolaine 4 ply	Pingouin Pingolaine 4 ply or mail order
Poppleton Guernsey 5 ply	Poppleton Guernsey 5 ply	Mail order
Sirdar Majestic 4 ply	Sirdar Majestic 4 ply	any 4 ply
Sirdar Majestic DK	Sirdar Majestic DK	any DK
Sirdar Talisman DK	Sirdar Talisman DK	any DK
Sunbeam Aran Bainin	Sunbeam Aran Bainin	Mail order
Sunbeam Aran Tweed	Sunbeam Aran Tweed	Mail order
Sunbeam Wool 3 ply	Sunbeam Wool 3 ply	Mail order or any 3 ply
Templeton's H & O Shetland Fleece	Templeton's H & O Shetland Fleece	Mail order
3 Suisses Gaelic Bainin	3 Suisses Gaelic Bainin	Mail order
3 Suisses Suizy DK	3 Suisses Suizy DK	Mail order
Twilleys Double Gold	Twilleys Double Gold	Twilleys Double Gold
Wendy Shetland DK	Wendy Shetland DK	Wendy Shetland DK or any DK
Yarn Store Cable Cotton	Mail order	Mail order
Yarn Store Cashmere	Mail order	Mail order
Yarn Store Natural British Wool	Mail order	Mail order

Canada	S. Africa
Mail order	Mail order
Mail order	Mail order
Mail order	Patons Beehive DK or mail order
Emu Filigree	Emu Filigree
Emu Scotch Superwash Wool 4 ply	Any 4 ply
Emu Shetland DK	Elle Shetland DK
Mail order	Mail order
Hayfield Brig Aran	Hayfield Brig Aran
Hayfield Gaucho	Hayfield Gaucho
Hayfield Grampian 4 ply	Hayfield Grampian 4 ply
Jaeger Alpaca	Mail order
York Fingering 3 ply (Patons)	Silver Sheen 3 ply (Patons)
Jaeger MatchMaker DK	Jaeger MatchMaker DK
Jaeger Naturgarn	Patons Nomad
Jaeger Wool-Silk	Any 4 ply (without silky effect) or mail order
Lister-Lee Motoravia 4 ply	Lister-Lee Motoravia 4 ply
Lister Lee Motoravia DK	Lister-Lee Motoravia DK
Mail order	Mail order
Mail order	Mail order
Mail order	Mail order
Mail order	Mail order
Lady Galt Kroy 4 ply (Patons)	Patons/Jaeger MatchMaker 4 ply
Patons Beehive DK or Patons MatchMaker DK	Patons Beehive DK
Phildar Perle 5	Mail order
Phildar Sagittaire	Mail order
Phildar Shoot	Mail order
Picaud Laine et Coton	Mail order
Picaud Orient Express	Mail order
Pingouin Confort DK	Pingouin Confort DK
Pingouin Confortable Sport	Pingouin Confortable Sport
Pingouin Coton Naturel 8 fils	Pingouin Coton Naturel 8 fils
Pingouin Fil d'Ecosse no 5	Pingouin Fil d'Ecosse no 5
Pingouin Pingolaine 4 ply	Pingouin Pingolaine 4 ply
Mail order	Patons Totem or mail order
Sirdar Majestic 4 ply	Lister-Lee Lavenda Crisp 4 ply
Sirdar Majestic DK	Sirdar Wash'n Wear Double Crepe
Sirdar Talisman DK	Sirdar Wash'n Wear Double Crepe
Sunbeam Aran Bainin	Patons Capstan on 4½/5mm needles
Sunbeam Aran Tweed	Patons Capstan on 4½/5mm needles
Sunbeam Wool 3 ply	Mail order or any 3 ply
Templeton's H & O Shetland Fleece	Elle Shetland DK or mail order
3 Suisses Gaelic Bainin	Pingouin Monsieur
3 Suisses Suizy DK	Jaeger MatchMaker DK
Twilleys Double Gold	Twilleys Double Gold
Wendy Shetland DK	Wendy Shetland DK
Mail order	Mail order
Mail order	Mail order
Mail order	Mail order

USING THE CHART

Tension: all the patterns were knitted up and checked in the yarns listed in the first column. In many cases these are widely available, but where they are not, the nearest equivalent in both weight, character and appearance has been quoted. When using an equivalent yarn, it is *doubly* important to check your tension, in order to achieve perfect results.

Needles: unless otherwise stated in the chart, use the needle sizes quoted in the pattern.

Yarn: unless otherwise stated in the chart, yarn requirements are as given in the pattern. Individual tension variations may cause fluctuations in amount used.

Addresses: should you have difficulty in acquiring yarn, or want to order by post, the addresses to write to are listed on pages 166–168.

NEEDLE CONVERSIONS

U.K. and Australia metric	U.K. and Australia original, Canada, S. Africa	U.S.A
2mm.	14	00
2¼mm.	13	0
2¾mm.	12	1
3mm.	11	2
3¼mm.	10	3
3¾mm.	9	4
4mm.	8	5
4½mm.	7	6
5mm.	6	7
5½mm.	5	8
6mm.	4	9
6½mm.	3	10
7mm.	2	10½
7½mm.	1	11
8mm.	0	12
9mm.	00	13
10mm.	000	15

AMERICAN TERMINOLOGY

Most knitting and crochet terms are identical in English and American usage. The exceptions to this are listed below, with the English term used in the book given first, followed by the American term.

Double crochet (d.c.) = single crochet (s.c.); stocking stitch (st. st.) = stockinette stitch (st. st.); yarn round needle (y.r.n.) = yarn over needle (y.o.n.); cast off = bind off.

Addresses

If you have any difficulty in obtaining yarns, you can write to the address given below for the head office or agent of the yarn spinner for stockist information. Where there is no agent the address of sole or main stockists are given. Where the yarn is available only by mail order, this address is given.

A.N.I.

Head Office and mail order

A.N.I.

7 St. Michael's Mansions
Ship Street
OXFORD OX1 3DG
U.K.

U.S.A. sole stockist

Textile Museum
2320 S Street
WASHINGTON D.C.
U.S.A.

CHAT BOTTE

U.K. agent

Groves of Thame Ltd.
Lupton Road
Industrial Estate
THAME
Oxon.
U.K.

U.S.A. agent

Armen Corporation
P.O. Box 8348
ASHEVILLE
NC 28814
U.S.A.

Canada agent

Districan III
Rue du Port
MONTREAL
Quebec
CANADA

Mail order

Chat Botté
BP 34959056
ROUBAIX
CEDEX I
FRANCE

ELLE

S. Africa

Mr J Norris
Consolidated Woolwashing
   and Processing Mills Ltd.
P.O. Box 12017
JACOBS 4026
S. AFRICA

EMU

U.K.

Customer Service
Emu Wools
Leeds Road
Greengates
BRADFORD
W. Yorks
U.K.

U.S.A. agent

Merino Wool Inc.
20th Floor
230 Fifth Avenue
NY 10001
U.S.A.

Australia agent and mail order

Mrs R Mallett
The Needlewoman
308 Centrepoint
Murray Street
Hobart
TASMANIA 7000

Canada agent

S R Kertzer Ltd.
257 Adelaide Street West
TORONTO M5H 1Y1
Ontario
CANADA

S. Africa agent

E. Brasch & Son
57 La Rochelle Road
Trojan
JOHANNESBURG
S. AFRICA

CHRISTIAN DE FALBE YARN

Mail order only

Christian de Falbe
97 Wakehurst Road
LONDON SW11 6BZ
U.K.

HAYFIELD

U.K.

Hayfield Textiles Ltd.
Hayfield Mills
GLUSBURN
Nr. KEIGHLEY
W. Yorks BD20 8QP
U.K.

U.S.A. wholesaler

Shepherd Wools Inc.
923 Industry Drive
SEATTLE
Washington 98188
U.S.A.

Canada wholesaler

Craftsmen Distributors Inc.
4166 Halifax Street
BURNABY
British Columbia
CANADA

Australia wholesaler

Panda Yarns International Pty. Ltd.
17–27 Brunswick Road
EAST BRUNSWICK
Victoria 3057
AUSTRALIA

S. Africa agent

A & H Agencies
392 Commissioners Street
Fair View
JOHANNESBURG 2094
S. AFRICA

JAEGER see PATONS

LISTER-LEE

U.K.

George Lee & Sons Ltd.
Whiteoak Mills
P.O. Box 37
WAKEFIELD
W. Yorks
U.K.

U.S.A agent details

Fransha Wools
P.O. Box 99
Parkside Mills
BRADFORD
Yorks.
U.K.

Canada major stockist

Mrs Hurtig
Anita Hurtig Imports Ltd.
P.O. Box 6124
Postal Station A
CALGARY
Alberta T2H 2L4
CANADA

Australia

Mrs. R. Mallett
The Needlewoman
308 Centrepoint
Murray Street
Hobart
TASMANIA 7000

S. Africa

S.A. Pty. Ltd.
P.O. Box 33
RANDFONTEIN
S. AFRICA

KAREN NAISMITH-ROBERTSON YARN

Mail order only

Karen Naismith-Robertson
The Walled Garden
Rycote Park
MILTON COMMON
Oxon. OX9 2PE
U.K.

THE NATURAL DYE COMPANY

Mail order only

The Natural Dye Company
Stanbridge
WIMBORNE
Dorset
BH2 14JD
U.K.

PATONS and JAEGER

U.K.

Jaeger Handknitting *or*
Patons & Baldwins Ltd.
ALLOA
Clackmannanshire
SCOTLAND
U.K.

Mail orders

Woolfayre Ltd.
120 High Street
NORTHALLERTON
W. Yorks.
U.K.

U.S.A.

C J Bates and Sons Ltd.
Route 9a
CHESTER
Connecticut 06412
U.S.A.

Australia agent

Coats & Patons Aust. Ltd.
321–355 Fern Tree Gully Road
P.O. Box 110
MOUNT WAVERLEY
Victoria 3149
AUSTRALIA

Canada agent

Patons & Baldwins (Canada) Ltd.
1001 Roselawn Avenue
TORONTO
CANADA

S. Africa

Mr Bob Theis
Marketing Manager
Patons & Baldwins (S. Africa) Pty.
Ltd.
P.O. Box 33
RANDFONTEIN 1760
S. AFRICA

PHILDAR

Canada

Phildar LTEE
6200 Est.
Blvd. H. Bourassa
MONTREAL Nord HIG 5X3
CANADA

U.S.A.

Phildar Inc.
6438 Dawson Boulevard
85 North
NORCROSS
Georgia 30093, U.S.A.

Mail order Information

Phildar
4 Gambrel Road
Westgate Industrial Estate
NORTHAMPTON
NN5 5NS
U.K.

PICAUD

U.K. and mail orders

Browns Woolshop
79 Regent's Park Road
LONDON NW1 8UY
U.K.

Priory Yarns
48 Station Road
OSSETT,
W. Yorks., U.K.

U.S.A. agent

Merino Wool Co. Inc.
230 Fifth Avenue
Suite 2000
N.Y. 10001
U.S.A.

Canada agent

Innovations C.F. Ltd.
11460 Hamon
MONTREAL
Quebec H3M 3A3, CANADA

Australia agent

Olivier Aust. (Pty.) Ltd.
53 Liverpool Street
SYDNEY 2001, AUSTRALIA

PINGOUIN

U.K.

French Wools Ltd.
7–11 Lexington Street
LONDON W1R 4BU
U.K.

Head office and mail orders

Mr R Mesdagh
BP 9110
59061 ROUBAIX
Cedex 1, FRANCE

U.S.A agent

Pingouin – Promafil Corp. (U.S.A.)
P.O. Box 100
Highway 45
JAMESTOWN
S. Carolina 29453
U.S.A.

Australia stockist

The Needlewoman
308 Centrepoint
Murray Street
Hobart
TASMANIA 7000

Canada agent

Promafil (Canada) Ltd.
1500 Rue Jules Poitras
379 ST LAURENT
Quebec H4N 1X7
CANADA

S. Africa agent

Romatex/Yarns and Wools
P.O. Box 12
JACOBS 4026
Natal
S. AFRICA

POPPLETON

U.K. and mail order

Richard Poppleton & Sons Ltd.
Albert Mills
Horbury
WAKEFIELD
W. Yorks.
U.K.

U.S.A agent

Mr & Mrs F Gordy
315 West Court Street
P.O. 11672
MILWAUKEE
Wisconsin 53211
U.S.A.

SIRDAR

U.K.

Sirdar Ltd.
Flanshaw Lane
Alverthorpe
WAKEFIELD WF2 9ND
W. Yorks.
U.K.

U.S.A. agent

Kendex Corp.
31332 Via Colinas
107 Westlake Village
CALIFORNIA 91362
U.S.A.

Canada agent/distributor

Diamond Yarn (Canada)
Corporation
153 Bridgeland Avenue
Unit 11
TORONTO M6A 2Y6
CANADA

Australia agent

see Patons

Addresses

Continued

SUNBEAM

U.K.

Sunbeam
Richard Ingram & Co. Ltd.
Crawshaw Mills
PUDSEY LS28 7BS
W. Yorks, U.K.

U.S.A distributors

Phillips Imports
P.O. Box 146
PORT ST. JOE
Florida 32456
U.S.A.

Grandor Industries Ltd.
4031 Knobhill Drive
SHERMAN OAKS
California 91403
U.S.A.

Canada distributor

Estelle Designs and Sales Ltd.
1135 Queen Street East
TORONTO
Ontario
CANADA M4N 1K9

Mail order

Woolfayre Ltd.
120 High Street
NORTHALLERTON
W. Yorks
U.K.

TEMPLETON'S

U.K. and mail order

James Templeton & Son Ltd.
Mill Street
AYR KA7 1TL
Scotland, U.K.

U.S.A. stockists

The Little Mermaid
At the Castle
205 East Lawrence Street
APPLETON
Wisconsin 54911
U.S.A.

The Wool Gatherer Inc.
1502 21st Street
WASHINGTON D.C. 20036
U.S.A.

The Wool Shop
250 Birch Hill Road
LOCUST VALLEY
N.Y. U.S.A.

Canada stockist

House of Heather
Lord Elgin Hotel
OTTAWA KIP 5K8
CANADA

3 SUISSES

U.K.

3 Suisses
Marlborough House
38 Welford Road
LEICESTER LE2 7AA
U.K.

U.S.A and Canada agent

Bucilla
230 Fifth Avenue
NEW YORK
U.S.A.

Head office and mail order

Filature de L'Espierres (3 Suisses)
Blvd. des Canadiens
7760 DOTTIGNIES
BELGIUM

TWILLEYS

U.K.

H G Twilley Ltd.
Roman Mill
STAMFORD
Lincs. PE9 1BG
U.K.

U.S.A. agent

House of Settler
2120 Broadway
LUVVOCK
Texas
U.S.A.

Australia agent

Panda Yarns International Pty Ltd.
17–27 Brunswick Road
EAST BRUNSWICK 3057
Victoria
AUSTRALIA

Canada agent

S R Kertzer Ltd.
257 Adelaide Street W.
TORONTO N5H MI
Ontario
CANADA

S. Africa agents

S W Nyman Ltd.
P.O. Box 292
DURBAN 4000
S. AFRICA

Chester Mortonson Ltd.
P.O. Box 11179
JOHANNESBURG 2000
S. AFRICA

WENDY

U.K.

Wendy International
P.O. Box 3
GUISELEY
W. Yorks.
U.K.

U.S.A.

Wendy Yarns U.S.A.
P.O. Box 11672
MILWAUKEE
Wisconsin 53211
U.S.A.

United Notions
1314 Viceroy Drive
DALLAS
Texas
U.S.A.

United Notions
P.O. Box 43145
5560 Fulton Industrial Blvd.
ATLANTA
Georgia 30336
U.S.A.

Australia agent

The Craft Warehouse
30 Guess Avenue
ARNCLIFFE
N.S.W. 2205
AUSTRALIA

Canada agent

White Buffalo Mills
545 Assiniboine Avenue
BRANDON
Manitoba
CANADA

S. Africa agent

Woolcraft Agencies
P.O. Box 17657
2038 Hillbrow
JOHANNESBURG
S. AFRICA

THE YARN STORE

Mail order and shop

The Yarn Store
8 Ganton Street
LONDON W1V 1LJ
U.K.